Why do Buses Always Come in Threes?

Why do Buses Always Come in Threes?

The extraordinary maths behind 60 everyday phenomena

COLIN BEVERIDGE

CASSELL ILLUSTRATED

This work is also published in the UK under the title
The Maths Behind...

An Hachette UK Company
www.hachette.co.uk

First published in Great Britain in 2017 by Cassell,
a division of Octopus Publishing Group Ltd
Carmelite House
50 Victoria Embankment
London EC4Y 0DZ
www.octopusbooks.co.uk

ISBN 978-1-78840-016-9

A CIP catalogue record for this book is available from
the British Library.

Printed and bound in China.

10 9 8 7 6 5 4 3 2 1

Publishing Director: Trevor Davies
Senior Editor: Leanne Bryan
Art Director: Yasia Williams-Leedham
Designer: Simon Buchanan, Design 23
Illustrators: Kevin Williamson, Gary Lee and Martin Lee
Picture Research Manager: Giulia Hetherington
Production Manager: Sarah Kulasek-Boyd

Contents

Introduction

This book is an answer to the question "When would you ever use mathematics in real life?" Mathematics is an unreasonably effective tool for understanding the Universe – whether you are looking on an enormous scale and trying to understand space, looking on a tiny scale and trying to understand subatomic particles, or looking around you on a human scale and trying to understand why buses come in threes or how the supermarket judges the correct number of cabbages to stock.

From physics to football to fluttering to flying, mathematics plays a fundamental role in many aspects of life, culture and science.

Applied mathematics is not about the mathematics you probably think of as mathematics – long division does not show up anywhere in this book, and you are not expected to do any algebra. Instead, it is about taking elements of the real world and modelling them using mathematics – which could be anything from counting, to algebra, to differential equations, to Inter-Universal Teichmüller theory (which is currently understood by literally one person). It is about distilling the messy, noisy world into something that can be solved by a human or a computer. It is about (to paraphrase Einstein) making everything as simple as possible, but no simpler.

You are probably wondering: what level of mathematical knowledge do I need to read this book? The answer is: none. It is not as if there is a test. More seriously, the point of the book is not to make you feel stupid for not knowing something. It is to show you interesting applications of mathematics you can enjoy either as a spectator or as an active participant. Whether you prefer to read it and nod along saying "I'd never thought of that!" or get your pen and paper out to dig deeper into the theory is entirely up to you. Both are perfectly valid ways of enjoying the book.

The Maths Behind takes a look at just some of the situations that can be better understood using mathematics, and the book is split into seven very broad sections.

We start in **The Human World** with some examples of how mathematics can be applied

in the interpersonal and political arenas, such as finding your ideal partner, why elections are inherently flawed and (putting ethical dilemmas to one side) whether and when you should break the rules.

Mathematics doesn't just apply to humans: in **The Natural World**, we learn about some of the zoological, geological and astronomical phenomena that yield to mathematical thought, including the life cycles of predators and their prey, how to measure earthquakes and why hexagons are everywhere from beehives to the Giant's Causeway.

Mathematics also underpins computers, in obvious and not-so-obvious ways. In **Technology**, we assess how the history of computing intertwines with the history of mathematics, how advanced algebra keeps your credit card information safe and how filters keep at least some of the spam out of your inbox.

While I am pretty sure Novak Djokovic is not solving differential equations (at least not rigorously) when he decides where to aim his first serve, tennis is just one of the **Sports** that has plenty of mathematics in it. Why do balls swerve when you spin them? How do you perform a perfect ski jump? And how did mathematics revolutionize the game of baseball?

Even in the **Entertainment** world, there is plenty to analyze: from the most efficient way to play Monopoly, to making decisions on game shows, to the patterns of the Alhambra Palace in Granada, Spain.

More obviously, there is mathematics to be found any time you try to get from A to B. In **Getting Around**, we can barely scrape the surface of the mathematics behind maps and self-driving cars, the mysterious "jamiton" effect that makes traffic back up without any obvious cause, and the navigational challenges of getting to Jupiter.

Finally, we come to the maths of the **Everyday** – or at least, some days. How do you pick your lottery tickets to maximize your chances of winning? Why don't you fall off the rollercoaster? How and why does the length of the day change throughout the year? And what do they mean when they say there is a 30% chance of rain?

There is only enough room in a book this size to cover a tiny fraction of the real-life topics where mathematical thinking either makes a thing possible, or allows it to be understood in a different way. If you would like to suggest themes to explore in the future, please feel free to get in touch!

The Human World

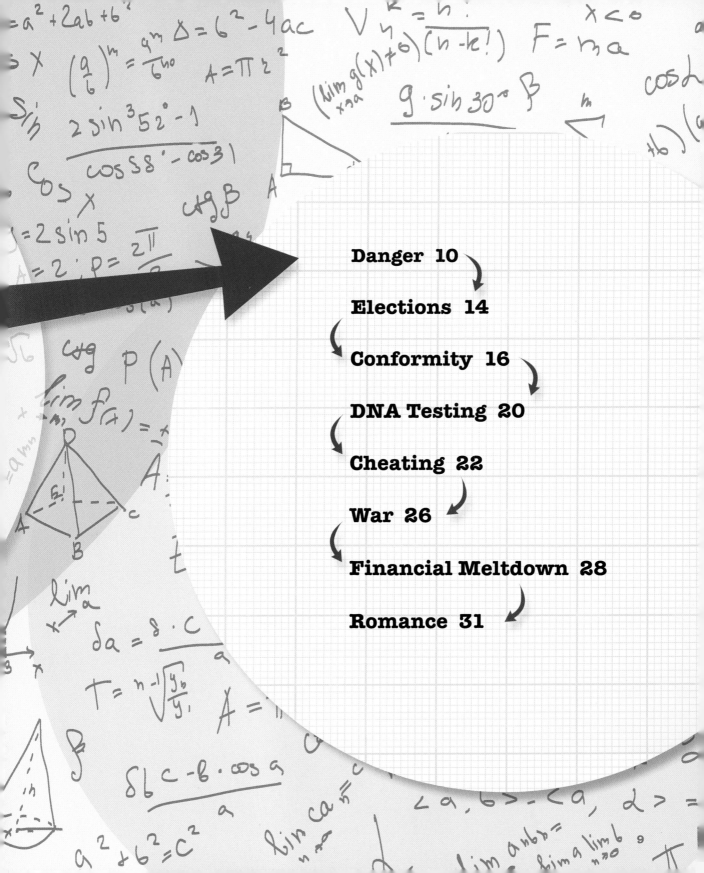

Danger

Even the most risk-averse person in the world takes risks. Their ethically sourced spinach in a green smoothie has a risk of containing salmonella. Their Prius is just as likely to wreck as any other car.

Pretty much everything you do, from climbing the stairs to bed, to crossing the road, to jumping on your motorbike, to doing a parachute jump, carries some degree of risk. Some of these things are clearly riskier than others – but the rewards for each of them vary as well. There is usually a trade-off between risk and reward.

So it makes sense to ask: what risks are worth taking? How can you assess risk? And, if all of your friends jumped off a bridge, would you?

SHOULD YOU DRIVE OR FLY?

In the aftermath of the 9/11 attacks, people turned to their cars in droves. Air travel was, perfectly understandably, seen as extremely risky, and it was a risk fewer wanted to take.

While it was an understandable human reaction, it was also a very poor mathematical one. Since 1996, there has been no year with more than 1,500 civilian fatalities from air crashes, and the trend has been generally downward since the early 1970s. According to planecrashinfo.com, if you are travelling on a regular airliner, there are about 4 fatalities (from all causes) in every million hours of flying. At 600mph, that is fewer than 7 deaths per billion miles in flight. The corresponding figure for driving is 12 to 15 fatalities per billion miles.

It has been said that you are more likely to have an accident on the way to the airport than on your flight, but that is a little bit disingenuous. The vast bulk of car accidents are prangs rather than serious collisions, whereas if your plane has an accident, the chances are it will not be one where the pilot can jump out to demand the insurance details of the chump who has just flown into their plane's newly painted tail.

It is all very well talking about fatalities per billion miles, but it is a bit of a tricky concept to wrap your head around. If I drive to see my brother, 250 miles away, what are my chances of dying in a crash? Sure, I could work it out but I am not sure the answer would mean very much to me. What we need is the *micromort*.

12,000 miles by plane = 1 micromort

250 miles by car = 1 micromort

WHAT RISKS ARE WORTH TAKING?

When Ronald A Howard, a professor in the field of decision analysis at Stanford University, talks about the probability of a catastrophic event, he measures things in micromorts. A micromort is a one-in-a-million chance of dying while undertaking an activity.

The chance of meeting an unnatural and untimely demise as you go about your day-to-day existence is somewhere about 1 micromort (in 2012, about 48 people in England and Wales died every day from things other than natural causes, out of a population of 56.5 million – so the probability of not surviving a day is 48/56,500,000, or about 0.0000008. It is simpler to compare that to other things if you write it as 0.8 millionths – or 0.8 micromorts. In the US, it is a bit more (1.6 micromorts, based on 2010 data; the difference is due to a higher chance of dying in a car accident). This varies depending on your age: if you are a newborn baby in the UK, your first day carries 430 micromorts of risk, although that drops to an average of about 17 over your first year.

With that baseline, you can gauge how dangerous different activities are. A marathon carries a risk of about seven micromorts and a sky dive for charity carries about nine micromorts – so the two activities (one of which is seen as super-healthy and the other as a crazy risk) are broadly comparable in danger.

You can also assess the safety of forms of transport in a simple and intuitive way: a 6-mile motorbike ride carries a risk of 1 micromort, and so does a 250-mile drive in the car. Motorcycling is about forty times as dangerous as driving (over all drivers and motorcyclists). However, travelling by plane is safer still: it takes a thousand miles of jet travel to rack up a micromort due to *accidents*, so cars are four times as risky as planes. As for terrorism, you would need to fly 12,000 miles for it to add up to a micromort.

RISK MEASUREMENT
A micromort is a one-in-a-million chance of dying while undertaking an activity

Running a marathon carries a similar level of risk (7 micromorts), to sky diving (9 micromorts)

MICROMORTS

By age & gender
Baseline mortality (chance of dying from any cause at this age)

- **1** 30 years female
- **2** 30 years male
- **4** 45 years female
- **6** 45 years male
- **1** 18 years male
- **0.5** 18 years female
- **15** 60 years female
- **23** 60 years male
- **0.5** 7 years male
- **<0.5** 7 years female
- **105** 75 years male
- **15** 0 years male
- **12** 0 years female
- **69** 75 years female

By activity

- **1** Skiing
- **8** Hang gliding
- **5** Scuba diving
- **0.5** Horse riding

$$v = \sqrt{2as}$$

HOW FAR CAN YOU FALL AND SURVIVE?

Oh no! The building is on fire! I am trapped two stories above the ground! The fire brigade will not be here before the house burns down – I suppose I had better jump. But first, let me get my calculator out and figure out how likely I am to survive the fall.

If I just stepped out of the window, 4.6 metres above the ground, I would accelerate under gravity at about 9.8 metres per second per second. I would hit the ground with a speed of $v=\sqrt{2as}$, where a is the acceleration and s is the distance to fall. So the speed I hit the ground would be somewhere in the region of 34 kilometres per hour (about 21 miles per hour). Thinking about car/pedestrian accidents at that speed, that is probably a "hospital rather than morgue" sort of fall, although obviously many other factors come into play: after all, there are people who fall out of planes and survive, and others who fall out of bed and do not – my personal health and the softness of the landing will come into play too.

I can mitigate the effect of falling if I dangle from the window-ledge rather than stepping straight out. If my upper-body strength is good enough to keep me steady by my finger-tips, my toes are only 2.4 metres (8 feet) from the ground, and I would land at about 24 kilometres per hour (15 miles per hour) instead – an impact I could probably limp away from.

If I wanted to give myself the best chance of surviving a fall from a building, I would consider the following options:

If I can lower my height, by dangling, dropping onto an awning or balcony, or fashioning a rope out of bedsheets, every foot I move closer to the ground improves my odds.

If I can increase my air resistance with a makeshift parachute (or better, a real one), this will also slow down my impact.

If I can find a soft landing spot, persuade people to catch me, bend my legs as I land, or otherwise make sure I meet the ground with a groan rather than a splat, then my injuries should be less severe.

REDUCE YOUR RISK OF INJURY

4.6 m (15 ft)

34 kph (21 mph)

2.4 m (8 ft)

24 kph (15 mph)

1. **Lower yourself from the window ledge**

2. **Increase air resistance**

3. **Make a rope from bedsheets/curtains**

4. **Choose a soft landing area such as a shop awning**

Elections

A short disclaimer before we begin: I always vote if I can. I vote even if my preferred candidate is on a hiding to nothing (which they normally are).

WHEN IS IT WORTH VOTING?

A perfect, selfish mathematician would vote only if it was worth it. They would calculate the value of voting as:

(the estimated benefit of their preferred candidate winning) × (the probability of an extra vote changing the result)

So if a candidate would make the voter $1,000 better off, and had a 1/1,000 chance of needing an extra vote to win the election, the value to the mathematician of voting would be $1. If the cost (in time and transport) of traipsing down to the polling station was more than that, they would stay home or do something else.

In practice, the smaller the election, the more likely your vote is to make a difference by breaking a tie: in my last local council elections, the winning candidate won by just 11 votes out of about 700; the chances of a tie between two evenly matched candidates in those circumstances is $\frac{700!}{(350!)^2} \times 2^{700}$, which is about 3%. If you live in Florida, where the turnout is typically around eight or nine million, the chances of your vote making a difference to the presidential race is about 0.03% – much higher than I expected! (See the graph on the right.)

WHY ARE ELECTION BOUNDARIES WEIRD?

It is surprisingly difficult to divide a country or a state up into electoral regions that give both a fair representation of the population and competitive races (at least in a winner-takes-all system.) It is also very easy, if you happen to have partisan boundary commissions, to create voting districts that give an advantage to one party over another.

The practice of drawing boundaries for your own advantage is called gerrymandering, after the Massachusetts governor in the 1810s,

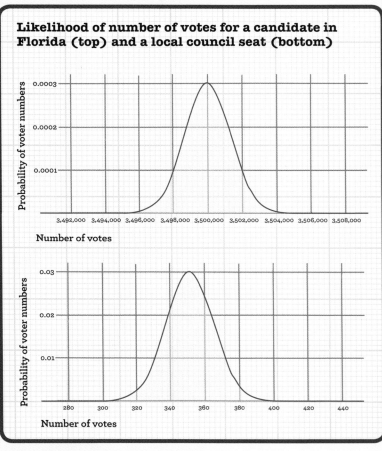

Likelihood of number of votes for a candidate in Florida (top) and a local council seat (bottom)

Elbridge Gerry. He signed a bill creating odd-shaped districts that favored his Democratic-Republican Party. One was reputed to look like a salamander. "You mean," said a journalist, "a Gerry-mander!" and the name stuck.

For example, suppose there are 100 voters in a state, equally split between two parties, and there are ten congressional districts to apportion. If the commission were so inclined, it could arrange the boundaries so their preferred party won 8 of the districts 6–4, and lost the remaining two 9–1. By grouping your opponent's

The binomial distribution provides a good first approximation for an election process.

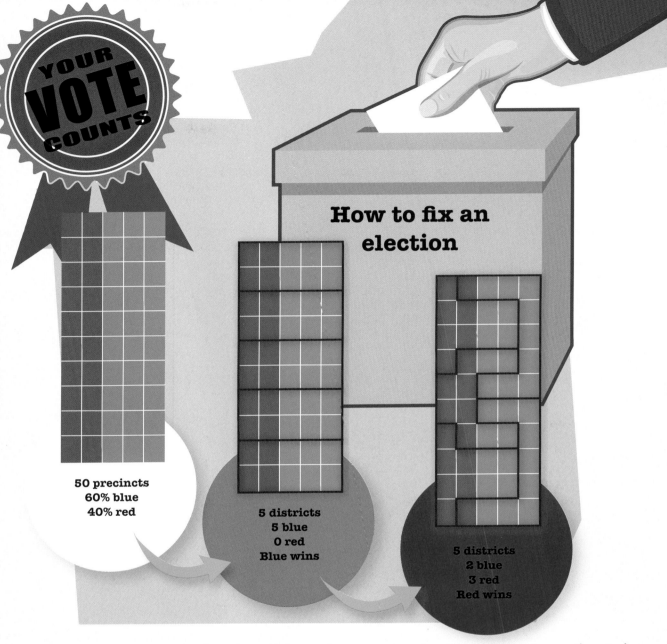

YOUR VOTE COUNTS

How to fix an election

50 precincts
60% blue
40% red

5 districts
5 blue
0 red
Blue wins

5 districts
2 blue
3 red
Red wins

voters together in huge numbers, and your own voters with slim (but reliable) majorities, you can create a wildly biased result – here, 8–2 as opposed to the more reasonable 5–5.

The most logical ways to guard against gerrymandering are either removing control of boundaries from the political parties, or implementing a more proportional voting system that skews the results less than first-past-the-

post does. Better still, agreeing a mathematical procedure to determine fair and equal districts would stop the practice altogether!

Obviously, there is a small problem with any of these suggestions: they all rely on the parties giving up some of their power. And the chances of them doing that are as slim as the part of Illinois's 4th congressional district that follows I-294 for purely constitutional reasons.

Conformity

Why do buses come in threes? Why do political parties generally have such similar policies? Why are there more Smiths in America than Millers, but more Müllers in Germany than Schmidts? Why is there a Starbucks on every corner? And, most pressingly, why do hipsters all look the same?

• •

THE MATHEMATICS BEHIND CONFORMITY AND CLUSTERING

In a fair and just world, English words would be evenly spread through the dictionary: there are 26 letters, so each letter deserves a little under 4% of the words. That is not the way it is though: the top five letters (T, A, S, H and W) together begin more than half of the words. The bottom half of the letters (X, Z, Q, K, J, V, U, Y, R, G, E, N, P and D) only begin 18.3% of words – compared with 16.6% starting with T alone. Why *aren't* the words uniformly distributed? There are many possible explanations – most of them linguistic rather than mathematical. For example, the easier a letter is to say to an English speaker, the likelier it is to start a word, and the more combinations a letter can appear in, the more common it is as an initial – S, for example, can be easily followed by C, E, H, I, K, L, M, N, O, P, Q, T, U, W or Y.

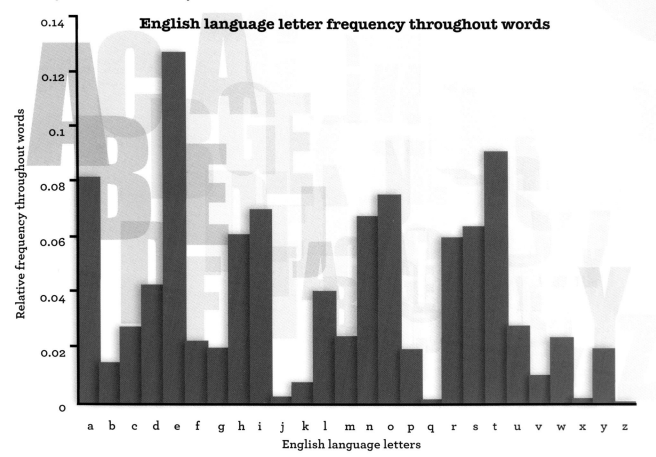

English language letter frequency throughout words

Relative frequency throughout words

English language letters

THE MATHEMATICS BEHIND THE SAME OLD POLITICS

"I don't vote," says my neighbour. "They're all the same." I sigh, deeply (some, I say, are significantly more awful than others), but recognize that there is an element of truth in what he says.

Let us start with a very simple model of politics. Everybody is somewhere on a spectrum of left-wing to right-wing (or liberal to conservative, or socialist to capitalist, as you prefer. The important thing is that there is a scale.) Each candidate has a set of policies that lie somewhere on that scale, and each voter votes for the candidate closest to his or her position. It might look something like the diagram above.

In an efficient system, the parties would be evenly spaced out across the political spectrum, but unfortunately, that is not the way things work. Imagine you are in charge of the Purple Party in the situation above. If you move your party's policies along the scale to the right, more people will consider you to be the closest party to their opinions. Similarly for the Orange Party,

moving policies to the left increases their share of the vote. This process repeats until the two parties (in principle) have virtually the same set of policies.

This simple model can be extended fairly easily to more than two parties and more than two dimensions (and even more complicated ideas than "vote for the closest party") with the same conclusion being reached every time: whenever you move towards the centre ground, you tend to pick up votes.

The only exception I know of is when ideologically fixed parties at the extremes gain some publicity. These parties are more interested in their position than in their popularity. In these cases, parties that had bunched up in the centre may begin to separate again in search of the fringe voters they are losing to the fixed parties. However, this effect is generally softened because most of the electorate tends to be fairly moderate; there is a trade-off between gaining a few voters at the extremes and potentially losing more voters in the centre.

Each candidate can appeal to more of the electorate by moving their position closer to their opponent's. This results in a tendency of candidates to have similar policies.

WHY IS THERE A STARBUCKS ON EVERY CORNER?

The same reasoning explains why gas stations or coffee shops tend to be clustered together. If customers tend to go to the nearest shop, the best place to start your shop is next door to the one that is there already, taking half of its customers. Of course, other effects come into play here too; if I have to walk halfway across town to get my cappuccino, walking next door is not going to make much difference to me! There is a gap between shops where the difference in convenience becomes a factor.

This is not why outlets of big chains tend to be close together; that is more of a dirty strategy. If you are a multi-million dollar megachain, you can afford to have the odd under-performing store for a while. So, if you open two new shops on the same block as an existing cafe, neither of them is likely to make much profit at first. However, the existing cafe will almost certainly take a hit – and, depending on its customer loyalty and profit margins – it is liable to go out of business. At which point, the big chain can close one of its stores (if it needs to) and be the only coffee retailer on the block.

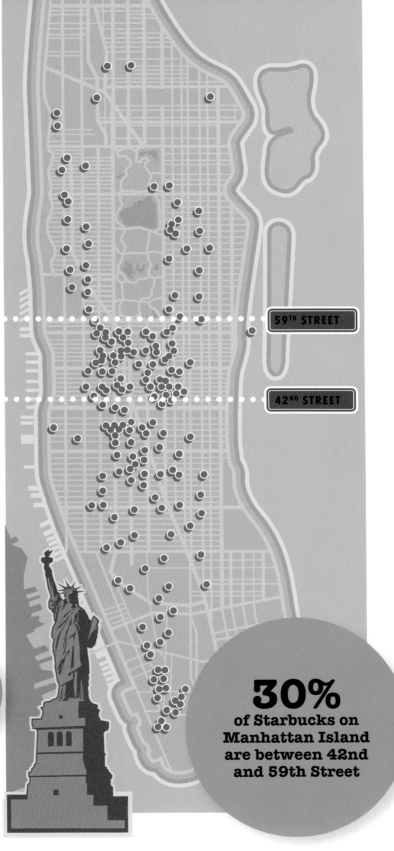

59TH STREET

42ND STREET

284 stores in Seoul

277 stores in New York

202 stores in London

30% of Starbucks on Manhattan Island are between 42nd and 59th Street

THE MATHEMATICS BEHIND MILLERS AND SMITHS

Suppose you have a population of 128 families with different surnames. Each family produces two offspring, each of whom marries someone from another family to form a new family. In a marriage in this population, one or other of the partners takes the other's surname – no double-barrelling here, I am afraid! What happens to the surnames?

Well, in the first generation, about a quarter of the surnames will die out completely. Half will now show up in just one family, and a quarter will now be in two families each. We are down to 96 names. **(Table 1)**

In the second generation, the one-family names will carry on in the same vein as before – a quarter will die out, half will be in one family, and a quarter will belong to two families. The two-family names are more interesting. For every 16, one will die out, four will belong to one family, six to two families, four to three families and one to four, and now we have only 78 names. **(Table 2)**

More interestingly, after just two generations, a quarter of the families share only ten of the original more-than-a-hundred names. The more families share a name, the more likely it is a) to survive into the next generation and b) grow. A one-family name has a 25% chance of growing, and 50% chance of remaining stable in numbers; by contrast, a ten-family name grows 41% of the time, and maintains its numbers 18% of the time. Even if it declines, it is a million-to-one shot that it will die out in the next generation.

These factors together mean that however the original population of surnames is arranged, some will come to predominate – typically the ones with higher numbers to begin with. If every medieval village had a forge but only some a mill, there will be more Smiths than Millers. If the tradition is to name families after people rather than jobs (Williams and Johnson, for example), the more common forenames become the most common surnames. The variations in naming traditions, jobs and even geography across different countries account for the differences in the distributions of surnames.

Table 1: First generation	
Names in two families	32
Names in one family	64
Extinct names	32

Table 2: Second generation		
Names in four families	2	(8 families in group)
Names in three families	8	(24 families in group)
Names in two families	28	(56 families in group)
Names in one family	40	(40 families in group)
Extinct names	40	(0 families in group)

WHY DO HIPSTERS ALL LOOK THE SAME?

To express their individuality, of course. They've been doing it since before it was cool.

DNA Testing

The computer in the forensics lab flashes up "MATCH CONFIRMED" and the absurdly good-looking and unflustered detectives high-five and say "we got him!" Another case closed by the magic of DNA testing.

But is it really so reliable? How can they be so sure that they have fingered the right perp? In reality, there is a bit more to it than that.

THE HUMAN GENOME

Every cell in your body contains DNA (deoxy-ribonucleic acid), an extremely complicated molecule made up of smaller molecules called *nucleotides*; there are four types of nucleotide in DNA: cytosine (usually denoted as just a C), guanine (G), adenine (A) or thymine (T).

DNA is arranged into structures called *chromosomes* and, in principle, if you had a sample of cells from someone's body, you could transcribe all of the nucleotides in each of the chromosomes and have a complete map of the human genome.

We do not usually do that (although the Human Genome Project did, it was a two-decade undertaking – and far too costly to do for every suspect). The full human genome would take about 6.5 billion characters to write it all down. For comparison, this book has only about 300,000 characters – your genetic book is 20,000 times as long, although it uses a smaller alphabet and is a less interesting read.

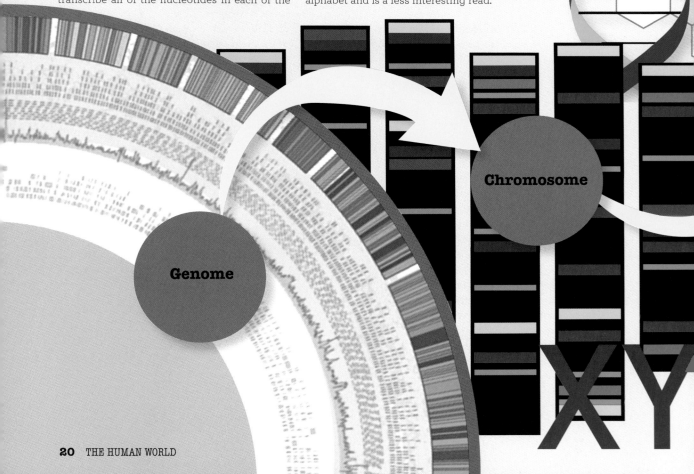

Genome

Chromosome

Crime scene match

| Crime scene |
| Suspect 1 |
| Suspect 2 |
| Suspect 3 |
| Suspect 4 |

Short tandem repeats (STRs)

THE GENETIC FINGERPRINT

Instead of comparing all of those billions of characters, a DNA test looks at a small number of regions of DNA with some useful properties:

they are "junk" DNA, part of the genetic code that does not have any obvious effect on development;

they have short strings of nucleotides that repeat over and over again – for example, TACATACATACATACA – known as short tandem repeats (STRs);

the number of times the strings repeat varies between people;

the number of STRs in one region does not affect the number of STRs in the other – they are *independent*.

If you are watching *CSI*, the DNA test is based on the FBI CODIS database, which uses 13 regions; if you are watching *Silent Witness*, they would use the UK standard of 10. In either case, the suspect's DNA is reduced to a sort of numerical fingerprint – simply the number of STRs in each of the regions.

THE PROBABILITY OF A RANDOM MATCH

Knowing the prevalence of a certain number of STRs in each location (it might be that 20% of people have ten STRs at one of the regions) and that these numbers are independent, you can not only compare the genetic fingerprint, but work out how likely it is that someone else shares it, simply by multiplying the probabilities together.

If 20% of the population shared the suspect's number of STRs at just one of the locations, the UK database would tell you that about one person in ten million has exactly the same fingerprint. The American test would call it a one in a billion chance.

$$\text{UK: } 0.2 \times 0.2 \times \ldots 0.2 = 0.2^{10} \approx 10^{-7}$$
$$\text{US: } 0.2^{13} \approx 10^{-9}$$

So, have we definitely caught the bad guy once the computer flashes its results? Sadly, it is not so simple. Because there is a risk of errors and contamination in the lab (not to mention identical twins and other long shots), the detectives would normally need more evidence before they could bring the case to trial.

Cheating

$$P(d) = \log_{10}(d+1) - \log_{10}(d) = \log_{10}\left(1 + \frac{1}{d}\right)$$

I think it is fair to say that none of us is 100% scrupulous all of the time – whether we kid ourselves that the traffic light had not *quite* turned red, or that the receipt was definitely for a justified business expense, or that it is OK to tell our toddlers that the favourite toy they left on the plane has gone off on an adventure and will be coming home to tell them all about it soon. Each of us has an idea of when it is OK to bend the rules a little bit.

Here I am not talking about bending the rules a little bit. I am talking about cheating of the flagrant and terrible sort, like copying someone else's essay, completely fabricating your accounts, or systematically altering your body chemistry in the pursuit of sporting glory. How can mathematics help catch the baddies?

HOW CAN YOU TELL IF SOMETHING IS PLAGIARIZED?

In the past it was easier for students to get away with copying their work off each other or using online essay-writing services. In those dark days, there were not too many tools to stop it. The poor graduate students marking the work were not paid enough to spot similarities between submissions, let alone check each handwritten document against the whole of the internet.

Luckily, today's essays are largely submitted electronically, and practical tools have been developed in the last couple of decades to make the grad student's life easier.

One of the most common tools is the *fingerprint*. Every document has a fingerprint, typically based on sequences of words called *n-grams*. For example, **(one, of, the, most)** is a 4-gram. You could list every sequence of four words in the document, and compare how many of the patterns match precisely or approximately with a reference collection of fingerprints. At its most basic, if more than a certain percentage of n-grams show up in an essay and a document elsewhere, the essay may warrant further scrutiny.

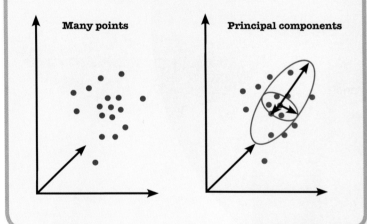

Principal component analysis is a technique used for finding the most useful vectors to describe a data set. At each iteration, the vector giving the largest variance is selected, subject to the condition that it is at right angles to any vectors already selected.

Many points

Principal components

Another smart example is citation analysis – checking the sequence, proximity and origin of references marked within the text. This gives an idea of structural plagiarism, rather than simply copying someone's work word for word.

The most interesting plagiarism-catching technique (mathematically speaking) is *stylometry*, which uses statistical methods to compare the style of one document to another – meaning that if a student's writing style in exam conditions is significantly different to their style in other submissions, there may again be cause

Stylometry: Marlowe–Shakespeare Word Frequency

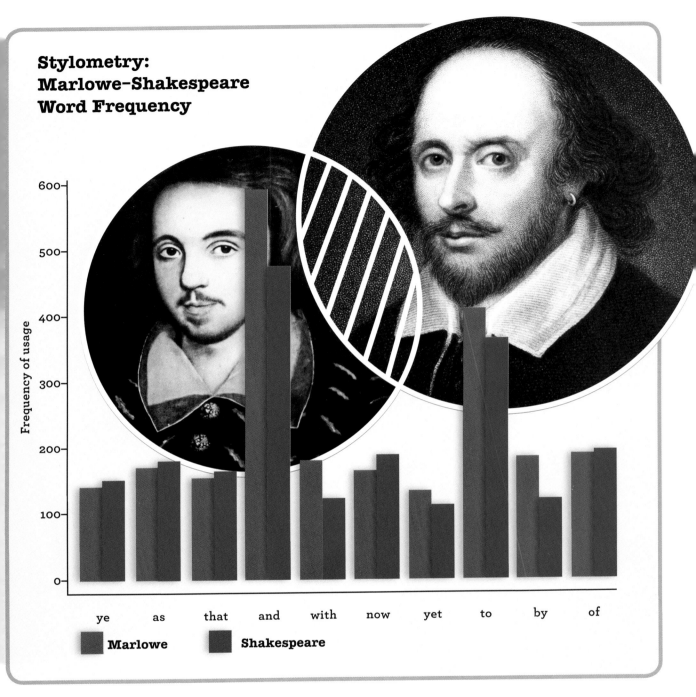

Frequency of usage

600 — 500 — 400 — 300 — 200 — 100 — 0

ye   as   that   and   with   now   yet   to   by   of

◼ **Marlowe**   ◼ **Shakespeare**

to investigate further. For example, the *writer invariant* technique considers the fifty most common words used by a writer. In each chunk of the document, those words are counted, giving an identifier of 50 numbers for each bit of text. The method then uses *principal component analysis* to find the plane of best fit for all of the identifiers; if the planes match up between two documents, it is very likely they share an author. Stylometry is a very neat trick, as it can also catch people who use essay-writing services, and hopefully prevent them from prospering.

Several stylometric analyses have suggested that some of Shakespeare's plays were at least co-authored with Christopher Marlowe.

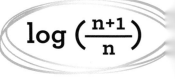

$$\log\left(\frac{n+1}{n}\right)$$

CAN YOU SPOT FAKE DATA?

Of course, it is not just in writing that cheating takes place. There is also a wide range of numerical fraud that mathematics can help catch. One of the simpler tools available is a process known as *Benford's Law*.

Take a large list of measurements – the only criterion is that the largest needs to be at least 100 times as large as the smallest. You might, for instance, pick the areas of the lakes in Michigan, of which Wikipedia lists about 200. The largest, Lake Superior, has an area of more than 20 million acres; the smallest listed right now is Lake Ligon, at 5 acres,

so it meets the criterion. Now, if you look at the first digit of each of the areas, you might expect to see about a ninth of the areas starting with 1, a ninth starting with 2, and so on. But that is not what you see at all: there are 29% starting with 1, 17% with 2, dropping down to only 5% of the areas beginning with 9.

Surprisingly, that is almost exactly what Benford's Law tells you to expect: in any naturally occurring data set, about 30% of the numbers will start with 1, 18% with 2, 13% with

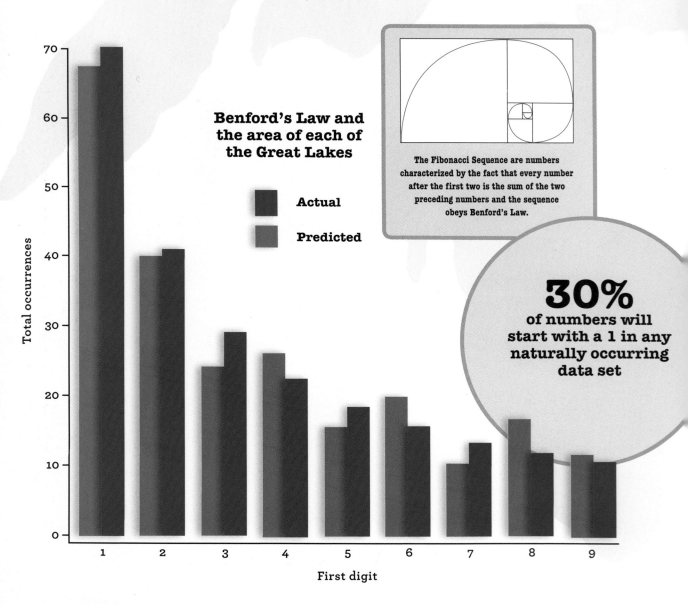

Benford's Law and the area of each of the Great Lakes

■ Actual
■ Predicted

The Fibonacci Sequence are numbers characterized by the fact that every number after the first two is the sum of the two preceding numbers and the sequence obeys Benford's Law.

30% of numbers will start with a 1 in any naturally occurring data set

Total occurrences (y-axis)

First digit (x-axis)

3 and so on. Mathematically, the probability of a number in such a list starting with n is $\log((n+1)/n)$. There is no simple explanation for why Benford's Law holds, although there are several complicated ones.

In any event, Benford's Law can also be used to detect fraud in several ways. For example, a forensic analysis of the macroeconomic data originally sent to the EU by the Greek government as it tried to join the Eurozone showed the hallmarks of made-up numbers. However, this did not come to light until much later, by which time the damage was done.

Similarly, the results of the 2009 Iranian general election do not obey Benford's Law as they should: for example, the number of votes in each precinct for fourth-placed candidate Mehdi Karroubi began with a 7 much more often than would be expected from a fair election. (In fairness, there were many other reasons to suspect fraud, including the number of cities in which more than 100% of the electorate voted, and a strong negative correlation between the number of invalid votes and the number of votes for the incumbent, Mahmoud Ahmadinejad, which is consistent with widespread ballot-stuffing.)

Cheats: Nations at the Rio 2016 Olympics with athletes serving doping suspensions indicated in red.

WHEN IS CHEATING WORTH THE RISK?

As we said earlier, everybody has a different idea of what constitutes serious misconduct and what constitutes bending the rules. A perfectly rational human would weigh up every decision as a balance between risk and reward: how much do I stand to gain from this? How much do I stand to lose if I get caught? What is the probability of getting caught?

If (reward) > (risk) × (probability), then ignore the rules; otherwise, follow them.

We are not perfectly rational, though. Most of us would not commit a crime, even if we knew we could get away with it. I do not have a good mathematical answer to why that is. It could be that there is a cost to breaking the rules, even if you are not caught. Perhaps social norms are a useful thing to keep society functioning after all.

War

The second half of the 20th century was characterized not by war, but by the threat of it. Both the USA and the Soviet Union had vast stockpiles of devastating nuclear weapons, and spent vast amounts on monitoring each other in case of a first strike. And both employed mathematicians to ensure they were adopting the optimal strategy.

● ●

The nuclear standoff resembles a classic problem from the relatively new field of *game theory*, known as the *Prisoner's Dilemma*.

Two criminals are arrested for a serious crime on flimsy evidence. If both stay silent, the police will only be able charge them with a minor offence, carrying a one-year prison term. If one incriminates the other, he will be freed while the other is imprisoned for 20 years. If each incriminates the other, they both get 15 years.

The *payoff matrix* for each of the prisoners looks like **Table 1**.

The best overall outcome for the pair is to remain silent (they end up with a total jail time of two years), but that is not what happens.

The first criminal reasons: if my accomplice incriminates me, I get a lighter sentence if I incriminate him also. If my accomplice stays silent, I also get a lighter sentence by incriminating him. So, whatever he does, my best choice is to incriminate. The accomplice reasons in the same way; both end up giving evidence against the other, and they end up with the *worst* possible outcome, spending a total of thirty years in jail.

The Prisoner's Dilemma relates to a one-off decision. The nuclear war problem relates to a decision made over and over again and that changes the logic. The *iterated* Prisoner's Dilemma problem does not have an analytical best solution. The best solution found in simulations is tit-for-tat: stick to the "nice" option until the other side picks the "nasty" option, then retaliate.

This is what the mathematicians on both sides realized: knowing that a first strike would meet with an immediate and devastating response, both refrained from attacking the other. The doctrine of *Mutually Assured Destruction* (the acronym is not accidental) prevented a nuclear war.

Russia: 7,000 nuclear weapons

USA: 6,000 nuclear weapons

China: 250 nuclear weapons

Table 1: The Prisoner's Dilemma and nuclear war. At first glance, the nasty option appears optimal.

	He incriminates me	He stays silent
I incriminate him	-15	0
I stay silent	-20	-1

Better option

	They attack us	They don't attack
We attack them	-15	0
We don't attack	-20	-1

Better option

Global nuclear arsenal

North Korea	<10
Israel	80–20
India	80–100
Pakistan	90–110
UK	225
China	250
France	300
USA	6,000
Russia	7,000

WHO WILL WIN A BATTLE?

If you are a general you want to make sure you only engage in battles you are likely to win. Surprisingly, it was not until World War I that Frederick Lanchester devised a simple set of formulas for predicting the outcome of a battle.

In hand-to-hand fighting, the bigger army almost always wins. *Lanchester's Linear Law* predicts that if the bigger army has B soldiers and the smaller army has S soldiers, then the bigger army will have B-S soldiers still standing when the smaller army is wiped out. An army twice as big is twice as powerful.

However, modern wars are not fought hand-to-hand. Instead, armies fire indiscriminately at each other and this dramatically increases the advantage for the larger army. Suppose the bigger army is twice the size of the smaller army: it has an attacking advantage (many guns firing on few enemies) and a defensive advantage (fewer guns firing on many comrades). In combination, this means an army twice as big is four times as powerful, and it turns out the number of soldiers still standing at the end of the battle is $\sqrt{B^2 - S^2}$. This is *Lanchester's Square Law*.

LANCHESTER'S LAWS

$$\frac{\partial B}{\partial t} = -\beta S \qquad B(0) = B_0$$

$$\frac{\partial S}{\partial t} = -\sigma B \qquad S(0) = S_0$$

where $\boldsymbol{\beta}$ is the bigger army's efficiency, and $\boldsymbol{\sigma}$ the smaller army's. B_0 and S_0 are the initial sizes of the armies. The ∂ symbols refer to partial derivatives – the rate of change of one variable with respect to the other. For example, $\partial B/\partial t$ is how the bigger army's size changes as time goes on.

1 In hand-to-hand combat the bigger army wins proportionally

2 In modern warfare an army twice as large has four times the power over the smaller force

Financial Meltdown

In the second half of September 2008, the banking world – which had been showing cracks for some time – fell apart. In the space of two weeks, a number of unexpected things happened.

$$\frac{1}{\sqrt{2\sigma^2\pi}}\, e^{-\frac{x-\mu}{2\sigma^2}}$$

Banking giants Lehman Brothers filed for bankruptcy, HBOS was forced into a merger with Lloyds TSB, Goldman Sachs and JPMorgan Chase left the field of investment banking, while two more banks, Wachovia and Washington Mutual, collapsed. Over the next few weeks, Iceland's banking sector simply stopped working as the three biggest banks went under; Fortis, a huge Belgian/Dutch/Luxembourg banking and finance company was partially nationalized; in Germany the Bundesbank had to help Hypo Real Estate, a Munich-based holding company; and even some Swiss banks had to be bailed out.

Nearly a quarter of a million Americans lost their jobs that October and the Dow Jones plummeted by more than a third in 2008. Argentina, Bulgaria, Estonia, Hungary, Latvia, Lithuania, Pakistan, Romania, Russia, Serbia, South Africa, Turkey and Ukraine were all in financial difficulties because they could not borrow money. Practically the entire world was in recession by the end of the year.

The reasons for the crash are complicated. In this section, I give a flavour of some of them.

HOW THE STOCK MARKET MOVES

In the early 1900s, the French mathematician Louis Bachelier suggested a relatively simple model for the movement of stock markets, based on the physical behaviour of gases known as *Brownian motion*. Bachelier's idea was that prices of stocks moved approximately at random, with the proportional amount they moved drawn from a *normal distribution*.

The normal distribution follows a distinctive bell-shaped curve which has the equation given at the top of this page. The parameters μ and σ are the mean – in this context, the most likely outcome – and the *standard deviation*, which is a measure of how wide the curve is. In financial terms, the mean represents your expected return from the stock, and the standard deviation represents the stock's *volatility* – a low volatility means a smooth and predictable curve, while a high volatility means wild swings up and down.

A stock with an annual expected return of 2% and a volatility of 1% would (in principle), increase by 1-2% about a third of the time, 2-3% about a third of the time, and suffer more extreme movements, in either direction, the remaining third of the time. In 19 years out of 20, the return would be between 0% and 4%.

Bachelier used this model to evaluate the price of *financial derivatives*, another key ingredient of the meltdown.

Sub-prime mortgage crisis

Global credit crunch

Global liquidity crisis

DERIVATIVES

The traditional way to invest in the stock market is to buy and sell shares in a company. However, it is not the only way.

Derivatives allow an investor to buy and sell rights, rather than assets. For example, a *put option* is an agreement giving its buyer the right (but not the obligation) to buy a specific stock for a specific price (the strike price) at a specific point in the future. If the stock price is higher than the strike price at maturity, the option owner exercises the option and gains the difference between the prices.

$$V(P,S,x) = \begin{cases} -x, & x < S \\ P-x & x \geq S \end{cases}$$

V is the return from a put option, P is the price of the underlying asset at maturity, S is the strike price and x is the price of the option.

Options are a powerful tool in several respects: for example, it is possible to use them as insurance against catastrophic drops in your assets' values, but more importantly, they allow you to benefit – or suffer – from fluctuations in a stock's value on a much greater scale. When you combine this with the practice of *leveraging* – borrowing to invest – gains and losses are magnified many times over.

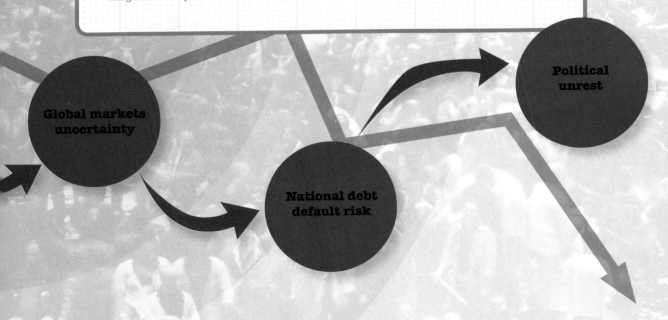

Global markets uncertainty

National debt default risk

Political unrest

THE BLACK–SCHOLES EQUATION

In 1973, Fischer Black and Myron Scholes developed a formula based on Bachelier's work that allowed for a rational way to price a derivative before its maturity. It is:

$$\frac{1}{2}\,\sigma^2 S^2 = \frac{\partial^2 V}{\partial S^2} + rS\,\frac{\partial V}{\partial S} + \frac{\partial V}{\partial t} - rV = 0$$

V is the unknown value of the derivative, *S* is the current price of the underlying asset, σ is the volatility, *r* is the risk-free interest rate and *t* is time. (Each ∂ means the rate of change of one variable with respect to another – so $\partial V/\partial t$ is how much the value changes per unit of time.)

This is not a simple formula – it is a second-order partial differential equation, and usually requires numerical methods to solve. As long as the underlying asset follows Bachelier's model – its expected return and volatility are constant – and a few other conditions are met, it is perfect, and even if they are only approximately met, it is still pretty good.

The trouble comes when the conditions are not met. In particular, when an asset stops following the normal distribution, things go very badly wrong.

INDEPENDENCE

When you take out a mortgage or a loan, your debt is usually packaged up with other loans and sold on to someone else. The principle is one of not keeping all of your eggs in one basket: if you own one loan with a certain probability of defaulting, you will either get all of the payments or there will be a default; if you own a fraction of many independent loans with similar default probabilities, you can give a much tighter *confidence interval* on your returns. In fact, the more loans in the package, the more it resembles a normal distribution, the less volatile an investment it ought to be, and the better a fit for the Black–Scholes equation (and similar models) it is.

Unfortunately, loan defaults are not independent events. This is especially true when talking about *sub-prime mortgages*, where the borrower has less than stellar credit and, in many cases, less than perfect understanding of the terms of their loan. In the early 2000s, sub-prime mortgages became increasingly prevalent, and were packaged in the same manner as other mortgages.

When the economy slowed down, there were suddenly huge numbers of people unable to make their payments – and the value of the derivatives based on the packaged mortgages was suddenly not just much lower, but not even well-defined. Not only were the losses enormous, nobody was quite sure *how* enormous.

Share prices in banks plummeted. Governments intervened in some cases, propping up the US mortgage backers Freddie Mac and Fannie Mae, but not in others, leaving the heavily leveraged Lehman to fail, and others like dominos behind it.

More to the point, when banks do not know how much they owe, it is impossible for other banks to trust them with loans. As a result, lending between banks came to a complete halt, and lending *from* banks practically stopped as well – the credit crunch – stopping the economy in its tracks.

Romance

Many modern couples meet online, saving their eyes the trouble of meeting across a smoky room, or however these things were done in the olden days. Aside from eliminating some of the awkwardness of dating, online dating sites have some pretty cool mathematics behind them.

• •

One such site is OkCupid. The people behind OkCupid were not the first to dream up using mathematics to help people find partners, of course, but the mathematics of romance is a relatively modern development. I now explore some of the problems of the heart that have been tackled as problems of the calculator.

FINDING A MATCH

When you sign up for OkCupid, you are asked to answer a selection of questions which could be anything from the very personal ("Have you ever cheated in a relationship?") to the extremely mundane ("Do you take sugar in your tea?"). Some are yes/no questions like these, others are multiple choice.

You do not just answer the question, though, you also say how you would prefer a potential partner to respond – which could be the same way ("What kind of movies do you prefer to watch?") or differently ("What's your least favourite household chore?") – and how important their response is to you.

To find out how good a match you are for someone, the site takes all of the questions you have both answered, and determines for each of you how happy the other's answers would make you. This is weighted by the importance you attach to each question: if your potential match has answered a "very important" question acceptably, they get 250 points; a "somewhat important" question counts for 10, "a little important" just 1 point, and "irrelevant", unsurprisingly, 0.

Online Dating Magazine estimates that there are over 2,500 online dating services in the US alone, with 1,000 services opening every year

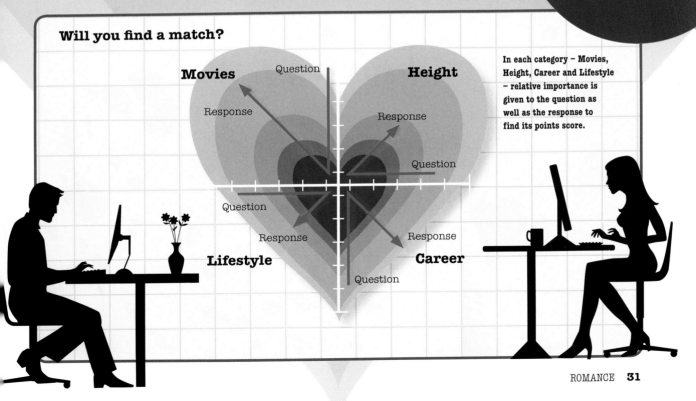

Will you find a match?

In each category – Movies, Height, Career and Lifestyle – relative importance is given to the question as well as the response to find its points score.

Movies
Question
Response
Height
Response
Question
Question
Response
Lifestyle
Career
Response
Question

Their score is simply the percentage of the total possible points they could have picked up. For instance, if they have answered a "very important" question well, a "somewhat important" question poorly and a "little important" question well, they would have scored 251 points out of a possible 261, or 96.2%.

To find the match percentage, their score and your score are multiplied together and square-rooted (this is known as the *geometric mean*). This figure tells you how well-matched you and the potential partner are.

Of course, there is a margin of error in such things. If you have only answered one common question that is "little important" to both of you, but both of your answers please the other, it is not likely that you are a 100% match. So, the computer subtracts a "reasonable margin of error", crudely worked out as 1/(the number of common questions you have answered) – so the match percentage OkCupid reports is somewhat on the conservative side.

It is just about the simplest thing that could possibly work – and, at least in some cases, it does!

33%
of people who use online dating services have never gone on a date

20%
of online daters get a friend to help with their profile

WHEN SHOULD I SETTLE DOWN?

A famous – although, as originally proposed, terrifyingly sexist – model of choosing a partner was mooted by the mathematician Merrill M Flood in 1949: suppose you have some number of potential matches, and are going to evaluate them one by one; at the end of each evaluation, you must either say "no" and lose your opportunity forever – potentially rejecting your perfect match, or "yes", and stop the search – potentially not even meeting the best candidate partner.

In this restricted version of dating, what is your best strategy for making decisions?

Surprisingly, it does not matter how the candidates are arranged or what the scoring system is, the strategy that maximizes your chances of saying "yes" to the ideal person is the same: give scores to the first roughly 37% of the candidates, and then pick the next person to beat the current best score.

If Jackson Browne was trying to decide between the seven women on his mind in his song *Take It Easy*, he ought to check out the first three (3/7 is about 43%), then accept the next person with the best score. A quick simulation shows that Jackson will make the correct choice about 40% of the time, a suboptimal choice 16% of the time, and die lonely about 42% of the time.

HOW LIKELY AM I TO MEET MY SOULMATE?

There is a school of thought that says there is one person, somewhere on the planet, who is your perfect soulmate, the one person you are destined to be with forever and ever.

Let us suppose that this idea is completely true: each person has one soulmate, the feeling is reciprocated, the attraction is immediate and obvious, and everyone spends their time searching the world for this special someone until they find them. How likely is it that you will ever meet them?

Let us suppose you can meet 100 people a day, every day, starting at your 18th birthday. How long would it take you to scope out all of the earth's 7,000,000,000 people?

(It could be that you are only interested in half of them. That's fine, there's nothing wrong with that.)

Well, you can estimate it with simple division: 7 billion people divided by 100 people a day is 70,000,000 days, which is about 200,000 years. It is not quite such bad news, though: you only need about 70% of that time to have a 50–50 chance of romantic success.

If everyone has a 1/70,000,000 chance of meeting their partner on any given day, though, only 100 romances would blossom every day, or a bit less than 40,000 per year. By contrast, 55 million people die each year. To keep the world's population constant, each of the lucky couples would need about 1,400 babies over their lifetimes.

HACKING OKCUPID

If you are of a particularly mathematical bent, like PhD student Chris McKinlay, you could turn your hand to hacking OkCupid to optimize your chances of finding true love.

You would need to find out what questions were important to people in your target demographic – which, if you are a mathematician, you can do with a bit of programming. However, you would need to avoid looking like a robot (several of his test accounts were quickly closed down). You would need to figure out what might appeal to that kind of person (McKinlay used text-mining to find clusters of women with similar interests: artistic twenty-somethings and professional creatives were the groups he found most interesting) and optimize your profile to highlight things you would expect to appeal to them. You would need to look at their profiles systematically, so they would be notified of your existence (again, a clever script could do this for you).

And then you would have to go out on dates and meet people. For McKinlay, it was date 88 before he met The One, which probably goes to show that the most important mathematical skill is not cleverness, but perseverance.

Couples who meet online are three times more likely to divorce

The Natural World

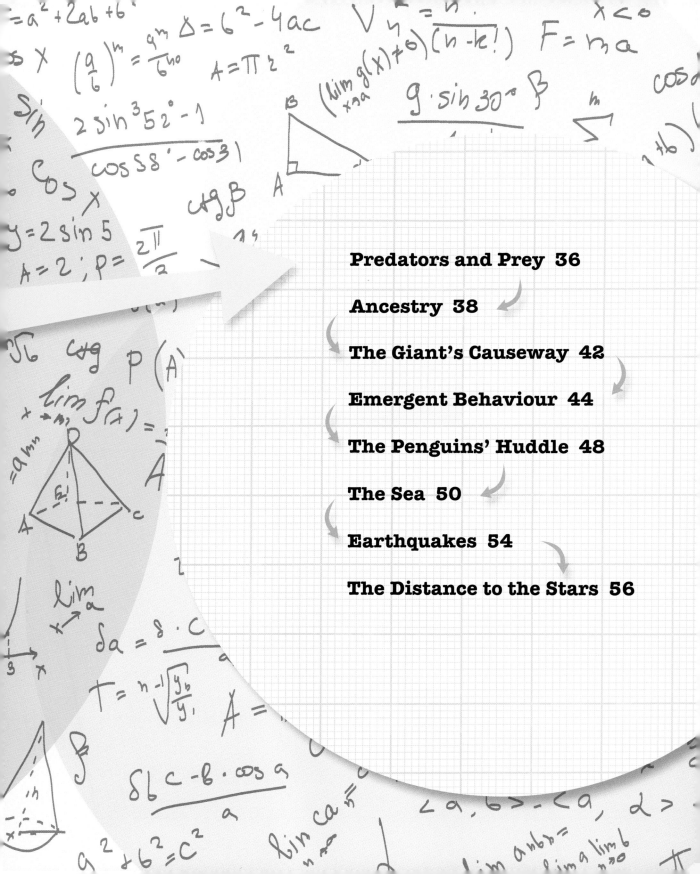

Predators and Prey

$$pG-q\ln(G)+sL-r\ln(L)=k$$

Throughout nature, there are examples of predators and prey: lions and gazelles, owls and mice, whales and plankton, to name but a few. We will look at some of the ways the populations interact.

One approach for examining this interaction is the *Lotka–Volterra* model, which makes some sensible simplifying assumptions about the predators and prey:

The predator population increases when a predator catches some prey; the probability of this happening is proportional to the product (multiplication) of the populations.

However, too many predators means there are fewer prey to go around, so the population decreases in proportion to itself.

The prey population decreases every time a predator catches one of them.

It also increases in proportion to itself by way of breeding.

Mathematically, the system can be written as a pair of coupled differential equations – let us use lions and gazelles as our animals, and call their populations L and G, respectively:

$$dL/dt=pLG-qL$$

$$dG/dt=rG-sGL$$

where p, q, r and s are constants that depend on the specific situation.

These equations are tricky to solve analytically for L and G as a function of time

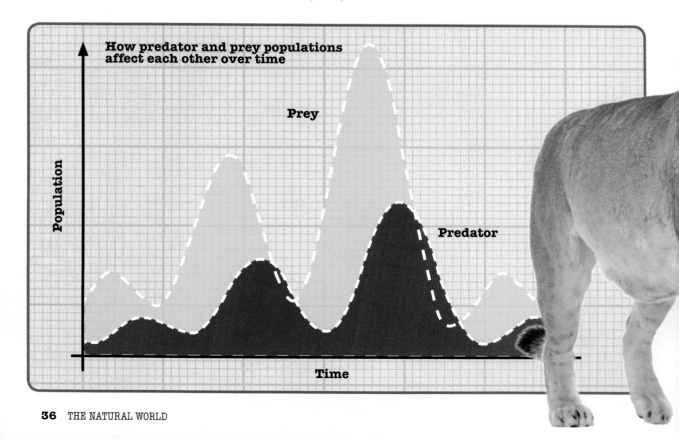

How predator and prey populations affect each other over time

Population

Prey

Predator

Time

– except in certain special cases, you cannot write down an explicit solution for the lion or gazelle population at a future point in time – although you can solve them numerically using computer simulations to get an approximate answer. You find that the predator and prey populations periodically increase and decrease – with peaks and troughs somewhat out of phase with each other. When there are large numbers of gazelles, the lion population increases – at which point, the gazelle population begins to drop. Now there is a comparative shortage of food for the lions, and their population drops in turn. With fewer lions around, the gazelle population begins to grow, and the situation returns to where we started.

What you *can* do analytically is find how the populations change with respect to each other: they satisfy the equation

$$pG - q\ln(G) + sL - r\ln(L) = k$$

for a constant k that depends on the initial values of G and L.

We can plot these equations on a *phase plane diagram*, showing what happens for various initial values. The populations follow closed curves, meaning that for any initial value, the model predicts that the populations will eventually return to those values.

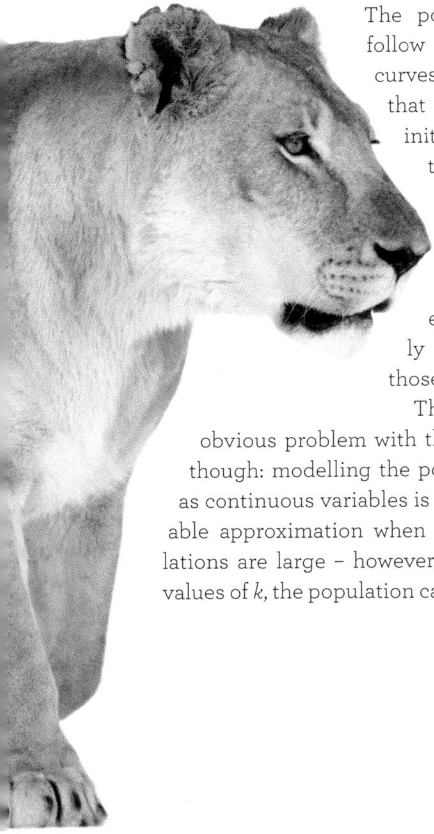

There is an obvious problem with this model, though: modelling the populations as continuous variables is an acceptable approximation when the populations are large – however, for some values of k, the population can become extremely small. Below 100 individuals, for example, there is very little chance of recovery in the real world; below 2, the chances of recovery are effectively zero – but the model says populations should rebound, even when populations reach tiny fractions of an animal. This discrepancy between what the model predicts and what would happen in reality is known as the *atto-fox problem*.

One way around this is to add a small random error term to the equations – in situations where the populations are large, the solutions are very similar to those discussed above; when populations become small, the solutions can easily "jump" to another curve – in likelihood, one where small populations remain small.

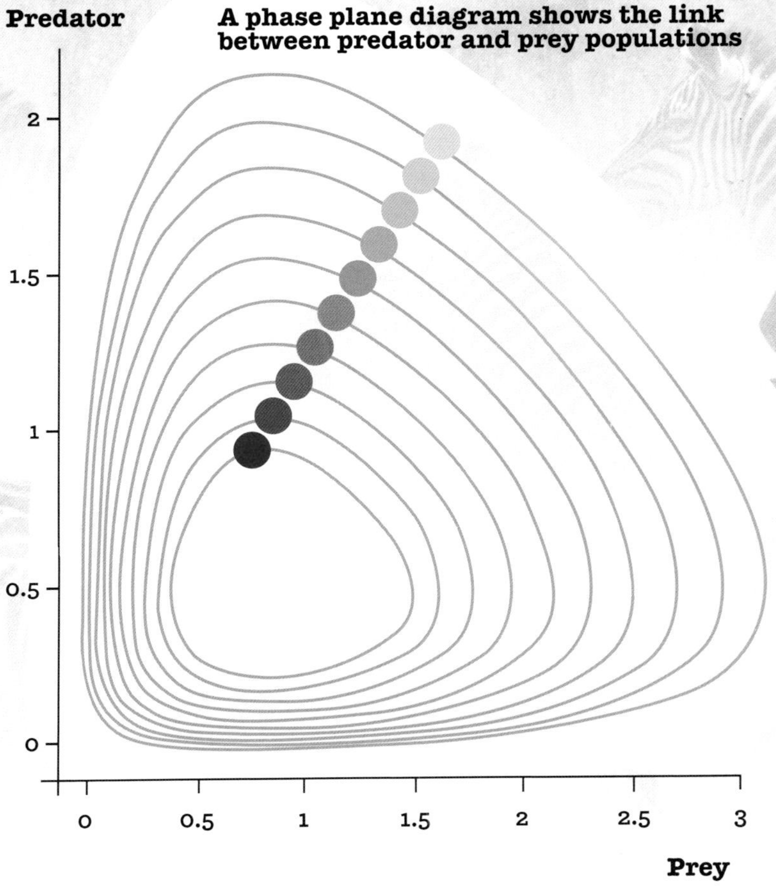

A phase plane diagram shows the link between predator and prey populations

Predator

Prey

With different initial numbers of predator and prey, the populations fall into different cycles.

Ancestry

$$P_t = 7.5 \times 10^9 e^{-\frac{t}{300}}$$

How can something as perfect as a mathematician evolve by chance alone? A famous creationist argument that life cannot possibly have evolved goes something like this: the probability of all of the elements of cellular life assembling in the correct order is roughly the same as that of a tornado sweeping through a junkyard and assembling a Boeing 747.

On the face of it, the argument has some merit: cellular life depends on at least 2,000 enzymes being thrown together, each of which is in itself wildly improbable – each enzyme has something on the order of 1,000 amino acids linked together in order. Fred Hoyle (who originated the junkyard tornado argument) suggested that the probability of it all coming together was something like 1 in $10^{40,000}$, which is a tiny number – something in the order of winning the lottery every week for 100 years.

Fortunately, that is not how evolution works: Hoyle might as well have calculated the probability of a tornado sweeping through a haystack and assembling a straw man. What Hoyle has worked out is the probability of the ingredients for life being put together in one place, completely at random, first time lucky.

Instead, it is a gradual and cumulative process: over many years of continual mixing, the mixtures that tend to stick together hang around longer than those that do not; the mixtures that tend to persuade other chains into the same shape tend to predominate; and so on over time, each slight increment in a tendency to survive propagating. And these mixtures are taking place all over the earth, all at the same time. There is an enormous number of evolutionary "experiments" all going on at once.

Moreover, to take Hoyle's analogy further, a 747 is not the only option for a flying machine: there are infinitely many variations on airplanes, any of which would have been just as remarkable.

As statistician R A Fisher is reported to have said, natural selection is a mechanism for generating extremely small probabilities.

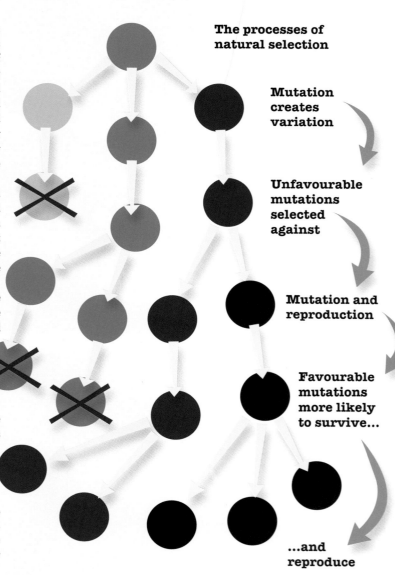

The processes of natural selection

Mutation creates variation

Unfavourable mutations selected against

Mutation and reproduction

Favourable mutations more likely to survive...

...and reproduce

THE HARDY–WEINBERG PRINCIPLE

In a simple population, it is possible to model the probabilities of various genetic make-ups using the *Hardy–Weinberg Principle*, named after mathematician G H Hardy (one of the central characters in the film *The Man Who Knew Infinity*) and biologist Wilhelm Weinberg, who discovered it independently.

If a gene location has two possible *alleles*, call them **A** and **a**, which occur with probabilities P and p (respectively), the probability of having a genotype of **AA** is P^2. Similarly, the probability of having a genotype of **aa** is p^2, while the probability of having a genotype of **Aa** is $2Pp$, because **Aa** and **aA** are the same, so far as we know.

Why is this useful? It can help estimate the prevalence of carriers of a genetic disorder such as cystic fibrosis. In populations of North European descent, the probability of a child being born with CF is about one in 3,000. Because it is a recessive trait, this corresponds to having both alleles in the genotype the same, so $p^2 = 0.0003$ – which means p is the square root of that, roughly 0.018. So, according to the Hardy–Weinberg principle, roughly 1 in 54 people carry the corresponding gene. (Research suggests it is about 1 in 25, which is not all that far off: it is in the "few per cent" range.)

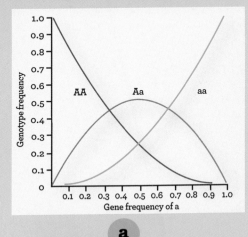

Genotype AA
Non-carriers who neither suffer nor pass on

Non-sufferers who could pass on

Non-sufferers who could pass on

$\dfrac{1}{3,000}$
sufferers

HOW CLOSELY RELATED ARE WE?

If you drew out your family tree, you would notice a pattern in the numbers of your biological ancestors: you have two parents, four grandparents, eight great-grandparents, and so on, doubling each time. Supposing generations start about 25 years apart, you can estimate the number of ancestors of your age you have at any point in the past as $2^{y/25}$, with y being the number of years ago. For example, 100 years ago, your sixteen great-great-grandparents would have been roughly your age.

If we go back 750 years, this model says you would have a little more than a billion ancestors of your age. However, there is a problem with that: most estimates of the world population in the 11th century put it at around 300 million. Where did all your extra ancestors go?

There is one key difference between the model and reality: it assumes that your ancestors are all distinct individuals, which is evidently not the case (Albert Einstein, to pick a famous example, married his cousin, meaning their children would have had six great-grandparents rather than eight).

This complicates the model dramatically, especially as you go further back: the more ancestors you have, the more likely they are to be the same person.

A fairly naive model of ancestry takes the world population to be exponential

$$P_t = 7.5 \times 10^9 e^{-\frac{t}{300}}$$

where t is the number of years ago and the number of ancestors at time t is double the number of ancestors in the previous generation, adjusted for the probability of two of them being the same person:

$$A_t = 2A_{t-25} \left(1 - e^{-\frac{P_t}{2A_{t-25}}}\right)$$

This is not simple to solve analytically. However, numerically, it turns out that the proportion of the world population who are also your ancestors remains below 1% until about 600 years ago, and then increases quickly to 35% at 700 years ago, and 80% at 800 years ago, where it stays in the long term. (The other 20% have lines which die out. If someone alive in the 1200s has descendants alive today, it is almost certain you are one of those descendants.)

The model has several weaknesses. One is that it assumes each partnership is selected completely at random from the entire global population – ignoring that historically, people have tended to select mates from nearby and to live close to their families. It also fails to take into account age differences: generations are nothing like as well separated as the model makes out!

However, it is a fair first effort for estimating how related two random people are. If you each have A ancestors out of a population of P, you expect to have A^2/P of them in common; using that as the mean of a *Poisson distribution*, you would need to go back 300 years (12 generations) to have a more than 1% chance of having a common ancestor, but going back 400 years would give you nearly 90%. Under the model's assumptions, you and a random stranger anywhere on the planet are likely to share an ancestor from the 1600s.

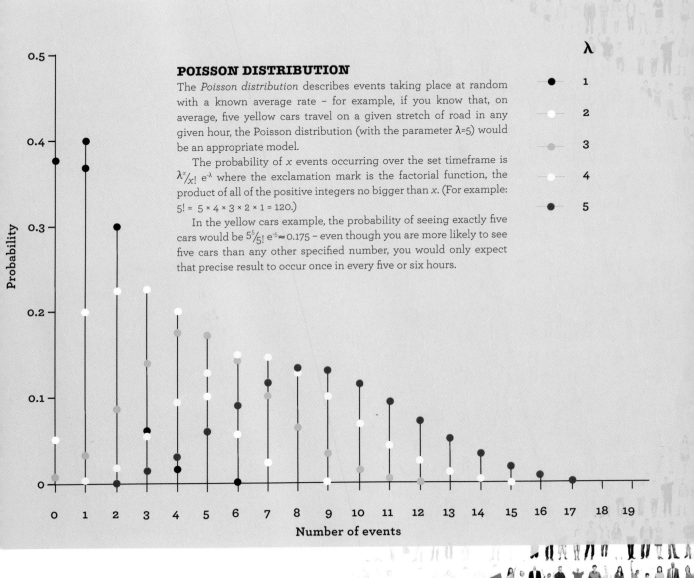

POISSON DISTRIBUTION

The *Poisson distribution* describes events taking place at random with a known average rate – for example, if you know that, on average, five yellow cars travel on a given stretch of road in any given hour, the Poisson distribution (with the parameter λ=5) would be an appropriate model.

The probability of *x* events occurring over the set timeframe is $\lambda^x/x! \; e^{-\lambda}$ where the exclamation mark is the factorial function, the product of all of the positive integers no bigger than *x*. (For example: 5! = 5 × 4 × 3 × 2 × 1 = 120.)

In the yellow cars example, the probability of seeing exactly five cars would be $5^5/5! \; e^{-5} \approx 0.175$ – even though you are more likely to see five cars than any other specified number, you would only expect that precise result to occur once in every five or six hours.

λ
● 1
○ 2
● 3
○ 4
● 5

Probability

0.5
0.4
0.3
0.2
0.1
0

Number of events

0 1 2 3 4 5 6 7 8 9 10 11 12 13 14 15 16 17 18 19

The Giant's Causeway

According to legend, the Scottish giant Benandonner challenged the Irish giant Finn MacCool to a fight, and Finn built a path across the Irish Sea to enable the two of them to have it out. The geological account is a bit less rich in storytelling.

Around 50 million years ago, volcanic activity around what is now County Antrim in Northern Ireland pushed molten basalt through the chalk beds. As the lava cooled, it contracted and cracked, leaving behind it tall, mainly hexagonal pillars of rock. A similar process on the Scottish side of the sea led to the idea that the pillars had once been linked – and hence the name "The Giant's Causeway."

Mathematicians obviously do not care about the giants – we care about the hexagons. Why that shape?

The answer is: it is all to do with energy. Researchers at the Dresden Institute of Technology, led by Martin Hoffman, simulated the behaviour of lava as it cools, more quickly at the exposed surface than below. As lava cools, it usually contracts in a way that releases as much energy as possible. On the surface, it turns out that the most efficient mechanism is to crack at a 90 degree angle, making for rectangular columns, spread at random across the lava field. However, as the cooling permeates further into the forming rock, the most efficient angle for cracking widens to 120 degrees, making hexagonal structures.

2.31 perimeter-to-area ratio of hexagons

Random cracks

4 perimeter-to-area ratio of squares

6.93 perimeter-to-area ratio of triangles

VORONOI DIAGRAMS

Suppose you want to split up a land mass, apportioning each block of land to the nearest big city. You would create something called a Voronoi diagram, named after Georgy Fedosievych Voronyi, who studied them in the 1900s, but which were discovered long before (perhaps by René Descartes). Given enough randomly scattered points, the Voronoi cells turn out (in most cases) to be predominantly hexagons, although other shapes are often found, and the hexagons themselves are only close to regular if the "big city" reference points are quite regularly spaced.

A Voronoi diagram was famously used by physician John Snow to track down the source of a cholera outbreak in London in 1854. Using the locations of water pumps as the reference points, he showed that the vast bulk of the victims of the epidemic had the same pump, on Broad Street, as their closest water source (this was in a time before the general acceptance of germ theory; the idea that cholera was caused by something in the water was considered outrageously disgusting). The authorities, faced with the evidence, removed the handle of the pump to put it out of use, and the outbreak petered out.

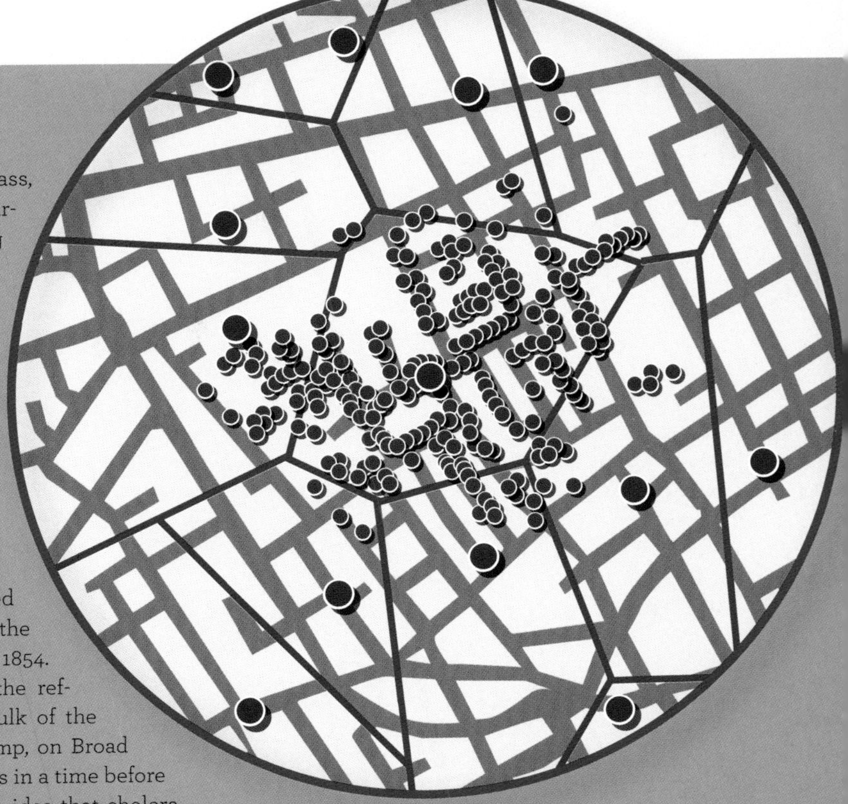

Why is this the most efficient mechanism? Hexagons have several properties that make them good candidates:

Random cracks spreading downwards through a rock tend to meet in threes, and symmetry arguments suggest that equal angles in these triads would be most efficient. If you stick 120 degree angles together, you end up with hexagons.

Relatedly, hexagons tessellate nicely; of the regular shapes that tessellate (triangles, squares and hexagons), hexagons are the most circular, giving them the greatest perimeter-to-area ratio – meaning they cool down most quickly.

Even without Hoffmann's detailed model, hexagons make sense: a simpler model would suggest that each drop of lava eventually joins up with the nearest cool point on the surface. In this case, the structure follows a *Voronoi diagram*, which has a tendency to form hexagons.

You are probably wondering what happened in the fight. The story I heard is that MacCool, realizing Benandonner was *huge*, even for a giant, had his wife dress him up as a baby. When Benandonner saw the size of the "young" MacCool, he reckoned that the boy's dad must be ENORMOUS – so he hot-footed it back to Scotland, tearing up the causeway as he fled. A little bit of game theory to finish things off!

Emergent Behaviour

$$x_{n+1} = 4x_n(1-x_n)$$

Simple rules can cause complicated behaviour. Things like a community of ants, artificial life and even unpredictable weather events emerge from models that seem trivial. But can a butterfly really cause a hurricane?

A computer can, in essence, only do a handful of things: read and write 1s and 0s into a storage system, convert inputs into 1s and 0s, and convert 1s and 0s into output. Apart from the input/output element, the sophisticated piece of hardware on which I am writing a book, listening to music and occasionally talking to friends around the world on Twitter, follows pretty much the same rules as Turing's hypothesized universal machine from the 1930s. And it can *annihilate* me at pretty much any game it likes.

THE MATHEMATICS BEHIND CAUSING A HURRICANE

When many science journalists hear a complicated argument, they feel the need to distill it down to something that is simpler. And, in many cases, wrong.

The myth of "butterflies cause hurricanes" came from just this kind of simplification of a much more interesting result: the story goes that

Edward Lorenz was studying a simple computerized weather model, which was giving lovely results. He stopped it for some reason, dutifully typed the values back into the system, and started it up again... and instead of nice seasonal patterns, the weather went absolutely haywire. Droughts, blizzards and hurricanes everywhere.

It turned out that the printout he had typed the values in from had rounded them to a few decimal places, losing a small amount of accuracy. When Lorenz calculated the effect of this, it turned out to be a discrepancy about as large as a beat of a butterfly's wings halfway around the world.

It is not that butterflies cause hurricanes, it is that the weather system is incredibly sensitive to its initial conditions, and a small adjustment can lead to enormous consequences. This is the foundation of *chaos theory*, one of the 20th century's more important mathematical breakthroughs.

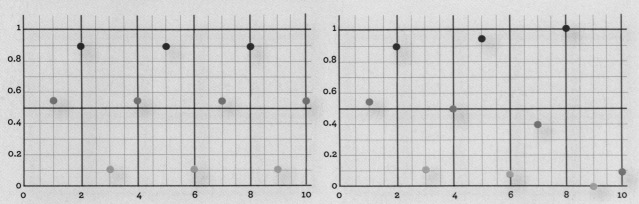

Chaos: critical dependence on initial conditions

Putting the value $x_0 = \sin^2(2\pi/7) \approx 0.6113$ into the formula $x_{n+1} = 4x_n(1-x_n)$ gives a regular, repeating pattern.

Putting $x_0 = 0.61$ instead makes the pattern completely unpredictable after about 10 iterations.

THE MATHEMATICS OF CHAOS

If the weather system is so chaotic, how can it be predicted at all? Well, I can look out of my window, spot that my neighbour's flag is billowing out towards the west, and over in the east there are some enormous and extremely dark clouds: I can forecast with some confidence that there is rain on the way. Over the short term, things behave more or less as they should. It is the "more or less" that is the problem. If I am tracking (let us say) a storm, and know that my model can predict where it'll be in one hour to within 2% of the distance travelled, that is fine for the first few hours. A five-hour forecast would be off by about 10%, which might be enough to say "Miami is unlikely to be affected overnight." The trouble comes when I try to do a one-day forecast: my error is now more than 250%, and pretty much useless.

In technical terms, a chaotic system has three properties:

It is extremely sensitive to initial conditions.
It is topologically mixing.
It has dense periodic orbits.

We have looked at the sensitivity aspect, but that is not enough on its own: for example, if you invest $10,000 over 30 years and get an 8% annual return, you will end up $1,500 better off than if you only got 7.5% – that half a per cent makes a large difference, but it is entirely predictable and not at all chaotic.

Topologically mixing means, in effect, that practically any situation can lead (eventually) to any other situation – and, more strongly, that any group of similar situations will eventually lead to any other group of similar situations. In weather terms, even if it is 40 below and blowing a gale, at some point in the future, you will end up being able to sit outside drinking margaritas in your Hawaiian shorts.

The phrase *dense periodic orbits* is a bit tougher: that means that, whatever conditions you are in, there is a nearby state that leads to a predictable, cyclic state (such as, say, snow today, rain tomorrow, then gorgeous sunshine, a windy day and back to snow, repeating every four days). Because of sensitivity, you are almost certainly not in such a cycle, but there is a very similar set of circumstances that is – remember, though, that the difference between states is butterfly-wing-flap wide!

Surprisingly simple-looking systems display chaotic behaviour: in as few as three dimensions, a setup such as:

$$dx/dt = s(y\text{-}x)$$

$$dy/dt = (r\text{-}z)x - y$$

$$dz/dx = xy - bz$$

(where s, r and b are constants) can lead to chaos.

THE MATHEMATICS BEHIND ARTIFICIAL LIFE

If simple rules lead to complex behaviour, does that mean you can program unpredictable things? Well, if you have ever tried coding, you will know that *every* program does unpredictable things, but I know that is not what we are talking about. The answer, unsurprisingly, is "of course you can."

One of the first such programs was John Horton Conway's *Game of Life* (not to be confused with the board game of the same name). You start with a rectangular grid of arbitrary size, and each cell on the grid follows certain rules, depending on the status of its eight neighbours (including diagonally):

For an empty cell, if three of its neighbours are full, it becomes full; otherwise it remains empty.

For a full cell, if two or three of its neighbours are full, it remains full; otherwise it becomes empty.

Most starting configurations are fairly dull, either dying out or settling down into stable patterns like the boat, the block, the beehive or the loaf, or oscillators like the blinker or the toad. However, others are more interesting. Every so often you come across a structure that repeats as it moves – a glider or a spaceship – and in some cases, you can find structures that create or destroy gliders.

If you are persistent, you can combine these structures to build computers, and even computers that can play the *Game of Life*. And if you were really persistent, you could build structures in that *Game of Life*...

It might be more interesting, though, to play with the rules: what happens if the conditions for life change? What happens if there are more than two states? What if you change the shape of the cells so they are hexagonal or some other combination of shapes? What happens if you change the topology of the board and play on a Möbius strip or a donut? How about in three dimensions? The possibilities are endless.

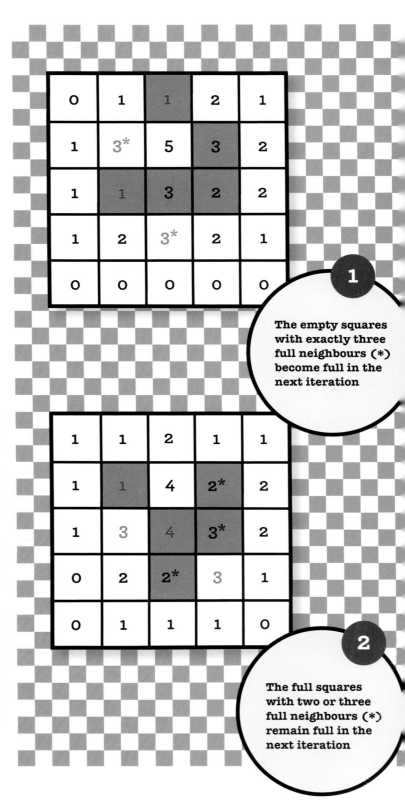

1 The empty squares with exactly three full neighbours (*) become full in the next iteration

2 The full squares with two or three full neighbours (*) remain full in the next iteration

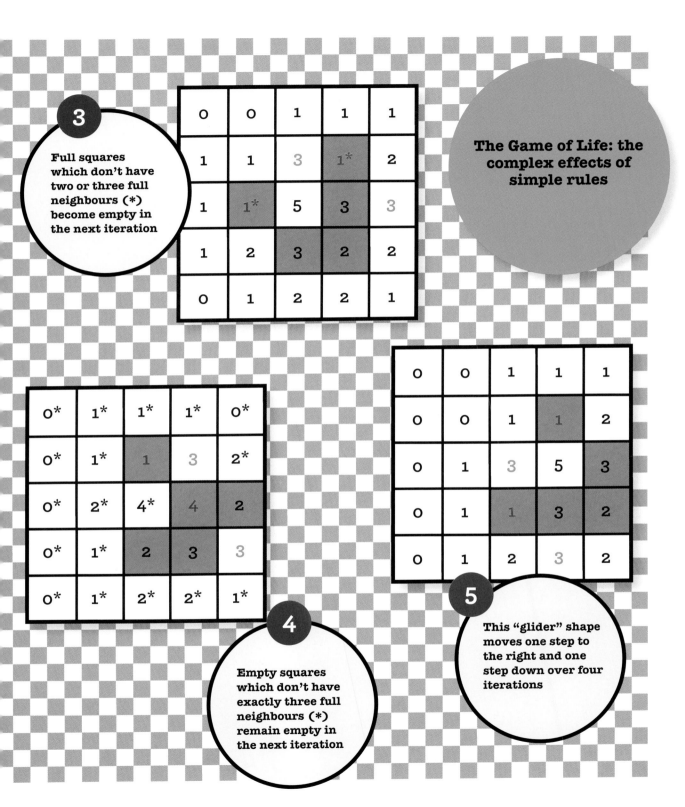

3

Full squares which don't have two or three full neighbours (*) become empty in the next iteration

0	0	1	1	1
1	1	3	1*	2
1	1*	5	3	3
1	2	3	2	2
0	1	2	2	1

The Game of Life: the complex effects of simple rules

0*	1*	1*	1*	0*
0*	1*	1	3	2*
0*	2*	4*	4	2
0*	1*	2	3	3
0*	1*	2*	2*	1*

4

Empty squares which don't have exactly three full neighbours (*) remain empty in the next iteration

0	0	1	1	1
0	0	1	1	2
0	1	3	5	3
0	1	1	3	2
0	1	2	3	2

5

This "glider" shape moves one step to the right and one step down over four iterations

The Penguins' Huddle

Antarctica. The world's most hostile environment. In the depths of winter, the temperature rarely rises above –20° celsius in the never-ending darkness.

$$W = 20\,Pe$$

Alone, no penguin would survive any length of time; instead, the male emperor penguins form an enormous huddle while the females have sensibly gone to sea to hunt, leaving their partners to guard and warm the eggs.

Huddling tightly together is mathematically astute because it reduces the surface area of penguins exposed to the elements. This is excellent if you are in the middle of the huddle, but not so great if you are at the edge. So how do the most exposed penguins survive?

The average mathematician would tell you straight away that the best shape for a huddle is a circle: it is the shape with the smallest perimeter, given a certain area. However, it is only ideal if there is no wind. If you are in an environment with hundred-mile-per-hour gusts,

like Antarctica, wind chill becomes a factor, and this causes the circle to stretch out.

Many models suggest that a huddle of penguins ought to look like a cigar, but according to Francois Blanchette, an applied mathematician from UC Merced, that does not reflect the reality he has observed from the careful watching of penguin movies.

Luckily, because he is an applied mathematician, he has tools he can use to approach the problem. He created a model where each penguin tries at each moment to move to a warmer spot – those most exposed to the wind at the front of the huddle move to more sheltered spots downwind, while the luckier, more central ones have no incentive to move: there is little room to waddle in the middle of the

Emperor penguins use thick layers of body fat and feathers to keep warm. These layers are such effective insulators that large parts of the surface of a penguin are even colder than the ambient Antarctic conditions.

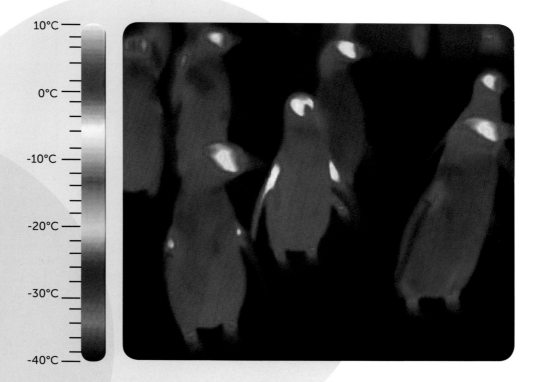

10°C

0°C

-10°C

-20°C

-30°C

-40°C

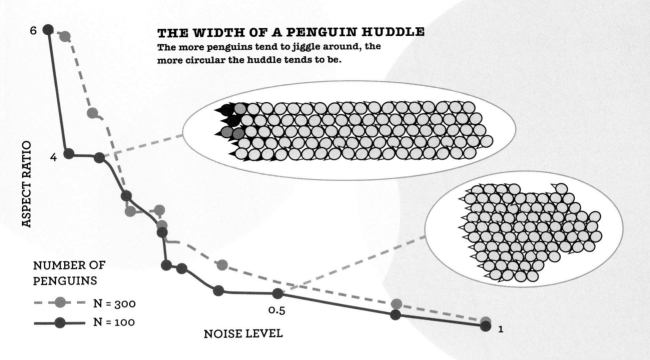

THE WIDTH OF A PENGUIN HUDDLE
The more penguins tend to jiggle around, the more circular the huddle tends to be.

ASPECT RATIO

6

4

NUMBER OF
PENGUINS

— ● — ● — N = 300

——●—— N = 100

0.5

NOISE LEVEL

1

model huddle. However, as the penguins at the front peel off, these penguins find themselves getting progressively closer to the wind.

His original result was a huddle agreeing with previous simulations – long, thin bands of unrealistic penguins. The width of the shape depends on the *Péclet number* (Pe), which is the ratio between thermal energy lost to convection and that lost to conduction – if Pe is small, it is important to minimize the perimeter, so the huddle is nearly circular; if it is larger, it is more important to reduce the number of penguins facing the wind, so you get a longer, thinner huddle.

The shape also depends on the number of penguins in the huddle: for small numbers of penguins, it may be that keeping as close together as possible is more beneficial than getting the best cross-section; for larger numbers, the shape settles down to a characteristic aspect ratio, still depending on Pe.

Blanchette's breakthrough was to add noise to the heat loss function for each penguin – if some feel colder than others, the simulated penguins form huddles that look much more like the ones in real life: just slightly on the oval side of circular, with the occasional gap forming in the interior.

This leads to a surprisingly fair outcome: even though each penguin is behaving entirely selfishly by trying to avoid the cold, the whole group shares the heat loss nearly evenly.

There is still room for improvement in the model – experts point out that there are fewer gaps in the model than there are in real life – but it gets many of the other key features of a huddle correct.

TURTLE FORMATION
Penguins exposed to the wind at the front of the huddle tend to take up less cold positions further downwind.

Wind

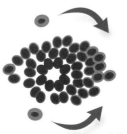

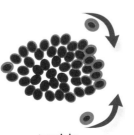

Lead colder penguins detach   and move round the huddle   to rejoin   at the rear

The Sea

$$\left(\frac{m_m}{m_s}\right) \div \left(\frac{d_m}{d_s}\right)^3$$

Mathematics and the sea have been linked since the first time someone on the coast realized there were roughly two high tides for every sunrise. The challenge of navigating vast bodies of water has been a major inspiration, and source of funding, for mathematicians for as long as there have been mathematicians – from crude maps, to astrolabes, to GPS.

We are going to look at the geometry of navigation, the length of the coastline and where the tides come from.

TIDES

There are two major causes for the tides: one is the Moon (which is quite small, astronomically speaking, but also not very far away), and the other the Sun (which is very big, but comparatively distant). But which has the bigger effect?

The answer is in Newton's *Principia*: the Sun does make a contribution to the tides, but it's rather smaller than the Moon's. We can check this by comparing the acceleration due to each body.

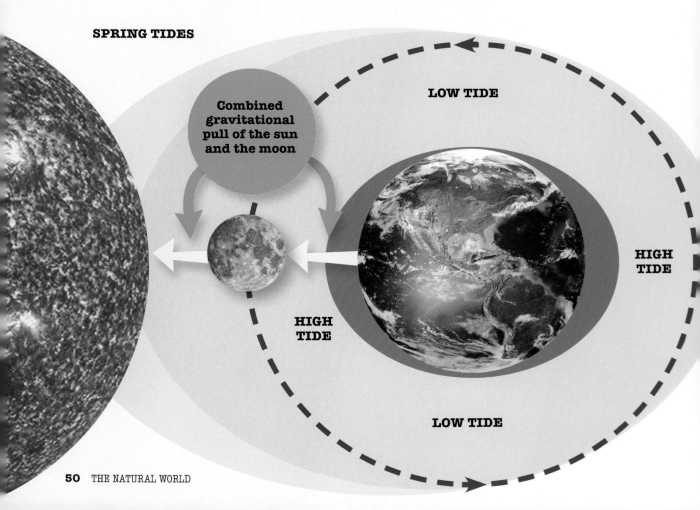

SPRING TIDES

LOW TIDE

Combined gravitational pull of the sun and the moon

HIGH TIDE

HIGH TIDE

LOW TIDE

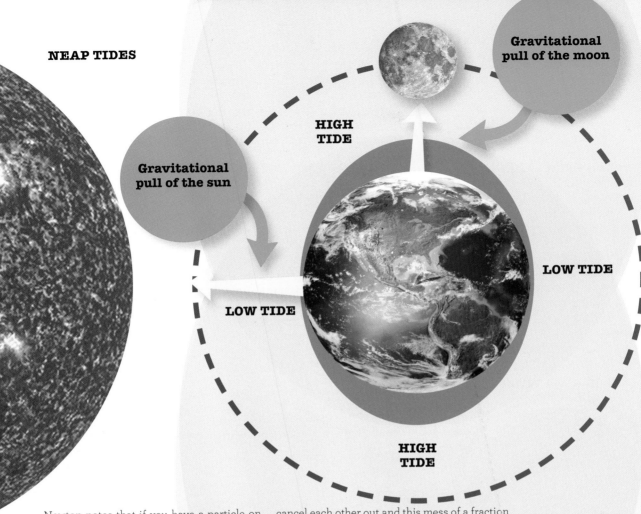

NEAP TIDES

Newton notes that if you have a particle on the surface of the earth, its acceleration due to a body of mass m at a distance d is:

$$\frac{2GmR_e}{d^3}$$

where G is the gravitational constant and R_e the earth's radius. What are those values? They are $6.7 \times 10^{(-11)} \, \text{m}^3 \text{s}^2 \text{kg}^{-1}$ and $6.37 \times 10^6 \text{m}$, since you ask, but we don't actually need them! Because we are only after the ratio of the two accelerations, we can work out:

$$\left(\frac{2Gm_mR_e}{d_m^3} \right) \div \left(\frac{2Gm_sR_e}{d_s^3} \right)$$

where m_m and m_s are the masses of the Moon and Sun, and d_m and d_s the corresponding distances. The 2, G and R_e in each fraction cancel each other out and this mess of a fraction simplifies to:

$$\textbf{\textit{(mass ratio)}/\textit{(distance ratio)}}^3$$

and now we can look up the numbers!

The Moon's mass is $m_m = 7.35 \times 10^{22} \text{kg}$; the Sun's is $m_s = 1.99 \times 10^{30}$, so the mass ratio is 2.71×10^7. There is a lot more mass in the Sun than in the Moon. But hold on: the Sun is $1.50 \times 10^{10} \text{m}$ away, while the Moon is $3.84 \times 10^8 \text{m}$, so the distance ratio is about 390. Cubed, that's 5.96×10^7.

The value of the fraction is about 0.45 – meaning the Sun's influence on the tides is only about 45% of the Moon's influence; the Moon has more than double the Sun's effect.

So the Sun is not insignificant in driving the tides, but it is certainly not the main driver.

THE COASTLINE

You might think it would easy enough to figure out how long a coastline is – just get a map and measure it.

There is a wrinkle, though: the length of the coastline depends critically on how you measure it. Taking, for example, the coastline of Norway, the *CIA World Factbook* claims a total length of about 16,000 miles. However, if you measure it with 60-mile long rulers, you find that the total is more like 1,900 miles. Seeing how that looks on a map, though, you notice that it misses a lot of detail – the estuaries and fjords are simply skipped over.

If your ruler is 30 miles long, you find the coastline is a third as long again – increased accuracy picks up a few more of the wrinkles. While the picture looks much better, a 15-mile long ruler would pick up even more wrinkles, and extend the length of the coastline still further.

In principle, you could continue with this refinement forever, and you may conclude that pretty much any coastline is infinitely long! However, there is a practical limit to how far you can take it (coastlines do not really have permanent features you would pick up with a foot-long ruler, for example).

But that is not good enough for mathematicians. This kind of structure, where looking more closely reveals further structure, is known as a *fractal*. Mathematicians do not consider a coastline as a one-dimensional curve or a two-dimensional shape, but somewhere in between.

The best way to explain this is with an example: if you start with a cube (let us say a centimetre on each side), and treble all of its dimensions to make it a 3 cm cube, each of the distance measurements (such as the edge length or the distance from one corner to the opposite one) is now three times as large. Each of the area measurements (such as the total surface area or the area of a face) is nine times as big –3^2. And its volume is 27 times as large, or 3^3. The powers in the ratios define the dimensionality of the shape: distances are one-dimensional, areas two-dimensional and volumes three-dimensional.

If you take a similar approach to the Norwegian coastline (and shrinking your ruler works out to be the same thing as making your shape bigger), you will find that doubling your resolution on average increases your measurement by a factor of $2^{1.52}$, which means that you *can* measure the length of Norway's coastline, as long as you don't mind doing it in miles[1.52]!

The length of the coast of Norway depends on the size of ruler with which it's measured

2,530 miles with a 30-mile ruler

1,900 miles with a 60-mile ruler

NAVIGATING AT SEA

Before there was GPS, navigating at sea was even more perilous than it is now.

Near the shore, it was simple enough to use known landmarks to triangulate your position: finding the angle between straight-on and three landmarks is enough to find your location and direction relative to them. For example, if one lighthouse is 30 degrees to the left of straight-on and another is 15 degrees to the right, and you know they are 14 miles apart, you can use the sine rule to determine a circle you must be on (it would have a diameter of $14/\sin(45°)$ miles, about 19.8 miles, and have its centre on the perpendicular bisector of the lighthouses). Repeating the trick with either lighthouse and a third landmark would give you a second circle; this intersects the first circle in two places – the common landmark and your position – and so you can precisely plot where you are (and where you are heading) on your chart.

Out on the ocean, far away from land, it is not so simple to triangulate: there are not many landmarks at sea. However, there *are* things you can often see to help you navigate – they are just in the sky rather than in the water.

If you know the angle H_o between the horizon and (for example) the Moon, and you know the Moon is directly above a particular point on the earth, you can limit where you are to a circle of radius approximately $60(90\text{-}H_o)$ nautical miles – again, doing this with several stars, planets or satellites gives you several circles, intersecting at your location.

The only trouble with this method is knowing where, exactly, the astronomical bodies are. Astronomers would publish enormous almanacs listing the positions of several easily identified bodies at given times – which was extremely helpful, as long as you knew what time it was. It was not until the 18th century that reliable ocean-going clocks were invented, at which point navigation became much easier.

USING A MARINE SEXTANT TO NAVIGATE AT SEA

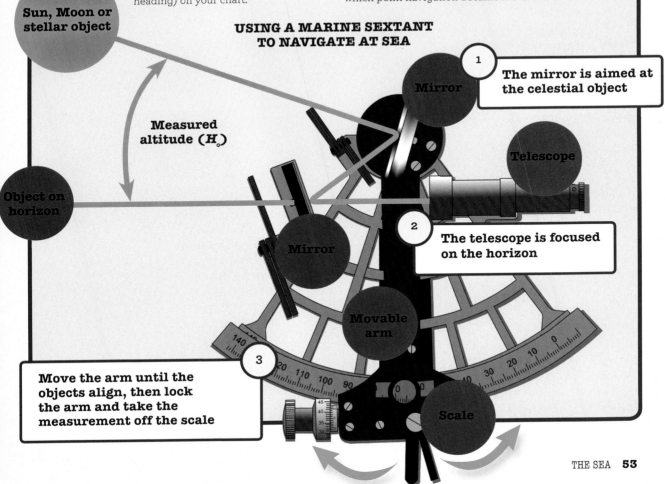

Sun, Moon or stellar object

Measured altitude (H_o)

Object on horizon

Mirror

1 The mirror is aimed at the celestial object

Telescope

Mirror

2 The telescope is focused on the horizon

Movable arm

3 Move the arm until the objects align, then lock the arm and take the measurement off the scale

Scale

Earthquakes

What causes an earthquake? When you hear on the news that Japan was hit with an earthquake nine in magnitude, how much bigger is that than one with magnitude six?

$$M_w = \frac{2}{3} \log_{10}(M_0) - 10.7$$

The earth's crust is made up of several enormous *tectonic plates* – seven or eight major ones, and dozens of minor ones – pieces that move around more or less together. For example, the Eurasian plate and the North American plate, which split the North Atlantic, are moving apart – most noticeably in highly volcanic Iceland. The Indian plate and the Eurasian plate are running into each other – which is why we have the Himalayas. And the North American and Pacific plates are sliding past each other extremely roughly – which is why San Francisco is prepared for the next enormous earthquake to strike at any time.

HOW ARE THEY MEASURED?

When the news says "Italy was struck by an earthquake with a magnitude of 6.5", it's not immediately clear whether that's a big or a small quake. (It is sort of medium-to-large: the 2011 Japan earthquake measured 9.0 in magnitude, but 6.5 is big for continental Europe.)

Given the numbers, it is easy to compare earthquakes qualitatively (the Italy earthquake was not as strong as the Japan one), but what about quantitatively? You would naturally assume the Japan earthquake was about half as big again as the Italy one, because 9 is about half as big again as 6.5. But it is more like **5,500** times as big.

Earthquake magnitude is measured on a *logarithmic scale* – each extra fifth of a point corresponds to roughly a doubling in intensity.

The simplest way I know to explain logarithms, is to talk about powers of 10. A million, or 1,000,000, has six zeros; $\log_{10}(1,000,000) = 6$. A thousand has three zeros and $\log_{10}(1,000) = 3$. The whole number part of a logarithm tells you roughly how long the number is. The decimal part tells you how far you are from the next power of ten – only that is not a linear scale, either.

A number with a log of 3.5 looks like it should be halfway between 1,000 (10^3) and 10,000 (10^4) and it sort of is. It is not the *arithmetic mean* (where you add them up and divide by 2) but the *geometric mean* (where you multiply them

> **1964, Prince William Sound, Alaska**
> **The largest earthquake to hit the US, 9.2 magnitude**

> **1960, Valdivia, Chile**
> **Site of the largest recorded earthquake worldwide, registered 9.5 by the US Geological Survey**

together and take the square root). The number with a log of 3.5 is 3,162.3 or so – in fact, it is $10^{3.5}$. That is not a coincidence.

Because the size of earthquakes varies quite dramatically – from tiny slips that simply do not register to enormous reconfigurations that cause tsunamis and level cities – reporting their size on a log scale makes sense: the smallest earthquakes you can feel are probably around 3.5 on the scale, while the biggest recorded ones are around 9; it is much easier to deal with those numbers than the corresponding *seismic moments*, which are 2×10^{21} and 3.5×10^{29} dyne-centimetres, respectively. (A *dyne-centimetre* is the work done by a force of one dyne (a ten-thousandth of a newton) over a distance of one centimetre. It is equivalent to one ten-millionth of a newton-metre.)

The seismic moment is a measure of how much energy is released by the movement of tectonic plates. A *seismometer* measures the energy in seismic waves, which is a small fraction of the total energy released by an earthquake, but enough to estimate the earthquake's size using various rules of thumb.

MMS SCALE

The moment magnitude scale (MMS) is related to, but not identical to, the Richter scale; the constants of the newer MMS were picked so that medium-sized earthquakes – those in the 5–7 range – would have similar scores, while giving more precision at the low end and no (theoretical) upper limit to readings.

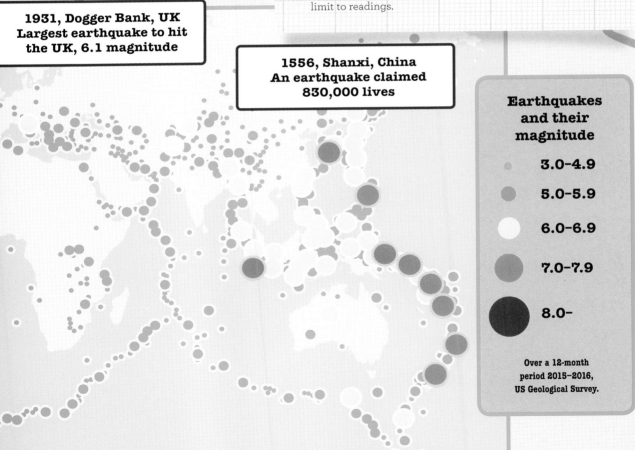

1931, Dogger Bank, UK
Largest earthquake to hit the UK, 6.1 magnitude

1556, Shanxi, China
An earthquake claimed 830,000 lives

Earthquakes and their magnitude

- 3.0–4.9
- 5.0–5.9
- 6.0–6.9
- 7.0–7.9
- 8.0–

Over a 12-month period 2015–2016, US Geological Survey.

The Distance to the Stars

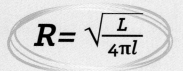

$$R = \sqrt{\frac{L}{4\pi l}}$$

According to *The Hitchhiker's Guide to the Galaxy*, "Space is big. Really big." So, how do we measure distances in space?

• •

There is a simple way, in principle, to measure how far away a star is from the Earth. One day, you measure the angle between a line pointing from you to some well-known, distant star, and a line pointing from you to the star you are trying to measure. Then do the same thing six months later. You know how far you have moved (twice the distance to the Sun), and can use trigonometry to work out the distance to your star.

Unfortunately, it is not so easy: compared to the distance to the Sun, the distance to stars is phenomenally large. The Sun is 8 light minutes away; Proxima Centauri more than 4 light *years* – about 280,000 times as far. You end up with really long, thin triangles, and the tiniest error in your angle observation, or in your knowledge of the distance to the Sun, means your distance estimate using this *stellar parallax* method will be wildly inaccurate. Imagine a penny placed three miles away. That is roughly as hard to measure as the apparent motion of Proxima Centauri, which is the nearest other star to our solar system.

This difficulty in measuring the angle was used for many years as an argument against the heliocentric model for the solar system: the stars did not appear to move relative to each other, which was consistent with the heavens being fixed in place! It was only in 1838 that the first successful stellar parallax observation was made, by Friedrich Bessel.

Even with today's technology, this method is only useful for stars within a thousand light years or so, but accuracy is improving all the time.

SIMILAR TYPES OF STARS

A method for finding the distance to more distant stars involves one of science's best graphs, the Hertzsprung–Russell diagram.

The horizontal axis shows the *spectral class* or *colour index* of stars – by examining the wavelengths of light emitted by a star, it is

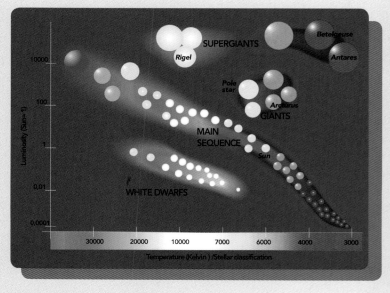

possible to deduce its temperature (the hottest stars are on the left of the diagram). The vertical axis shows the star's luminosity – how much light it emits (the brightest stars are at the top).

The vast majority of observed stars fall near a diagonal line on the graph, known as the *main sequence*, although some – the white dwarfs, the giants and the supergiants – lie on slightly different curves.

If you know a star's type and colour index, it is possible to figure out how far away it is. You use the H–R diagram to find out its luminosity – how brightly it shines and compare that to how bright it looks in the sky.

How much of a star's energy reaches the Earth is inversely proportional to the surface area of a sphere whose radius is the distance between the star and the Earth. This means that if the star emits L units of luminosity, and we (a distance of R away) receive l units, we know that $l = L/(4\pi R^2)$ – which we can rearrange to find the distance: $R = \sqrt{(L/4\pi l)}$.

The Hertzsprung-Russell diagram is a scatter graph of stars showing the relationship between the stars' absolute magnitudes (or luminosities) and their temperatures.

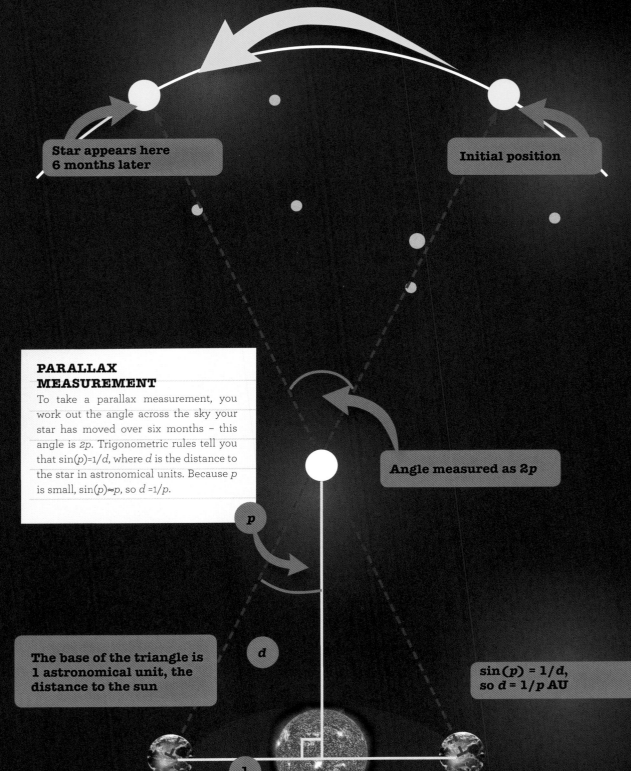

Star appears here 6 months later

Initial position

PARALLAX MEASUREMENT
To take a parallax measurement, you work out the angle across the sky your star has moved over six months – this angle is *2p*. Trigonometric rules tell you that sin(*p*)=1/*d*, where *d* is the distance to the star in astronomical units. Because *p* is small, sin(*p*)≈*p*, so *d* =1/*p*.

Angle measured as 2p

p

The base of the triangle is 1 astronomical unit, the distance to the sun

d

$$\sin(p) = 1/d,$$
so *d* = 1/*p* **AU**

1

ARE STARS IN CONSTELLATIONS RELATIVELY CLOSE TO EACH OTHER?

No. Or rather, not necessarily.

It's difficult, at least for me, to remember that the stars are not all the same distance away. (I have a similar problem with dinosaurs. For example, the triceratops lived closer to today than it did to the time of the stegosaurus.) Constellations do not take this into account at all.

Imagine that the earth is surrounded by a giant basketball, and each star is projected onto the inside of it. The constellations are 88 distinct "rectangular" regions of the basketball, and any star you can see in a straight line through that region is in that constellation. (I say "rectangular" because the lines that divide them are not straight – after all, they are on a sphere!) They are *supposed* to be vertical and horizontal, but the earth's axis is not static, so they have become slightly wonky.

Because stars are not fixed in the sky (each has its own orbit in the Milky Way), they can move within and between constellations. For example, when the zodiac was first conceived of, the Sun passed roughly evenly through the twelve zodiac constellations through the year. Now it all but misses Scorpius (Scorpio) and takes a short cut through Ophiuchus instead, and the traditional dates are *way* off.

Given enough time (several tens of millennia), the patterns you are used to seeing in the sky will be completely unrecognizable, which means the triceratops and stegosaurus would be completely unable to navigate by today's night sky, but in completely different ways.

HOW LONG WOULD IT TAKE TO REACH THE STARS?

As I am writing this, unconfirmed reports have arrived suggesting that a habitable planet may exist in orbit around Proxima Centauri, which is four light years away. How long would it take a spaceship to go there and check it out?

It is easy to put a lower limit on how long it would take: Proxima Centauri is 4.24 light years away, and nothing travels faster than light, so it would take at least 4.24 years to get there.

Unfortunately, we cannot travel at the speed of light. The fastest human-made object ever was Helios II, a West German probe examining the Sun, which in 1976 travelled about 70,000 m/s. The speed of light is 300,000,000 m/s, about 4,000 times as fast as that. Since light travels 4,000 times as fast as our fastest spacecraft, it would take us at least 4,000 times as long to get to the stars – a good 17,000 years! For comparison, it is only 10,000 years since humans developed the idea of farming.

UNITS IN SPACE

In most of science, distances are measured in metres, or simple multiples thereof: a kilometre is 1,000 metres; there are 1,000 millimetres in a metre. All very simple and straightforward.

In astronomy, though, the numbers get very big very quickly – even the Sun, the closest star to Earth, is 150,000,000,000 metres away (give or take). Instead, astronomers use a patchwork of measurements that make their lives easier.

The average distance from the Earth to the Sun is defined to be one *astronomical unit* (AU) – which is used mainly when talking about distances within the solar system. More commonly, distances are measured by the length of time it takes light to travel that far. The Sun is 8 light minutes away – that is how long it takes its light to reach us. A light year is about 9.5 quadrillion metres and the observable universe is nearly 50 billion light years across.

Astronomers also use the *parsec*, which is about 3.26 light years. This is related to the stellar parallax: an object one parsec from Earth, observed at times six months apart, would appear to have moved 1/3600 of a degree in the sky.

Andromeda Galaxy
2.5 million light years

Hercules Globular
25,000 light years

Alpha Centauri
4.4 light years

The Sun
8.3 light minutes

The Moon
1.3 light seconds

From Earth to. . .
At the speed of light
299,792 km/sec

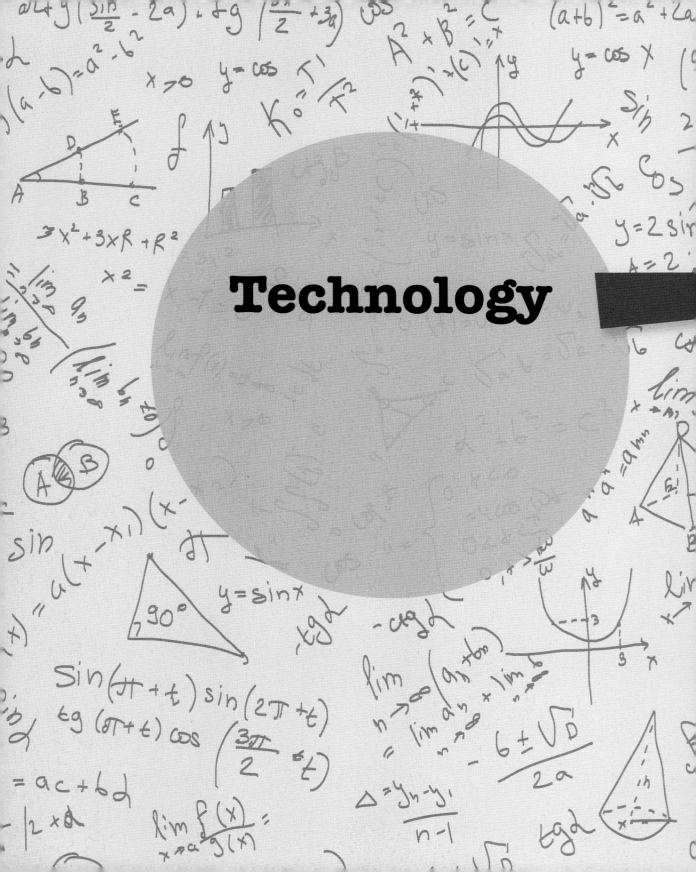

Technology

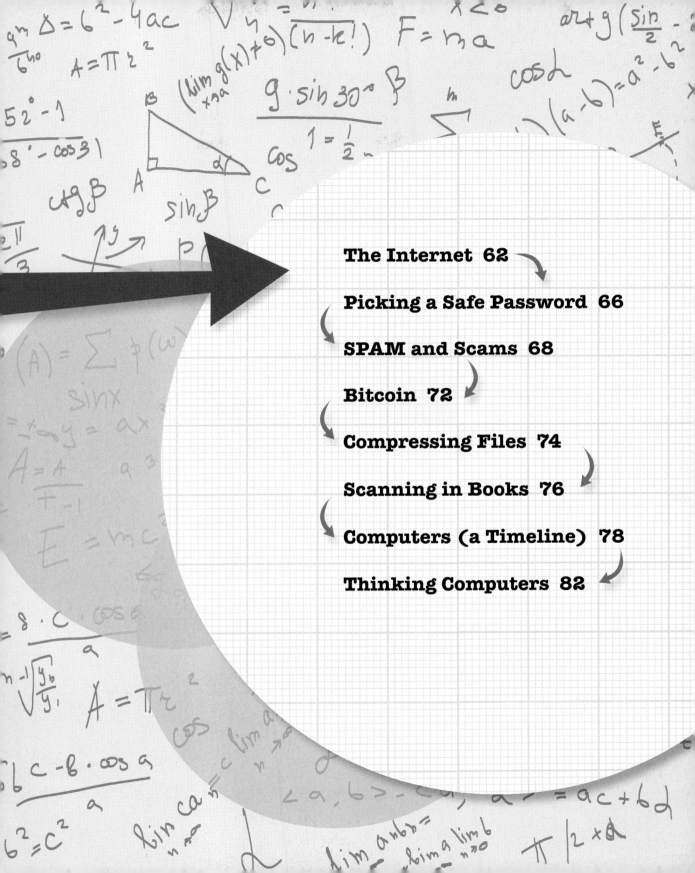

The Internet

In 1989, while a contractor at CERN, Tim Berners-Lee figured out a way to combine the ideas of hypertext, connection protocols and the system of domain names and (as he says): "ta-da! The World Wide Web."

There is a difference between the web – broadly speaking, the content we mean when we say "the internet" casually – and the internet, which is the infrastructure behind it: an network of networks connected both physically and wirelessly, designed to be *fault-tolerant* – that is, when connections are damaged or compromised, the network reorganizes itself to avoid the problem.

Here I focus on the internet, properly speaking: how it works, why it is designed the way it is, and why it is so difficult to draw it.

And there is *loads* of mathematics in that.

HOW DOES INFORMATION GET FROM A TO B?

"It's all 1s and 0s" is a cliché when it comes to computers, but there is an awful lot of truth in it. A piece of text is translated, letter by letter, into numbers (for example, in ASCII, "A" is represented by the number 65, and "q" by 113 – the word "Antique" would be transcribed as 65-110-116-105-113-117-101), and from there into binary (65 is 100 001 in binary, and 101 becomes 110 101), turning each character into a string of 1s and 0s. A bitmap image is split into pixels, each of which may have a value from 0 to 255 for the amount of red, green and blue showing. These can be represented as a string of numbers, converted to binary. Another string of 1s and 0s. (255 is not a random number: it is 11 111 111 in binary, the largest number you can make with eight binary digits, or *bits*.)

Modern files do not generally use ASCII or bitmaps – there are far more efficient schemata for translating text, images, sounds, videos and other documents into binary – but the principle remains the same: anything a computer can do can be represented as 1s and 0s, and this is excellent news for the internet. It means that, if you have a system of chopping strings of 1s and 0s up into small *packets*, a system for sending the packets through the system, and a system for reconstructing them at the other end, you can send just about anything just about anywhere.

And guess what? That is exactly the system we have.

Splitting files into standardized packets allows them to be sent reliably between different systems and reassembled at the other end.

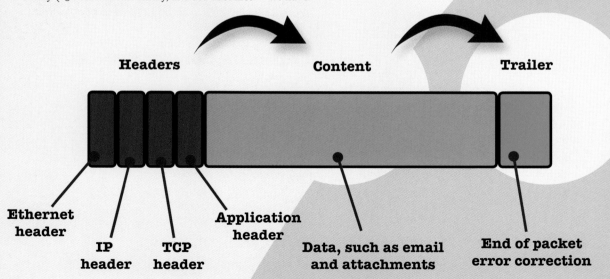

Headers — Content — Trailer

Ethernet header

IP header

TCP header

Application header

Data, such as email and attachments

End of packet error correction

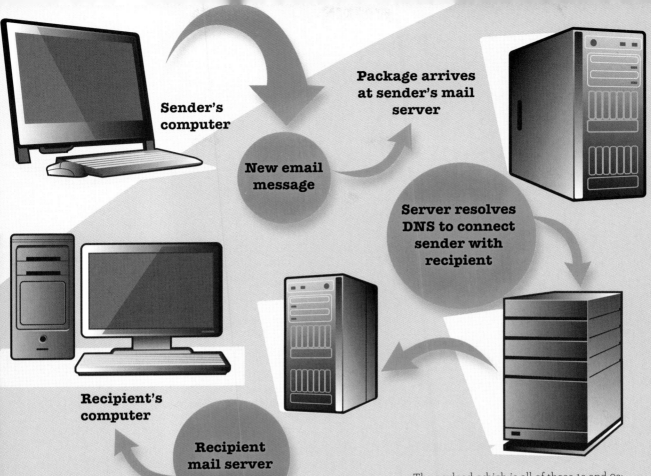

Sender's computer

New email message

Package arrives at sender's mail server

Server resolves DNS to connect sender with recipient

Recipient's computer

Recipient mail server

Chopping a file up is not especially hard. Looking on my desktop, I have a report stored as Microsoft Word file containing 125 kilobytes (kB) of information – a byte is 8 bits, so let us call it about a million bits. A typical packet can carry slightly less than 1000 bits, so this string of a million 1s and 0s is split into about a thousand numbered packets.

Each packet, a little like a real-life postal packet, consists of three parts:

A header, which says where the packet is from, where it is going, the protocol (what kind of packet it is – email, a web page, a video file, etc.), and which number in the series of packets it is; this roughly corresponds to the address label.

The payload, which is all of those 1s and 0s; this is the content of the packet.

A footer, which tells the computer where the end of the information is and has a check to make sure nothing has changed in the packet; I think of this as the packet's seal.

There are many ways to check the packet has been sent correctly; one of the simplest is to count how many 1s are in the packet before it is sent and send that number in the footer. If it matches the number of 1s that arrive in the payload, there is a fair chance it has arrived safely. If it mismatches, then there is definitely been an error.

Once the receiving end has picked up all of the packets, it is simply a case of arranging them into the correct order, extracting the payload from each of them, and putting the strings of 1s and 0s back together. You then have a file that is identical to the one that was sent.

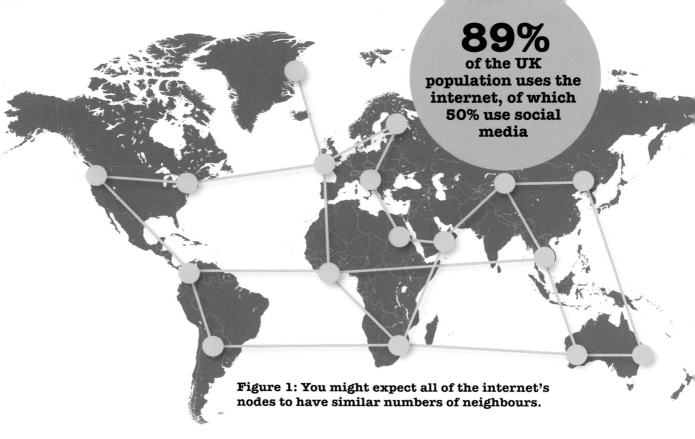

89% of the UK population uses the internet, of which 50% use social media

Figure 1: You might expect all of the internet's nodes to have similar numbers of neighbours.

THE SHAPE OF THE INTERNET

At first glance, it does not make much sense to talk about the shape of the internet. It is like talking about the colour of the interstate highway network or the weight of the space program. However, there are at least two ways in which it makes sense.

The first is its geographical shape of the connections which (rather interestingly) follows pretty much the same pattern as the telegraph did in the early 20th century, which in itself is pretty much the same pattern as the trade routes established over the preceding centuries. This makes some sense: after all, if New York and London already do a lot of business, you would want a decent communication connection between them.

However, that is not the mathematical shape. To look at it mathematically, we need to represent the internet as a graph. I do not mean the kind of graph you had to plot in high school, such as $y = x^2 - 4$, but a proper graph: all of the *nodes* (places where cables meet) and *edges* (cables connecting nodes).

You might expect the graph to look something like **Figure 1**, each node connecting nicely to its half-dozen or so neighbours. Of course that is not what happens.

Instead, it turns out to look something like **Figure 2**, you have a large number of "leaves" (nodes with only one connection). You have somewhat fewer nodes with two connections, fewer still with three and so on, until you have a few nodes with very many connections. This is structurally somewhat similar to the way airlines arrange their flights: a few regional hubs serve large numbers of airports, while most airports connect to only a few other cities.

Why is the shape of the internet important? It turns out that systems following this kind of pattern can be mapped using *hyperbolic geometry*. Using this kind of map (rather than a traditional geographic one), which takes into account the speed data can travel as well as physical distance, it is possible for messages to be routed more efficiently along the cables of the internet. That means your email gets to you faster – and your internet goes down less often!

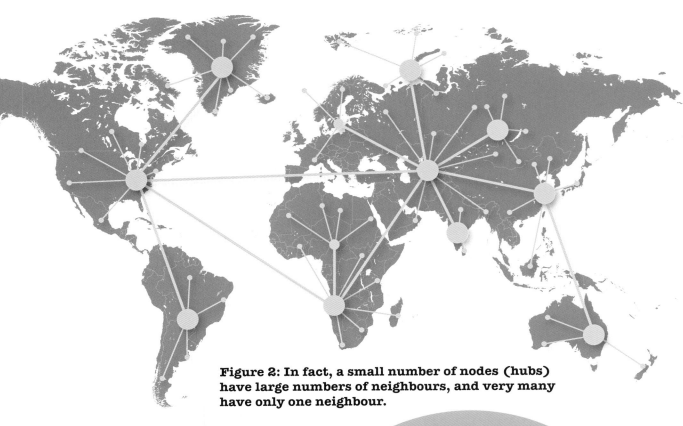

Figure 2: In fact, a small number of nodes (hubs) have large numbers of neighbours, and very many have only one neighbour.

HYPERBOLIC GEOMETRY

Hyperbolic geometry was one of the first non-Euclidean geometries to be discovered in the 19th century. In Euclidean geometry, it is assumed that if you have a line L and a point P that is not on the line, there is exactly one line through P that is parallel to L; in hyperbolic geometry, it is assumed that there would be at least two such lines. This can be understood as space having a particular kind of curvature. In fact, hyperbolic geometry is a much better description of the physical universe than Euclidean geometry.

In hyperbolic geometry, "lines" correspond to arcs, as shown. All three of the black lines through P are parallel to the red line l.

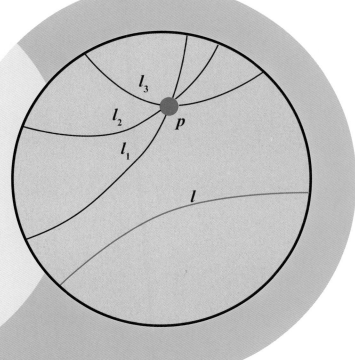

Picking a Safe Password

How safe is my password? It is a staple of movies: the hacker sits down at the computer and immediately guesses the master password. But how likely is that to happen in real life? The short answer is: it depends on how good your password is.

BIKE LOCKS AND PINS

The simplest password in regular use is a four-digit code – which you might use to secure something you would rather not lose, but it would not be earth-shattering if you did: your bike, your phone, or access to all of the money in your bank account.

The four-digit PIN is not a particularly secure way to lock something. You have ten possible choices for the first digit, ten for the second, and so on – multiplying these together gives 10,000 possible codes. A computer could check all of those in a blink of an eye, which is why debit cards and phones usually get locked if you enter the PIN wrong a few times in a row. (As for bike locks, if you can manage three guesses a second, you can expect to crack one in well under an hour.)

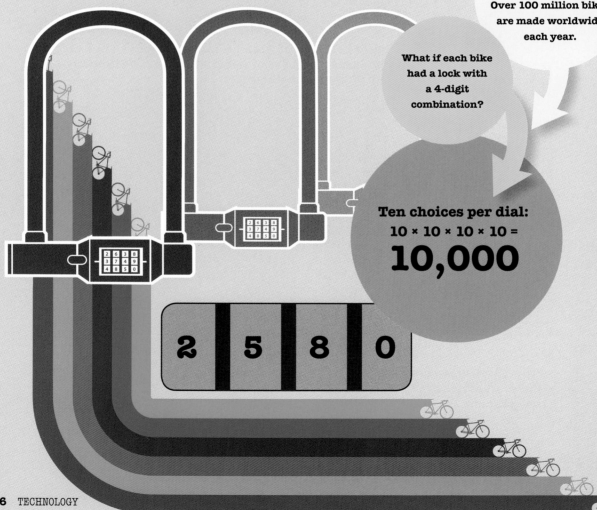

There are more than a billion bicycles in the world today. Over 100 million bikes are made worldwide each year.

What if each bike had a lock with a 4-digit combination?

Ten choices per dial:
10 × 10 × 10 × 10 =
10,000

2 5 8 0

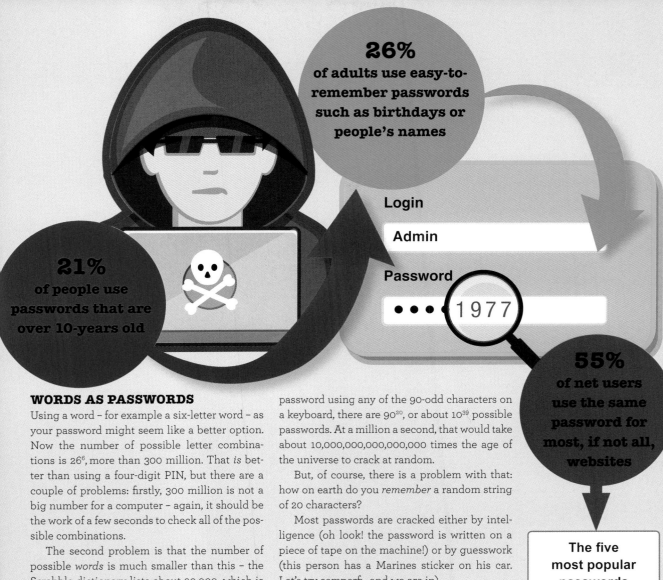

26%
of adults use easy-to-remember passwords such as birthdays or people's names

21%
of people use passwords that are over 10-years old

Login

Admin

Password

•••• 1977

55%
of net users use the same password for most, if not all, websites

The five most popular passwords

123456

password

12345

12345678

qwerty

WORDS AS PASSWORDS

Using a word – for example a six-letter word – as your password might seem like a better option. Now the number of possible letter combinations is 26^6, more than 300 million. That *is* better than using a four-digit PIN, but there are a couple of problems: firstly, 300 million is not a big number for a computer – again, it should be the work of a few seconds to check all of the possible combinations.

The second problem is that the number of possible *words* is much smaller than this – the Scrabble dictionary lists about 20,000, which is not *that* much more than the number of possible PINs. If you restrict your possible passwords to a predictable list, it makes them much more easy to guess! (This is also a problem with PINs: analysis by datagenetics.com found that more than one in six of the 3.4 million PINs they analyzed were either 1234 or 1111. Those are the first things hackers will try!)

EXTENDING THE ALPHABET

If you want to make your password harder to break with brute force, there are two things you can do: make it *longer* and use *a bigger alphabet*. If you are allowed to have a twenty-character password using any of the 90-odd characters on a keyboard, there are 90^{20}, or about 10^{39} possible passwords. At a million a second, that would take about 10,000,000,000,000,000 times the age of the universe to crack at random.

But, of course, there is a problem with that: how on earth do you *remember* a random string of 20 characters?

Most passwords are cracked either by intelligence (oh look! the password is written on a piece of tape on the machine!) or by guesswork (this person has a Marines sticker on his car. Let's try semperfi...and we are in).

THE TRADE-OFF

There is a trade-off in picking a password: you need something that is neither easy to find by brute-force (so short passwords are bad) nor easy to guess (password1234 is a dreadful choice) – but you also need something that's easy to remember (HSgD58fAR4 is secure, but good luck remembering it). The sweet spot lies somewhere in the middle. Comic artist Randall Monroe suggests that four random common words you can work into a story (such as "correct horse battery staple") are almost certainly at least as good as what you have at the moment.

SPAM and Scams

$$p = \frac{s_1 s_2 s_3 \ldots s_N}{s_1 s_2 s_3 \ldots s_N + h_1 h_2 h_3 \ldots h_N}$$

In 1978, the Digital Equipment Corporation sent out an email message advertising their computers to almost 400 users, a significant fraction of the internet users at that time. The message has gained notoriety: it was the first spam email.

While it is not known how successful the campaign was for DEC, the idea of making money from unsolicited emails quickly caught on, and remains a problem 40-odd years later. We will look at some of the mathematics behind spam, scams and other internet crime.

SPAM BLOCKERS

There are dozens of ways in which email services determine whether a message is likely to be spam, from the fairly straightforward to the extremely sophisticated. Here I will talk about one of the simpler versions, the *Naive Bayesian Classifier*.

Suppose your computer knows nothing about what you consider spam, and you train it by telling it what you think of each incoming email. A note from the library about your overdue books? You hit the green button, that is proper email. A message from Auntie Muriel about her planned visit next week? Green button. Something telling you you have won the Canadian lottery, despite not having entered? Red button, spam. A message from Ban Ki-Moon, saying the UN needs you to help transfer some money? Red button.

Now, the computer can analyze the words used in your emails to figure out the probability that the next incoming message is spam. The way it does this is to break each message down into individual words, determining the probability of a message being spam, given that it contains a particular word. "Lottery" might be 80% spam. "Secretary-General" might be 95%. "Bayesian" might be 2% (some spam emails litter their contents with random words to try to bypass the filters.) This number is the *spamicity* of the word.

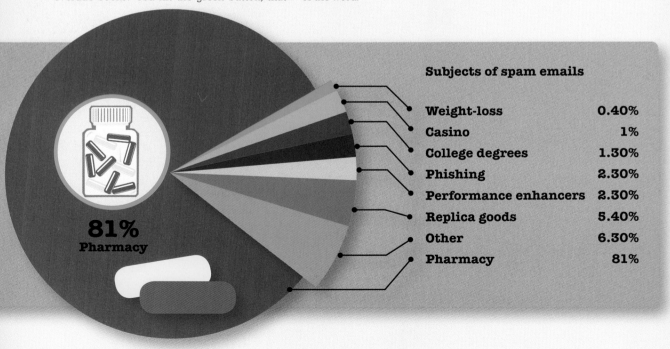

Subjects of spam emails

Weight-loss	0.40%
Casino	1%
College degrees	1.30%
Phishing	2.30%
Performance enhancers	2.30%
Replica goods	5.40%
Other	6.30%
Pharmacy	81%

81%
Pharmacy

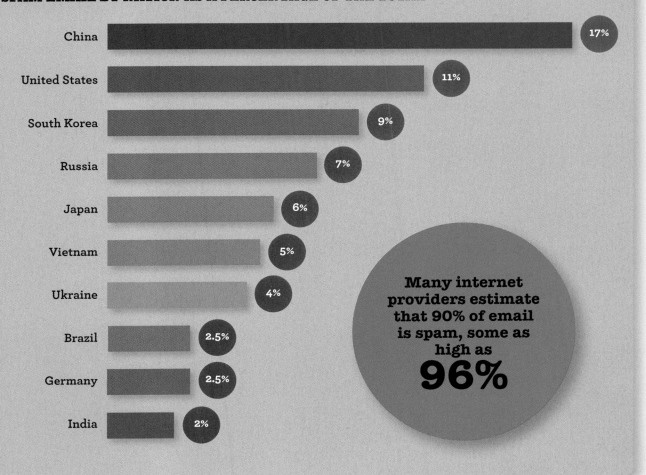

SPAM EMAIL BY NATION AS A PERCENTAGE OF THE TOTAL

- China — 17%
- United States — 11%
- South Korea — 9%
- Russia — 7%
- Japan — 6%
- Vietnam — 5%
- Ukraine — 4%
- Brazil — 2.5%
- Germany — 2.5%
- India — 2%

Many internet providers estimate that 90% of email is spam, some as high as 96%

To work out the probability of a particular message being spam, the computer calculates an overall spamminess value for it based on all of the words with enough data to provide a good probability estimate. This works out to be:

$$p = \frac{s_1\, s_2\, s_3 \dots s_N}{s_1\, s_2\, s_3 \dots s_N + h_1\, h_2\, h_3 \dots h_N}$$

where p is the probability of spamminess, all of the s_1, s_2 and so on is the spamicity of each of the N words we are looking at, and the h_1, h_2 and so on, the non-spamicity of each of the words (which can be worked out as $h_k = 1 - s_k$). If p is greater than some threshold, say 90%, the email system diverts the offending message into the junk folder; otherwise, it goes to your inbox. Beautifully, you can continue to train the system about what you consider spam as you go along, and improve its results!

This relies on the words in the email being independent, which they clearly are not (how often do you see the word Secretary-General in a context that does not also use the word UN, for example?), but the Naive Bayesian classifier is a pretty solid baseline for sorting messages into spam and non-spam.

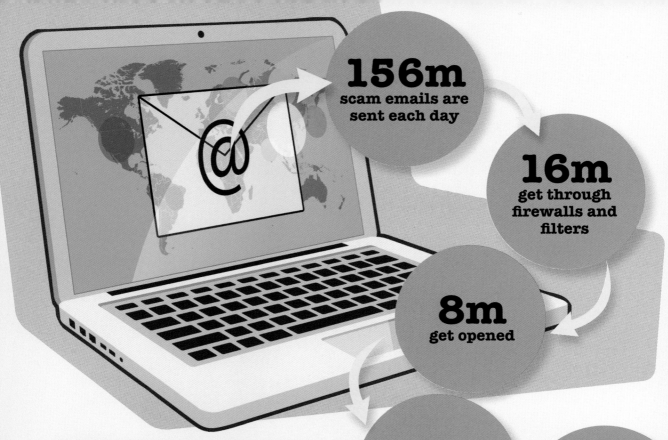

156m scam emails are sent each day

16m get through firewalls and filters

8m get opened

800,000 get clicked

75,000 users fall for a scam

HOW DO THEY MAKE MONEY, OR, WHY ARE THERE STILL EMAIL SCAMS?

You would think that only the most gullible of fools would fall for such a flagrant scam, standing out with poor use of English, an email address that has nothing to do with the sender's purported name, and an implausible story. And to an extent, you are right: the enormous majority of such emails go directly into the junk folder, never to be seen again.

However, there are two factors working in the scammers' favour: firstly, it costs practically nothing to send an email, or even to send thousands upon thousands of emails. The second is, they are not trying to find *you* – you are smart and discerning. You are the last person they want to engage with. They are looking for the kind of gullible fool who does not spot red flags, someone greedy and trusting enough to keep sending them money to iron out the escalating "little problems" until they are penniless. When you are emailing thousands – if not millions – of people, the chances of catching someone daft enough to fall for the scam increases dramatically.

Legitimate businesses often run email newsletters with details of sales and offers. They calculate the value of a newsletter as (*the size of the list*) × (*the proportion of people who respond*) × (*the average amount responders send*). Depending on the business, the size of the list can be anything from dozens to millions; the proportion of people who respond would typically be measured in a few per cent, and the average spend varies wildly depending on the business.

Spammers use the same formula: while the proportion of people who respond is minuscule, their lists are enormous (because they do not bother with pesky details like asking people to opt in) and the amount they spend is comparatively large. Estimates say that the average victim pays out US$20,000, and that around a quarter of a million scammers operate worldwide, making about $1.5 billion a year. (This means there are around 75,000 people a year who do fall for it.)

WHY PYRAMID SCHEMES COLLAPSE

Along with the typical so-called Nigerian scam, which involves sending money to facilitate a non-existent payment, one prevalent type of internet scam is the *pyramid scheme*.

A typical example may work like this: You are recruited to the scheme by a friend. You pay $10 to the friend and $10 to the person who recruited them. You are then invited to find six new people to recruit to the scheme under the same terms.

On the face of it, this is a great deal: you pay out $20, but you recoup that as soon as you get two new members on board. If you get six new recruits and each of those recruits six new members, you rake in $60 + $360 = $420 – a 2000% return on your investment!

Unfortunately, there is a snag: you very quickly run out of people to recruit. If there are 6 people in the first level of recruits, there are 36 in the second and 216 in the third. Level 10 requires more than 60 million people on top of the 12.5 million already in the scheme, and by level 13 you need more people than there are on the earth.

People in level n: 6^n
Total people up to level n: $6(6^{n-1})/5$
If a pyramid scheme asks for k people in the next level, the formulas are k^n and $k(k^{n-1})/(k-1)$, respectively.

While people in the high level of the pyramid can comfortably cash out a huge return on their investment, the structure of this scheme means there are always more losers than winners.

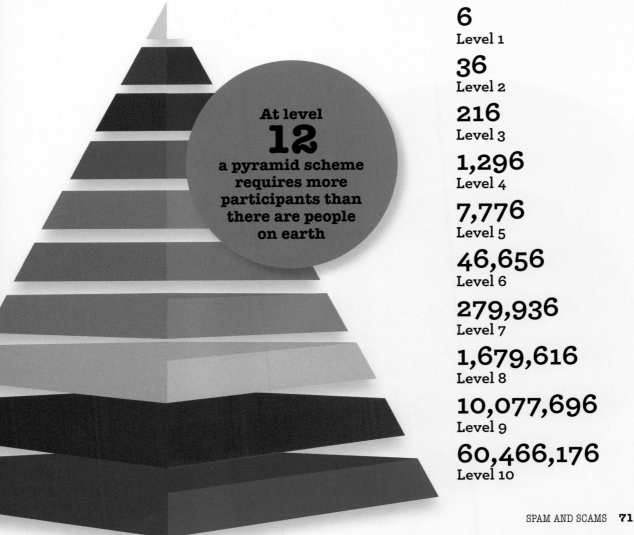

At level
12
a pyramid scheme requires more participants than there are people on earth

6
Level 1

36
Level 2

216
Level 3

1,296
Level 4

7,776
Level 5

46,656
Level 6

279,936
Level 7

1,679,616
Level 8

10,077,696
Level 9

60,466,176
Level 10

Bitcoin

In some circles, Bitcoin is the smart way to pay for things: secure, untraceable, convenient and low-fee. In others, it is a threat to proper banking, an unregulated and unpoliceable free-for-all, and a magnet for money-laundering and other criminal activity. In truth, it is all of those things (except, maybe, secure and untraceable). It is also pretty interesting mathematically.

HOW DOES BITCOIN WORK?

First suggested by a mysterious pseudonymous coder, Satoshi Nakamoto, in 2008, Bitcoin relies on a distributed database of transactions that is known as the blockchain. Every transaction is broadcast to the network, validated independently, added to the local copy blockchain, and rebroadcast by each node – making sure that the database remains synchronized. Every ten minutes or so, the list of transactions is accepted, pushed to every part of the network, and then frozen into history.

This is where the mathematics comes in. The "every ten minutes or so" bit of record-keeping is due to a *miner* somewhere striking lucky. A miner – someone with a computer – has to take all of the recorded transactions in the current block and add a series of symbols to the end. Unfortunately for the miner, this is only accepted by the system after it has run through a *one-way hashing algorithm*, and found to have a certain number of zeros at the beginning. (The number of zeros is adjusted every couple of weeks to make sure the "every ten minutes or so" is kept roughly constant.) Also unfortunately for the miner, there are many other miners trying to do the same thing. Whoever succeeds first earns a reward and ongoing transaction fees, and the other miners need to start all over again.

A hashing algorithm is a way of turning a bunch of symbols into a (usually quite large) number, but a number that requires significantly less storage space than the original bunch of symbols. However, the problem with one-way hashes is that it is very hard to work backwards –

hence the term one-way! The only practical way to find an acceptable series of symbols to add to the recorded transactions is to try a whole load and see if any of them work.

This so-called *proof-of-work* system, where you can only claim a reward and freeze things into the blockchain if you have done a significant amount of guesswork, makes it extremely hard to modify the blockchain retrospectively – for example, if you wanted to try to pretend you had not spent some of your money. To do that, you would need to get lucky and be the next miner to modify the blockchain. On average, you would need about 200 quadrillion tries (as of 2015; certainly many more by now) – the odds are hardly in your favour!

IS BITCOIN REALLY SAFE AND SECRET?

It is safer than cash (as long as you are careful with your Bitcoin addresses, it is very hard to steal; the cryptography behind Bitcoin is extremely strong), but somewhat less anonymous: after all, every transaction is recorded in the ledger! While it is anonymous, it is possible in some cases to look at spending patterns and make fair guesses about who people are. There are ways around this (for example, by using services which "join" coins together or by cleverness with your addresses), but these might seem intimidatingly complex to the average user.

It's as dangerous as cash, too: once it is spent or lost, it is gone forever. There is very little by way of consumer protection in Bitcoin world!

Alice has a message for Bob and wants to sign it so Bob knows it's from her.

Alice generates a *private* and a *public* key. Her private key **D** is a number between 1 and the curve order, and her public key **Q** is generated by multiplying an agreed base point by **D** – using *elliptic curve multiplication*. She keeps the private key secret but the public key can be made available.

1. Alice turns the message she wants to sign into a number **z** using a *hash function*.
2. Alice picks a random number **k** between 1 and the *curve's order*, **n**; she also works out **k**'s *multiplicative inverse modulo n - k⁻¹*.
3. She multiplies the *base point* **G** by **k**, using elliptic curve multiplication, to get a point with x-coordinate **x**, a whole number.
4. She finds the remainder from dividing **x** by **n** and calls the result **r**.
5. She works out the remainder from dividing **k⁻¹ × (z + r × D)** by **n** and calls the result **s**.
6. She sends **r** and **s** along with the message.

Bob receives the message and wants to check Alice really signed it.
1. Bob receives the message and the signature (**r**, **s**).
2. He applies the *hash function* to the message to turn it into a number **z**.

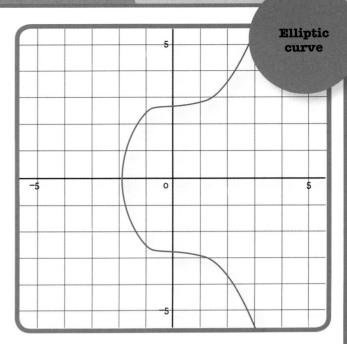

Elliptic curve

Public key cryptography based on elliptic curves underpins the security of Bitcoin.

3. He calculates **w**, the multiplicative inverse modulo **n** of **s**, and **v**, the multiplicative inverse of **r**.
4. He works out **u × G + v × Q**, where **G** is the base point and **Q** is Alice's public key – the **x**-coordinate of this is **x**.
5. If **x** and **r** give the same remainder when divided by **n**, the signature is good.

BASE POINT: an agreed point on the Bitcoin elliptic curve. It has an x-coordinate of 60,007,469,361,611,451, 595,808,076,307,103,981,948,066,675,035,911,483,428,688, 400,614,800,034,609,601,690,612,527,903,279,981,446,538, 331,562,636,035,761,922,566,837,056,280,671,244,382,574, 348,564,747,448.

BITCOIN ELLIPTIC CURVE: Bitcoin's cryptography is based on the elliptic curve $y^2 = x^3 + 7$.

CURVE ORDER: a number specifically chosen for the Bitcoin elliptic curve. For the record, it's 115,792,089,237,31 6,195,423,570,985,008,687,907,852,837,564,279,074,904,382,6 05,163,141,518,161,494,337.

ELLIPTIC CURVE ADDITION: to add two points on an elliptic curve, you draw a line through them and find where it crosses the curve again. The reflection of this

point in the x-axis is the sum of the two points. To add a point to itself, the line you draw is the tangent at that point.

ELLIPTIC CURVE MULTIPLICATION: to multiply a point on an elliptic curve by an integer, you add it to itself that many times using elliptic curve addition. This is a one-way function: given the start and end points, it's not usually easy to work out the number of times the start point was multiplied.

HASH FUNCTION: a function for converting a message into a number. Hash functions are typically one-way: you can't easily tell what the input was from the output.

MULTIPLICATIVE INVERSE MODULON: if you multiply a number by its *multiplicative inverse modulo n*, and divide the result by *n*, you get a remainder of 1. For example, the multiplicative inverse of 7, modulo 11 is 8 because 7 × 8 / 11 = 5, remainder 1.

Compressing Files

There's an old mathematical/philosophical conundrum that asks "What is the smallest number you can't describe in fewer than 65 characters?" There's no sensible answer to it: supposing such a number exists, you could describe it as "the smallest number you can describe in fewer than 65 characters," using only sixty-four.

$$\Sigma p_i \log_2 p_i$$

Shannon's information theory

• •

This sets up the idea that some numbers can be written more concisely than others. Not just using placeholders (calling 3.1415926535879… "π" doesn't really describe the number!), but for example, 10^{10} is a much more succinct way of writing 10,000,000,000. A computer might even code the string representation as "1*1,10*0" to represent "one 1 followed by ten zeros."

There is a theoretical lower limit to how much information can be compressed, discovered by Claude Shannon. If a message is written in an alphabet of some number of characters, and the relative frequency of each character is p_i, the message's *entropy* is $\sum p_i \log_2 p_i$. You cannot compress the message into fewer bits without losing information.

HUFFMAN CODING

One approach to compressing a message is Huffman coding, which assigns a one-or-more bit code word to each letter of the alphabet. The idea is that more common letters get short code words, while rarer ones get long ones.

For example, the message "WATCH OUT WHERE THE HUSKIES GO AND DO NOT EAT THE YELLOW SNOW" has twelve spaces, seven Es, six Ts and Os, and so on down to a single R, I, C, K and Y. To create a Huffman code, you recursively combine the groups with the lowest frequencies together, so the first set of groups might be: (space) (12), E (7), T (6), O (6), H (5), W (4), A (3), S (3), N (3), D (2), L (2), R/I (2), C/K (2), Y (1). See **Table 1**.

Table 1	
(Space)	12
E	7
T	6
O	6
H	5
W	4
A	3
S	3
N	3
D	2
(R and I)	2
(C and K)	2
Y	1

Table 2	
(Space)	12
E	7
T	6
O	6
H	5
W	4
A	3
S	3
N	3
(Y and C and K)	3
D	2
(R and I)	2

Lossless compression allows a file to be reduced in size and reconstructed exactly as it originally was; lossy compression allows greater reductions, but with a loss in quality.

LOSSLESS

100MB — Original

50MB — Mathematically lossless compression 2:1

100MB — Mathematically lossless decompression

LOSSY

100MB — Original

20MB — Visually lossless compression 5:1

2MB — Lossy compression 50:1

Table 3: Huffman coding reduces the number of bits required for the message from 464 to 211.

CHARACTER	CODE	Count	Bits	Total
(SPACE)	00	12	2	24
E	110	7	3	21
T	010	6	3	18
O	011	6	3	18
H	1001	5	4	20
W	1011	4	4	16
A	1111	3	4	12
S	10000	3	5	15
N	10001	3	5	15
D	10101	2	5	10
L	11100	2	5	10
Y	101001	1	6	6
R	111010	1	6	6
I	111011	1	6	6
C	1010000	1	7	7
K	1010001	1	7	7

TOTAL 211

As the groups get bigger, they move up the table, so combining Y with C/K makes **Table 2** (opposite bottom).

You might decide on the convention that every time you go left in the tree, you append a 0 to the code, and every time you go right, you add a 1, which would give the codewords to each character seen in **Table 3**. As you can see, the more common characters get the shortest codes. This encodes the message in 211 bits, compared to a theoretical minimum of 208.2. (Depending on which version you use, ASCII would require 406 or 464 bits, which shows that compression can reduce file sizes.)

There is a little more to Huffman coding (you normally need to specify which letter corresponds to which code-word, or else you can't easily reconstruct the text), but variations on the technique are used in many of the most common compression routines used in computing.

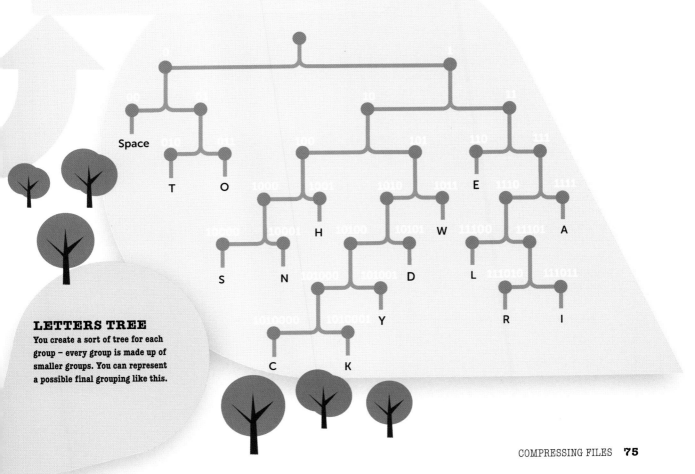

LETTERS TREE
You create a sort of tree for each group – every group is made up of smaller groups. You can represent a possible final grouping like this.

Scanning in Books

Modern books are generally written on computers, which makes it fairly easy to turn them into electronic form. However, for books written before the 1980s, it is very rare to have text files available – but you can still find searchable versions of many of them on Google, or at Project Gutenberg.

Nobody has gone through and retyped all of these books – instead, they have been scanned in and automatically converted to text. We will look at one possible way to do that.

1

DE-SKEW THE IMAGE

Whether the image is a scan or a photo, any page is unlikely to be perfectly aligned. One method to de-rotate the image is known as the *Hough algorithm*, which tries to find an estimate for the baseline of each line of text. Here is how:

Examine every point (x, y) which is coloured, but has a white point immediately below it. (This does not mean it *is* on the baseline of a line of text, but it is more likely to be so than a random coloured point.)

Parameterize all of the possible lines through that point in the form *(angle, perpendicular distance to the origin)*. In practice, "all of the possible lines" means infinitely many. We restrict the lines we store to those whose angle is a multiple of (say) 0.2 degrees, and store the distance correct to the nearest whole number.

Keep count of the number of times each line appears. Lines parallel to the base line will appear more often than others.

Find the N most common lines and calculate the mean of their angles, θ.

Rotate the entire image by $-\theta$ and it should now be aligned nicely!

2

TIDY UP THE IMAGE

We then need to clean up the image so it can be analyzed. We start by removing any noise that has been introduced, either positively or negatively, and then break the text up into a hierarchy – paragraphs made up of lines, made up of words, made up of *glyphs*, which could be letters, numbers or punctuation.

Making sure the text makes sense at each level of the hierarchy is one of the key ideas behind OCR (optical character recognition).

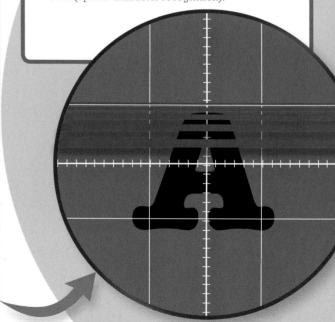

③

LETTER RECOGNITION

Sophisticated *feature-extraction* methods figure out which letter is which by analyzing things like whether each letter has a bulb, a stem or a tail. A more brute-force approach is to compare each glyph to a catalogue of known letters.

This *matrix-based* method involves turning your glyph into a grid, like the low-resolution A in the image. The program will then:

Take in turn each of the known glyphs it has stored;

Convert them to a grid of the same resolution;

Count how many pixels are different between your glyph and the stored glyph.

A simple approach is to take the highest-scoring glyph as the winner, but it is usually more sensible to assign a likelihood to each glyph: ones with many wrong pixels are less likely to be the correct glyph than ones with few.

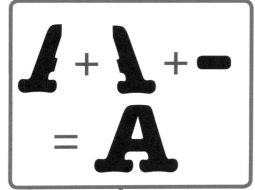

④

APPLY THE LEXICON

Once the glyphs have been analyzed, the software usually compares the potential guesses with a lexicon of allowed words – so a best-guess of "tbe" for a word would likely be "the." This also has potential drawbacks: what if your text uses words – proper nouns, for example – that are not in the lexicon?

This step uses a measure known as the *Levenshtein distance*, which (roughly speaking) counts how many simple edits you would need to turn one word into another. For example, to turn "Lewinsten" into "Levenshtein" would need two replacements (w to v and i to e) and two additions (and h and an i), so the Levenshtein distance between "Lewinsten" and "Levenshtein" is four. Generally, OCR software will favour the lexicon word with the smallest Levenshtein distance to be its best guess.

		L	E	W	E	N	S
	0	1	2	3	4	5	6
L	1	2	3	4	5	6	7
E	2	1	2	3	4	5	6
V	3	2	1	2	3	4	5
E	4	3	2	1	2	3	4
N	5	4	3	2	1	2	3

Computers (a Timeline)

Ask a mathematician what they think of computer science, and the answer will likely involve a scrunched up nose and a look of disgust. But this reaction hides one of the dirty secrets of mathematics: almost all of the development of calculating machines and computers is based on work done by mathematicians – many of them the most famous mathematicians of their time.

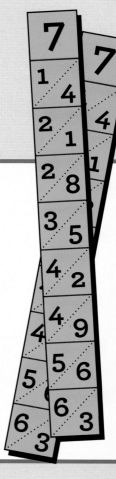

NAPIER AND HIS BONES

Aside from pretty much inventing the decimal point and the logarithm, for which generations of schoolchildren have cursed his name, the Scottish mathematician John Napier invented a tool now known as *Napier's Bones* – strips of ivory (in those days), wood or plastic (now) with the multiplication tables printed diagonally on them.

They do not really look like a computer, but they are an important part of the evolution of automated calculation. You can easily use them to work out large numbers multiplied by a single digit as shown: select the rods corresponding to the large number, and pick out the row corresponding to the small one. Working from the right, the total of the numbers in each diagonal corresponds to the units, tens, hundreds and so on in your answer. (You may need to carry a one over to the next diagonal – but that is not difficult.)

For example, to work out 372 by 7, you would take the 3, 7 and 2 "bones" and lay them out in that order. The 7th row reads 2/1 4/9 1/4, so your answer is [2] [5] [10] [4]; you would carry the 1 from the 10 onto the 6, making your answer 2,604.

Knowing how to perform that kind of calculation makes it possible (if not necessarily easy) to do long multiplication, long division, and even – with an extra, special bone – extract square roots.

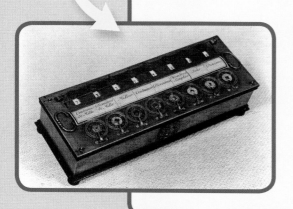

BLAISE PASCAL AND THE PASCALINE

The first real calculating machine was designed and built by Blaise Pascal (you may know him from such hits as Pascal's Wager, the SI unit for pressure and pretty much inventing probability) around 1643. You input numbers by twisting dials, and the machine added or subtracted them, as you preferred.

It was not designed as a mathematical machine so much as an administrative one: Pascal's father was a tax collector, and having a device to do some of the drudge work doubtless made his life more efficient. Pascal made around 50 Pascalines over the course of a decade.

GOTTFRIED LEIBNIZ AND THE CALCULATING MACHINE

In 1671, Gottfried Leibniz, a German diplomat best-known for a priority dispute with Isaac Newton over calculus (as Samuel Hansen says, Newton did it first, but Leibniz did it right), designed a calculating machine that did two better than Pascal's: the Step Reckoner, first built a couple of years later, could also multiply and divide. These operations took a bit of work (they did a mechanical version of the long multiplication and division methods I learned in school, more than 300 years later), but were still a leap forward in mechanical computation.

At least, it could do these sums in principle. In practice, the gear-work was too intricate for the 17th century, and a design flaw in the carry mechanism made the machine rather unreliable.

BABBAGE, LOVELACE AND THE ANALYTIC ENGINE

A significant advance in mechanical calculation was Charles Babbage's Difference Engine – which would have been able to compute polynomials to 31 decimal places, had it ever been built. However, Babbage and Joseph Clement, who was brought in to build it, fell out over costs and it was never finished; also, Babbage had become distracted by the idea of the Analytical Engine.

Inspired by the mechanical looms that were revolutionizing weaving in France, he designed a machine that would qualify as a computer today: rather than mechanizing algebra, it would be programmable by means of punch cards.

Famously, his collaborator Ada Lovelace published the first recognizable computer program around the same time, describing how to compute Bernoulli numbers.

The Analytical Engine was never built either.

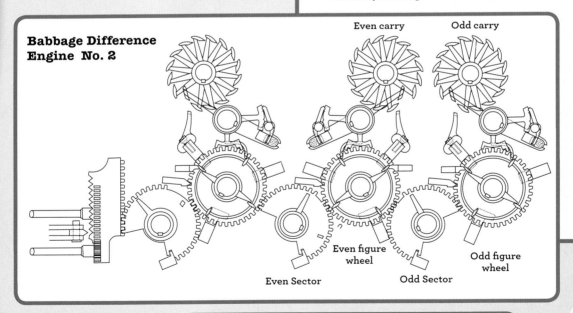

Babbage Difference Engine No. 2

Even carry · Odd carry · Even figure wheel · Odd figure wheel · Even Sector · Odd Sector

BERNOULLI NUMBERS

The Bernoulli numbers are a sequence of fractions used in the calculation of the tan and tanh functions, as well as in combinatorics, asymptotic analysis and topology. The first few terms are 1, -1/2, 1/6, 0, -1/30, 0, 1/42, 0 and -1/30.

GENAILLE-LUCAS RODS

An ingenious development of Napier's bones came in 19th-century France, where mathematician Édouard Lucas posed an arithmetic problem and railway engineer Henri Genaille created a set of rulers to solve it.

A complicated-looking grid of numbers and triangles, Genaille–Lucas rods make multiplication by one-digit numbers straightforward by eliminating the need for any mental work: all you do is arrange the rods like you would for Napier's bones, pick the top number of the row you are interested in, and follow the triangles back to the start. To compute 584 × 8, you would take the index, 5, 8 and 4 rulers and arrange them side by side. Starting with the top number of the 8th row of the 4 ruler, you would get 2, pointing to a 7 on the 8 ruler. This points to a 6 on the 5 ruler, pointing to a 4 on the index ruler, giving you 4,672 as a correct answer.

You can redesign these rods to make division possible, but it is probably more trouble than it is worth: Genaille–Lucas rulers were popular for a few years, but were soon replaced by other calculating devices.

SLIDE RULES

Slide rules are older than the mechanical calculators listed previously – they were first put together by William Oughtred in the 17th century, around the same time as Napier's bones. The idea uses Napier's idea of logarithms turning multiplication into addition and division into subtraction. By taking two rulers, with numbers logarithmically spaced on them, and sliding one past the other, multiplication and division of large numbers becomes a matter of reading numbers off a scale.

Adding inverse, trigonometric, logarithmic and exponential scales to a slide rule dramatically increases the number of potential calculations a skilled operator can do. The main limitations to slide rule mathematics are that you can only get answers as accurately as you can slide and read from the rulers, and that answers can go off the scale. The slide rule will usually give you the first few significant digits of what you are working out, but it is up to you to figure out whether 6.9 means 6.9, 0.069 or 6900!

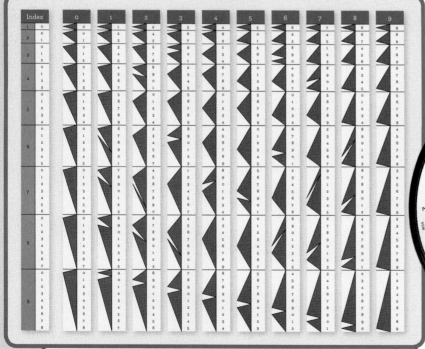

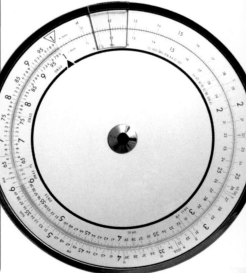

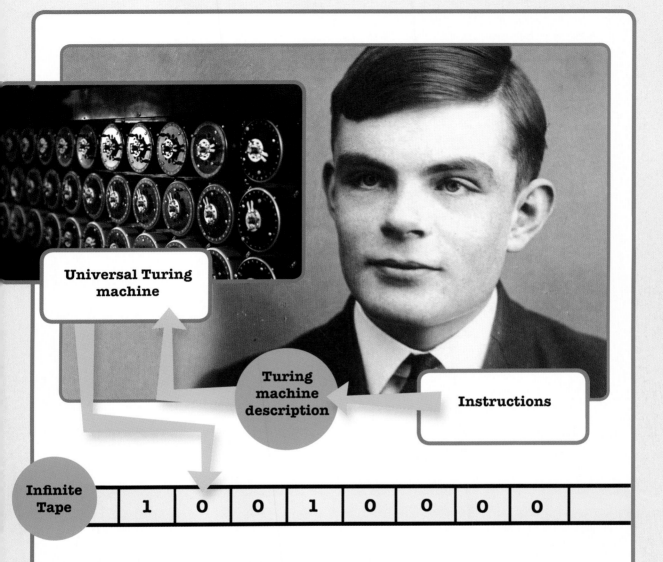

Universal Turing machine

Turing machine description

Instructions

Infinite Tape

| 1 | 0 | 0 | 1 | 0 | 0 | 0 | 0 | |

TURING, THE UNIVERSAL MACHINE AND WORLD WAR II

As part of a thought experiment about the *Entscheidungsproblem* – a problem posed by David Hilbert to determine whether an algorithm could classify every possible statement as "true" or "false" – Alan Turing came up with the idea of a Universal Machine. The Universal Machine would take a strip of paper, add and remove marks from it, and jump back and forth along it.

Again, this machine was not built – it was part of a thought experiment – but the idea of *Turing com-*

pleteness stems from it: in some sense, no computer language is any more powerful than the Universal Machine in terms of what it can theoretically achieve. Obviously, most are more practical.

Programmable computers were finally built during the Second World War, both at Bletchley Park in England (where Turing was serving as a code-breaker) and in the USA (the Manhattan Project, for example, made heavy use of new-fangled computers to simulate nuclear explosions).

Thinking Computers

Being able to say "Siri, I want to buy every book Colin Beveridge has ever written" and have the lot delivered immediately by drone would be amazing; at the same time, we all have nightmares of the "I'm sorry, Dave, I can't do that" variety.

• •

Artificial intelligence – computers which think for themselves – is simultaneously one of the most exciting and one of the most terrifying ideas in the modern world.

We will now look at some of the ways computers "think" and "learn", and discuss some of the implications.

HOW DOES GOOGLE KNOW WHAT I'M AFTER?

If there was ever a good anecdote to illustrate how doing your algebra homework makes your life and everybody else's a better place, it is the story of Larry Page and Sergey Brin. As part of a research project during their studies at Stanford in the 1990s, they devised an algorithm to determine which web pages were the most important ones. The whole of the web could (in principle) be modelled as a network of links, which could in turn be represented as a *transition matrix* showing where you would wind up next if you clicked at random. By iterating through the transitions over and over again, they could come up with a probability of landing on any given page, which they converted into a ranking – which they called PageRank.

And that was how Google got started. The basic idea is undergraduate-level mathematics, and yet it has grown in under two decades to be one of the largest corporations on the planet.

But does it *think*? That is a much harder question. What do we mean by think? A limited argument can certainly be made for it, at least for pure PageRank: it is making its own decisions based solely on the structure of the web and its pages, without human intervention (except at the level of trying to exploit the algorithm for personal gain or to embarrass

others). It discovers things unknown to its inventors. But at the same time, it has no notion of what it is actually doing, any more than a computer programmed to randomly create abstract art does.

TRANSITION MATRIX

The transition matrix shows the probability of moving from the page listed along the top to the page listed down the left-hand side. If you are on page A, you have a 100% chance of ending up on page B next, so the element in the transition matrix in the column corresponding to A and the row corresponding to B is 1. If you are on page B, you have a 50% chance of moving to C and a 50% chance of moving to D — so the corresponding elements are both ½.

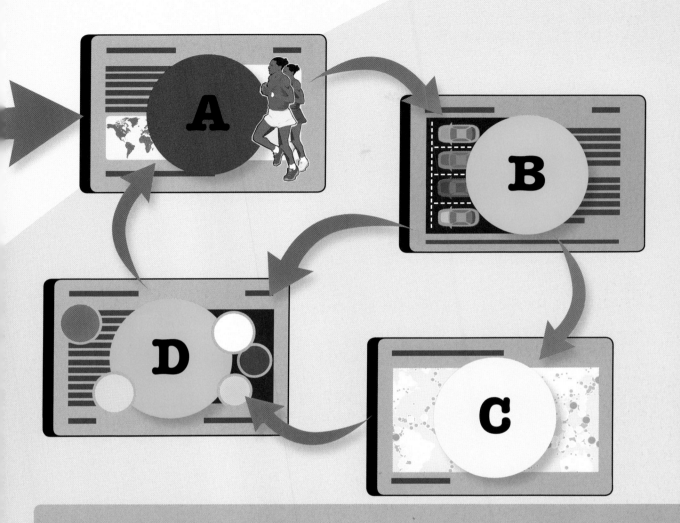

	END			
START	A	B	C	D
A	0	0	0	1
B	1	0	0	0
C	0	1/2	0	0
D	0	1/2	1	0

1
1
1/2
1

Linked Pages

Each column describes the fraction of links from one page to each of the others. The principal eigenvector of the resulting matrix gives the relative probabilities of ending on each page. Here, if you surfed at random, you're twice as likely to end up on A, B or D as you are on C.

WHY DOES AUTOCORRECT ALWAYS PICK THE MOST EMBARRASSING CORRECTION?

I am old enough to remember the days when, instead of using a virtual keyboard on a smartphone, sending a text message as simple as "On my way" would require you to type 666 66 0 6 999 0 9 2 999 on actual physical keys. Typing like this was a complete pain, and often led to garbled messages (and, in retrospect, it is perfectly understandable that text-speak abbreviations like "u" for "you" became commonplace; pressing 88 rather than 999 666 88 probably increased the life of mobile phones significantly).

At some point, somebody had an idea: how about, instead of having to press the keys one at a time, you just press them once and the phone can try to figure out what you mean? So, if you type 968, the keys with Y, O and U on, the machine can infer that you mean "YOU" rather than "ZOV" or, only slightly more plausibly, "WOT". This was a great innovation, and

in most cases, you did not need to put so much effort into checking you had pressed the keys the right number of times. You did not feel the *need* to check the message so carefully, because fewer of your messages were garbled. And this bred complacency: if you are not checking carefully, you can easily send a message confusing "RAIN" for "PAIN", or "DARN" for "FARM". Generally, though, there were (at most) only a few possible options for each set of keys and the phone would be correct most of the time – and if not, it would be clear enough what you meant. There is still very little thinking (or even mathematics) involved: the machine is simply matching a list of numbers against a list of words.

Enter the virtual keyboard, and things suddenly get much more complicated.

It is simple enough mathematically to figure out which virtual key someone pressed – every

ARE THE COMPUTERS GOING TO TAKE OVER AND ENSLAVE THE HUMANS?

In 1965, the co-founder of Intel, Gordon Moore, noted that the maximum density of transistors in computers had doubled every year since the invention of the transistor, and predicted that the trend would continue for some time. The observed rate has slowed slightly over time (Moore himself revised his estimate to every two years in the 1970s, and Intel suggested 2.5 years was the current rate in 2015).

Why does this matter? It turns out that transistor density is a proxy for computing power. Even ignoring the improvements in chip efficiency, the effect of doubling power every two years for five decades means that today's computers are several millions of times quicker and able than those of the 1960s. The effect of doubling every 30 months for the next five decades will mean another million-fold improvement.

This leads to a potential problem, known as *The Singularity*: at some point, in the not-too-distant future, computers will have more processing power than the human brain, at which point genuine artificial intelligence becomes almost an inevitability.

time you touch the screen, the event is registered with the relevant coordinates; if those coordinates lie within the outline of a key, that is the key you pressed. However, your phone is not a typewriter. It wants to come up with what you *meant* to do, not what you actually did. Instead of saying "you hit 'G'", the phone might think "you hit 'G' with a probability of 57%, 'F', 'T', 'Y', 'H', 'V', 'B' and 'C' with 5% each, and all of the other letters with probability 1%." (These are "for example" numbers – cell phone manufacturers do serious statistical analysis.) When you hit a sequence of keys between two spaces, the machine can check the likelihood of all of the words in its dictionary against what you actually typed, simply by multiplying the probabilities of all of the letters in each word, and chooses the most plausible option.

There is more to it than that, of course. The most plausible option also looks at the commonness of words (I am more likely to mean "Fire!" than "Fie!", because I am not texting a Shakespearean play most of the time) and of phrases (even if I type "NOOK" after "I'm writing my...", I would hope the phone would correct it to "BOOK").

So why does it get it wrong so often and so embarrassingly? The truth is, it *does not* get it wrong very often. We, as humans, get it wrong almost all the time, and autocorrect has to put it right. We are so reliant on it that we expect it to know what we mean.

As for the embarrassing typos? It is easy enough to make those on a computer without "autocorrect". Embarrassing miscorrections are pretty rare. It is just that when they *do* occur, they tend to get packaged into viral images and shared widely.

Sport

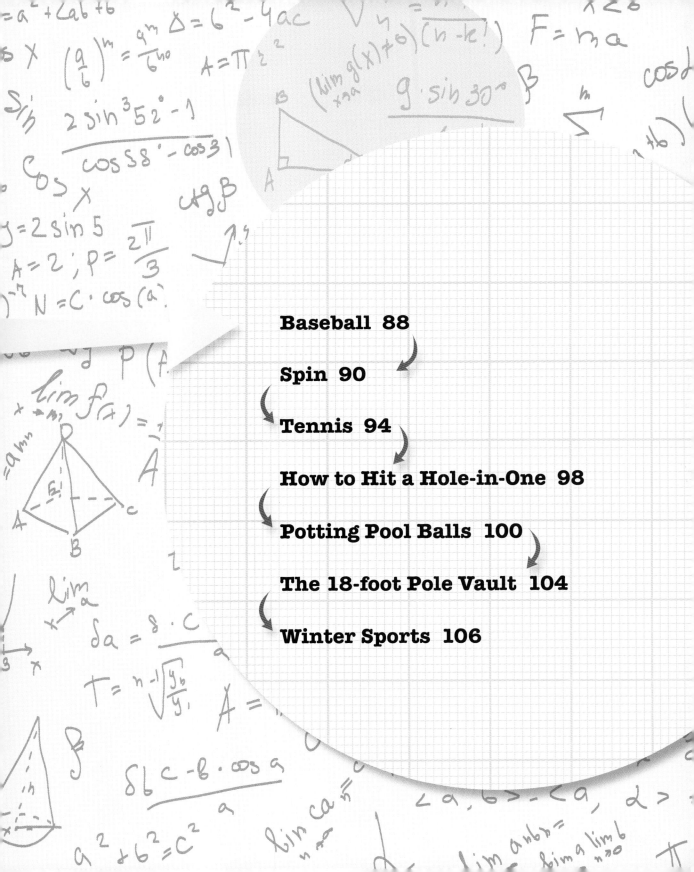

Baseball

$$SP = \frac{singles + 2 \times doubles + 3 \times triples + 4 \times home\ runs}{at\ bats}$$

In 2002, the Oakland A's were, let us say, at a "financial disadvantage". Compared to the top teams in Major League Baseball, their annual revenue was paltry – the Yankees, for example, brought in nearly three times as much, and only two teams in Major League Baseball had a lower payroll. So how could a team with so little money become competitive with the richest in the league?

Baseball has always been a statistician's game – it lends itself to comparing players' batting averages (how many hits they made divided by the number of times they came up to bat – 0.300 is generally considered very good), earned run averages (how many runs the pitcher would have been responsible for over the course of a game) and countless other comparisons.

In addition, scouts would typically test physical attributes like speed and strength before recommending players based largely on their gut feeling.

The A's, under the stewardship of Billy Beane, pretty much tore up those specific traditions in favour of a different way of making their picks: they deconstructed the game of baseball and figured out what things made them more likely to win.

A key finding was that the traditional statistics were a poor guide to a player's value to the team: characteristics like "getting on base" were found to be more important than raw batting average. This makes sense: the longer you can go without collecting outs, the more runs your team will tend to score.

Similarly, the A's valued *slugging percentage*, which is worked out as the total number of bases reached per at bat. Whereas the traditional batting average counts all hits the same, the slugging average counts a double for two points, a triple for three and a home run for four points.

$$SP = \frac{singles + 2 \times doubles + 3 \times triples + 4 \times home\ runs}{at\ bats}$$

Because other teams continued to base their signings on the old-fashioned stats and the scout's feel, the economic laws of supply and demand meant that the players the A's were after turned out to be much cheaper to employ than orthodox superstars. Despite their economic shortfall, the A's reached the playoffs in 2002 and 2003 – by which point the bigger teams had cottoned on to the benefits of a statistical approach and eroded Oakland's advantage.

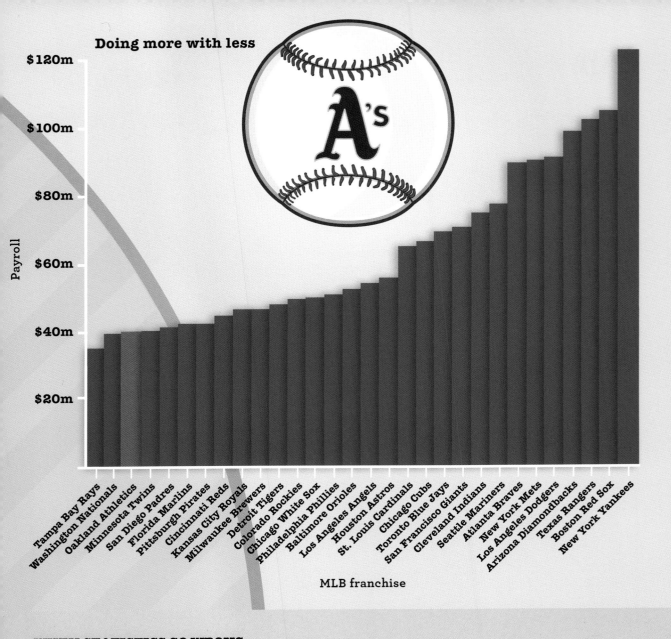

Doing more with less

Payroll

$120m
$100m
$80m
$60m
$40m
$20m

Tampa Bay Rays
Washington Nationals
Oakland Athletics
Minnesota Twins
San Diego Padres
Florida Marlins
Pittsburgh Pirates
Cincinnati Reds
Kansas City Royals
Milwaukee Brewers
Detroit Tigers
Colorado Rockies
Chicago White Sox
Philadelphia Phillies
Baltimore Orioles
Los Angeles Angels
Houston Astros
St. Louis Cardinals
Chicago Cubs
Toronto Blue Jays
San Francisco Giants
Cleveland Indians
Seattle Mariners
Atlanta Braves
New York Mets
Los Angeles Dodgers
Arizona Diamondbacks
Texas Rangers
Boston Red Sox
New York Yankees

MLB franchise

WHEN STATISTICS GO WRONG

"No more than three passes" was the catchphrase of one of soccer's first statistical analysts, Charles Reep. Reep spent the 1950s relentlessly documenting English matches, devising his own notation system and using a miner's helmet to help illuminate his notebook on a wet Wednesday night in the less pretty parts of England.

Reep's analysis determined that most goals scored were the result of moves of three passes or fewer – analysis that convinced many clubs of the benefits of the "long ball system," moving the ball as far down the pitch as possible, as quickly

as possible. As late as the 1990s, many teams still based their style of play on Reep's systems.

Sadly, those systems were awful. Not just in an aesthetic sense (using the long ball is a *very* dull way to play soccer) but in a statistical sense too: as soccer writer Jonathan Wilson points out, around 90% of all of the moves Reep analyzed comprised three or fewer passes, but only 80% of the goals came from such moves. Short moves (like long ball) produced many goals because they were common – but in fact, they were *less* likely to produce goals than longer moves.

Spin

Everyone who has ever watched a pitcher throw a curveball has experienced the effect of spin and swerve on a ball. But why do balls behave like that? The rule of thumb in determining how the spin of a ball determines its swerve boils down to a single phrase: the ball follows its nose.

$$\frac{F}{L} = 2\pi r^2 \omega \rho v$$

Applying top spin to a ball means the front of the ball is spinning downwards, and the ball will tend to dip. Throwing a ball forwards so it spins clockwise when viewed from the top means it will move to the right. Why is this?

An instinctive explanation is to imagine the air the ball is travelling through is made of tiny, light beads – as your ball spins and moves forward, it knocks the beads out of the way and moves them around.

First, let us think about what happens if we throw a ball without spin. The main effect is to push the beads in front of the ball together,

slowing the ball down as they push back. Some of the beads slip by the ball on either side – there is no reason for them to favour one side or the other, and the *pressure* – roughly, how densely the beads are packed – on either side is about the same.

If, instead, you add a little side spin as we did before, so as to spin the ball clockwise when viewed from the top, the beads on the left side of the ball are pushed together more forcefully than the beads on the right, which are being helped past the ball as it spins. There is a build-up of pressure not just in front of the ball, but even more so on the left-hand side, while the

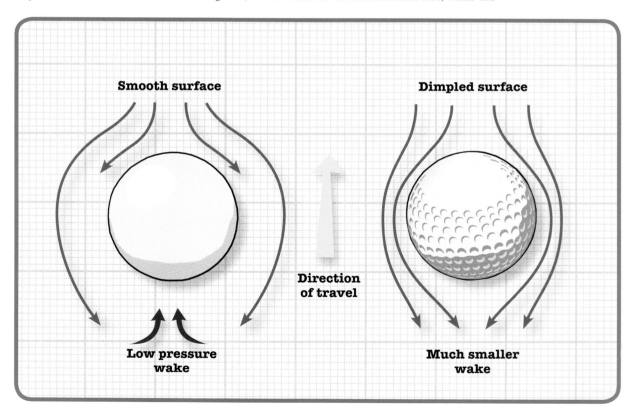

Smooth surface

Dimpled surface

Direction of travel

Low pressure wake

Much smaller wake

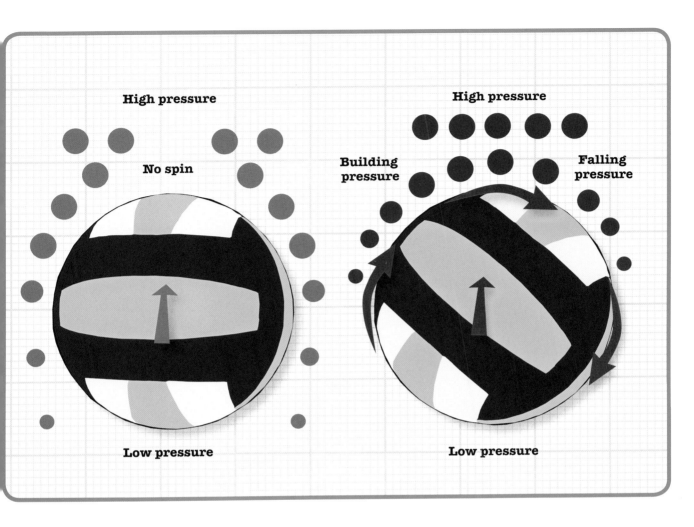

High pressure

No spin

Low pressure

High pressure

Building pressure

Falling pressure

Low pressure

pressure on the right-hand side drops. The combination of the two means the beads push the ball slightly to the right, in the direction the front of the ball is spinning.

The reasons spin affects the flight of a ball were deduced by Newton in the 17th century, but it was German physicist Heinrich Gustav Magnus who studied the mathematics of it in the 1850s. He determined that the force per unit length on a cylinder of radius r, moving forwards through a medium of density ρ with a speed of v, spinning around its axis at a rotational speed of ω, would be $F/L = 2\pi r^2 \omega \rho v$.

For a sphere, it gets more complicated, since there is more than one possible axis for

the ball to spin around. For top or back spin, the axis of rotation is horizontal, and parallel to the ball's forward motion, while for side spin, it is vertical. You could also combine these with spin parallel to the forward motion of the ball – in effect, the axis of rotation could be pointing in any direction!

The effect on the maths of a variable axis is to turn the scalar equation into a vector one; the change of shape also changes some of the scaling, and you end up with the following for the force vector:

$$\boldsymbol{F} = \pi^2 r^3 \rho \, \boldsymbol{\omega} \times \boldsymbol{v}$$

CURVEBALLS AND KNUCKLEBALLS

When you wind up and unleash a fastball, you almost certainly drag your fingers down the back of the ball as you release it, imparting back spin. If you are a curveball pitcher, you add some sideways spin as well to make the ball follow its nose one way or the other.

But there is another way to pitch that, done well, is more baffling than either: the knuckleball. It can veer dramatically from one side to the other, then change direction mid-flight. At 80mph, it takes about half a second to reach the batter – but the change in movement over the last third of that can be devastating.

The trick to throwing a knuckleball is to send it down with practically no spin. You hold the ball between your thumb and third finger, and place the fingernail of your index finger just behind the seam to keep the ball from spinning as you let it go with a push. Instead of rotating many times on its way to the batter, it spins maybe twice.

Rotating like that, the air resistance acting on the seam comes into play in an unpredictable way: the spin can be slowed down, stopped, and reversed just by the way the ball moves through the air. Going back to our beads model, adding a seam to the ball as it spins means the beads can push back against the spin, twisting the ball around the other way. It can even be reversed again later in the motion if the other side of the seam finds itself pushing against the air on the other side – which is what makes it swerve in different directions! (By contrast, the rotations of a rapidly spinning ball will just slow down slightly, rather than change direction.)

It is not all that hard to throw a knuckleball; the difficulty comes in throwing it fast and accurately. It is a much slower pitch than most, so if it does not move about in the air, it is easier for a batter to hit.

It is surprising that relatively slow spin makes such a difference, but even a couple of rotations between pitcher and batter give a significant deviation. Putting approximate values into the Magnus equation gives a force of about 0.2N – enough to move the ball eight inches either way over the half-second it is in flight.

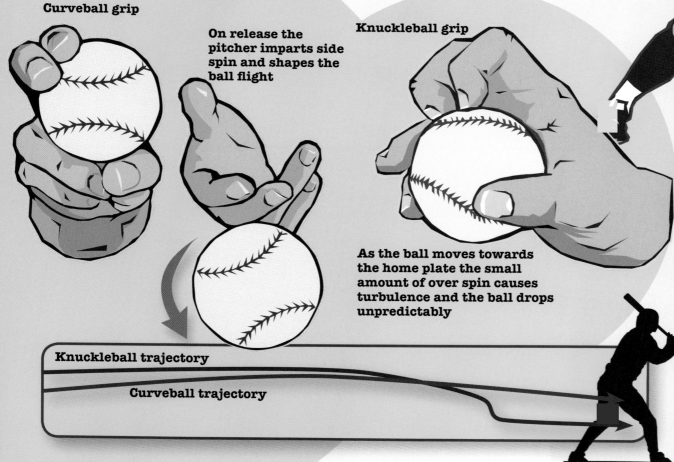

Curveball grip

On release the pitcher imparts side spin and shapes the ball flight

Knuckleball grip

As the ball moves towards the home plate the small amount of over spin causes turbulence and the ball drops unpredictably

Knuckleball trajectory

Curveball trajectory

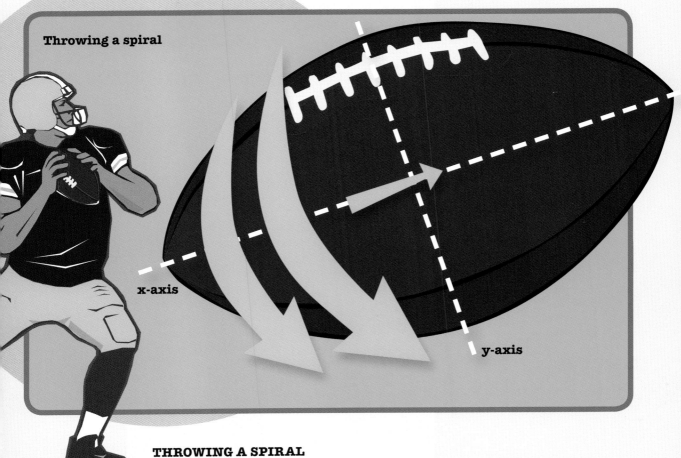

Throwing a spiral

x-axis

y-axis

THROWING A SPIRAL

If you are a quarterback, when you first learned to throw a football, you learned to throw a *spiral* – you would never throw the ball without a great deal of spin around its longest axis. But why would you spin a ball when you want it to go roughly straight?

There is a key difference between a spiral and a curveball: a curveball rotates around the vertical axis, which is at right angles to the way the ball is moving. A spiral spins around the axis moving in the same direction as the ball, which gives a completely different effect. Looking at the Magnus equation again, it contains a *vector product*, $\boldsymbol{\omega} \times \boldsymbol{v}$. Vector products combine the size of the two vectors involved with the sine of the angle between them. For a perfect spiral, the axis of rotation is parallel to the velocity vector, so the sine of the angle between them is zero, and there is no force at all due to the spin!

In fact, spinning it in that direction does not change the ball's direction at all: instead, it keeps the ball balanced and moving in the same direction as you threw it. That is important, because throwing the ball accurately long distances requires air resistance to be kept to a minimum, which means keeping the ball's cross-section as consistently small as possible. As soon as the ball deviates, the cross-section changes and the ball tends to move from its planned path, and to slow down – neither of which you want if you are trying to pick out a receiver some way downfield.

The mathematics behind throwing a spiral rather than a curveball is that the spiral's spin makes the ball *easier* to predict, while a curveball makes it *harder*. Which makes sense: in football, you are throwing to a team-mate; in baseball, to an opponent.

Tennis

$$v = \frac{\Delta fc}{2}$$

Bernard Tomic barely even saw it, let alone get his racket to it. John Isner, serving to stay in the third set of their 2016 Davis Cup rubber, unleashed a mighty serve straight down the line that clocked in at 157.2 miles per hour. But how do they know that?

SPEED GUNS

The trick is to use a radar gun pointed at the ball. If you send a beam of light at a moving object, depending on its direction of motion, the frequency of the light you receive back changes. This is known as the *Doppler effect* and can be heard by listening to, say, an approaching car: as the car passes you, the pitch of its engine appears to drop, and you hear a lower note. Exactly the same thing works with light waves, and even with pulses of light.

Mathematically, the change in frequency can be measured. The speed, v, of the moving object away from or towards the gun is (the proportional change in frequency, Δf) × (half the speed of light, c):

$$v = \frac{\Delta fc}{2}$$

There was a sudden increase in record serve speeds in the late 2000s as technology improved: early radar guns were only able to measure speed in the direction they were facing, so a serve to the corner (about 15 degrees away from straight-on, as far as the speed gun is concerned) would appear to be about 3.5% slower than one down the middle. Modern radar guns use pulses of light rather than a continuous stream, which allow the speed to be measured in any direction.

The speed itself is measured immediately after it leaves the server's racket, which is the fastest it travels on its journey to the other end of the court. Air resistance and bouncing mean that it is generally travelling about half the measured speed by the time it reaches the receiver.

Even so, a ball moving at 80 miles per hour... it's not something I would want to be in the way of!

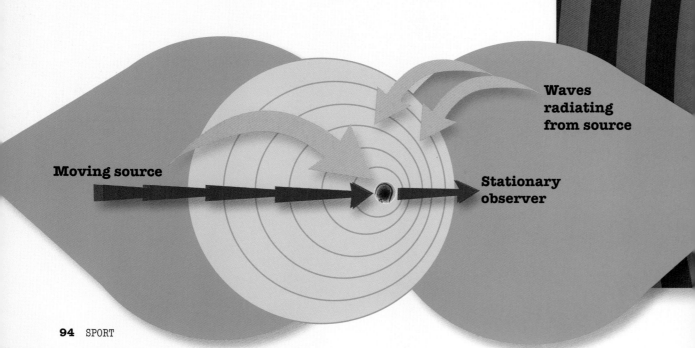

Waves radiating from source

Moving source

Stationary observer

RANKINGS

In the first round of the 1990 US Open, world number one Stefan Edberg was on the wrong end of one of tennis's biggest upsets. Against the unseeded Russian Alexander Volkov, so unfancied that he had booked his flight home for the evening of the match, Edberg went down 6–3, 7–6, 6–2.

Despite his capitulation – and it is hard to over-stress how awful a result this was – Edberg, bizarrely, retained his number one spot in the rankings.

How?

It comes down to the way the rankings are calculated. It has changed slightly over the last 30-odd years, but the basic principles remain the same. Every professional tennis tournament, from Grand Slams like the US Open and Wimbledon, where the winners can expect to pick up several million dollars, down to Futures tournaments with a total prize money in the tens of thousands, gives a number of points based on how far you progress. Winning a Grand Slam is worth 2,000 points. The semifinal of a Masters series match wins you 360. Reaching the round of 16 in a Futures tournament nets you a whole ranking point! Generally, the more important the tournament, and the further you progress through it, the more points you win.

There is a limit, though. Your total ranking score is restricted to your best 18 or 19 scores from the previous 52 weeks, so you cannot artificially inflate your score by playing more tournaments.

Perhaps surprisingly, this kind of ranking system in tennis has only been around since the 1970s. Before then, qualification for tournaments was pretty much arbitrary: the tournament directors and national tennis associations could invite whoever they liked to take part, meaning that some players who deserved to take part would be excluded for political reasons. After 81 players boycotted Wimbledon in 1973, the system was introduced to make sure of a level playing field.

It is a fairly simple system – so how could Edberg retain his crown while bowing out in the first round?

That is easy. The US Open was never his strongest tournament, and in 1989 he had reached the fourth round. His net loss due to the Volkov debacle only amounted to a few dozen points – and his nearest challengers for the title, Boris Becker and Ivan Lendl, had contested the final the previous year. Defending champion Becker obviously could not improve on that result, while Lendl was too many points behind to catch up with Edberg.

ATP rankings at the start and end of 1990

	1 January 1990				31 December 1990		
1	Ivan Lendl	TCH	2913 points	1	Stefan Edberg	SWE	3889 points
2	Boris Becker	GER	2279 points	2	Boris Becker	GER	3528 points
3	Stefan Edberg	SWE	2111 points	3	Ivan Lendl	TCH	2581 points
4	Brad Gilbert	USA	1398 points	4	Andre Agassi	USA	2398 points
5	John McEnroe	USA	1354 points	5	Pete Sampras	USA	1888 points
6	Michael Chang	USA	1328 points	6	Andrés Gómez	ECU	1680 points
7	Aaron Krickstein	USA	1217 points	7	Thomas Muster	AUT	1654 points
8	Andre Agassi	USA	1160 points	8	Emilio Sánchez	ESP	1564 points
9	Jay Berger	USA	1039 points	9	Goran Ivanišević	YUG	1514 points
10	Alberto Mancini	ARG	1024 points	10	Brad Gilbert	USA	1451 points

SHOULD YOU SERVE OR RECEIVE?

Suppose each player wins 90% of their service games – except when they are under pressure and know that losing the game will lose them the set, in which case it is a toss-up. Should you serve first or second?

The answer is a resounding "first" – if you serve first, the normal course of events is for the set to follow serve until you are leading 5-4, at which point your opponent is under pressure. Even if they keep their cool, you will then have a routine service game, be leading 6-5, and have another good chance to break serve and win the set.

Even though you and your opponent are evenly matched in skill, winning the toss and serving first would put your chances of winning before a tie-break at 58%, and your opponent's at 30%. Worse still for your opponent: because the serve continues to alternate, you will also be serving first in the next set about 63% of the time!

58%
better chance of winning by serving first

HOW MUCH BETTER MUST YOU BE TO WIN?

Tennis is a game of tiny margins: a failure on one critical point can easily become the difference between victory and defeat. To show how tiny, imagine you have a 55% probability of winning any point against me – you win on average 11 points out of 20. How likely are you to beat me over five sets?

Because of the scoring system – one player needs to score at least four points, with a two-point gap – I need more luck to beat you than you need to beat me. Your probability of beating me in any given game works out to be a bit more than 62%.

It gets more severe when it comes to the probability of winning a set: ignoring tie-breaks (although you could work them out, if you wanted to), your chance of winning at least six games with a two-game margin becomes something in the region of 82% – you would expect to win slightly more than four sets of every five.

That translates into a probability of winning a five-set match of nearly 96%. You would beat me in about 22 of every 23 matches we played, despite having only a relatively small technical advantage over me. Even if I trained until I won 49% of the available points, I would still beat you barely once in every three matches.

How to Hit a Hole-in-One

$$\arctan\left(\frac{2.125}{180}\right) \approx 0.67 \text{ degrees}$$

Miguel Ángel Jiménez watched his tee shot spin back into the cup, held his arms aloft, holstered his club and danced a little jig. His ace at Wentworth's 148-yard second hole in 2015 was his tenth of his 28-year professional career: nobody has hit more holes-in-one on tour than Jiménez.

"PLAY ON SHORT HOLES – BUT NOT TOO SHORT!" AND OTHER NONSENSICAL ADVICE

According to the National Hole-In-One Register, the most likely holes on which to hit an ace are not the very shortest holes: around half of holes-in-one are made with six to nine irons. Details of their statistical analysis are surprisingly lacking. I would not be very surprised to find that the distribution of holes-in-one owes more to the number of holes of that length than to the accuracy of the clubs!

With most holes-in-one, including Jiménez's, the ball lands some way beyond the pin and rolls back into it. If you land the ball 4.57 m (15 feet) beyond the flag on a flat green, and the ball has a 10.8 cm (4.25 inch) wide target, the direction it needs to roll back is about two-thirds of a degree either side of the line to the middle of the hole. The pace on the ball also needs to be right, or else it may fall short or overshoot the hole.

$$\arctan\left(\frac{2.125}{180}\right) \approx 0.67 \text{ degrees}$$

The better a player you are, the more likely you are to hit a hole-in-one, but it is unlikely even if you're a pro! A pro can expect an ace every 3,000 rounds or so, while a low-handicap golfer might hit one every 5,000. A duffer like me would need to play more like 12,000 rounds before sinking one off the tee.

5-IRON 8%

6-IRON 11%

7-IRON 14%

Percentage of holes-in-one hit by each club

8-IRON 14%

9-IRON 12%

PITCHING WEDGE 7%

Rounds of golf per hole-in-one

12,000

5,000

3,000

Professional

Low-handicap player

Duffer

DON'T DO IT IN JAPAN

While your chances of hitting a hole-in-one are slim, the consequences of doing it in Japan can be devastating: the local custom is for anyone who hits an ace to throw a huge party for everyone at the course.

Or at least, that is what the insurance companies tell you. In the 1980s, only the wealthiest of Japan's population could afford to play the game. Surely only a cynic would suggest that an insurance company started the "tradition" as something to offer insurance against, bringing their company to the attention of potential clients?

THE FORMULA FOR THE PERFECT PUTT

Researchers at various Scottish universities have developed a formula describing the putting technique of several golfers. Here it is:

The perfect putt

$$V_c = 2D\left(\frac{1}{T}\right)\left(\frac{P_T}{k}\right)\left(1 - P_T^2\right)\left(\frac{1}{k}\right) - 1$$

where V_c is club speed, D is the amplitude of forward swing, T is the time of the forwards swing, P_T is the proportion of time before the ball is hit from the top of the swing and k is "a figure used by psychologists to denote how golfers' internal guide couples with the timing of the shot." If you believe this will help you with your putting, the researchers are also reported to have a bridge for sale.

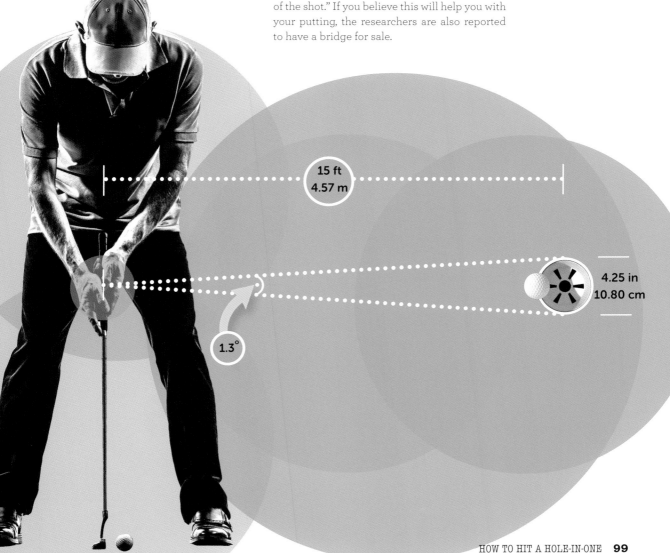

15 ft
4.57 m

4.25 in
10.80 cm

1.3°

Potting Pool Balls

$$\tan^{-1}\left(\frac{2.9}{96}\right)$$

Mathematically, you won't be wasting time playing pool. It involves some really cool geometry. Like, how hard is it to pot a pool ball and why is it easier to do it straight on?

THE GEOMETRY OF POTTING

How hard is it to pot a pool ball?

Naturally, it depends on the setup, but some things remain the same. An American pool ball is 5.7 cm (2¼ inches) in diameter, while the mouths of the corner pockets are roughly double that – between 11.4–11.8 cm (4½ and 4⅝ inches) wide; the side pockets are usually another 1.3 cm (half-inch) wider. A standard table is 2.7 m (9 feet) long by 1.4 m (4½ feet) wide. Let us suppose we want to pot a ball that is midway between a corner pocket and a side pocket, as pictured. How much leeway do we have?

A perfect shot would put the ball exactly in the middle of the pocket, but "in the pocket" is good enough! Because the pocket is double the width of the ball, we can afford for the middle of the ball to be half a ball-width away from the

centre of the pocket – so we can be up to 2.9 cm (1⅛ inches) off in either direction.

We are trying to pot a ball that is 68 cm (27 inches) from the cushions. Pythagoras's theorem tells us that the distance to the corner is the square root of $68^2 + 68^2$, or about 96 cm.

If we need to travel 96 cm and arrive within 2.9 cm of where we planned, we can work out how big an error in the angle we can allow: it's $\tan^{-1}(2.9/96)$ which is about 1.7 degrees.

Looking at the pool ball in the middle, that means there is a 3.4 degree sweet spot on it – if we can hit the ball in that sweet spot (and hard enough, but not too hard), it should drop nicely into the pocket. That is a little less than 1% of the ball – we have got a target that is roughly 0.18 cm (0.07 inches) wide.

WHY IT'S EASIER TO POT FROM STRAIGHT ON THAN FROM AN ANGLE

Depending on where you play the white ball from, the sweet spot can appear larger or smaller. The more straight-on the angle, the less accurate you need to be!

In the example, the sweet spot is 0.18 cm wide, and if you are shooting from straight on, it looks pretty much 0.18 cm wide. If instead you are shooting from a 45 degree angle, it looks smaller, but not by *that* much – you have still got about 0.13 cm to play with. What about if you are trying for an ultra-fine cut, at right angles to the pocket? It is a shot to nothing. You have only 0.0026 cm to aim at, and the slightest error on the wrong side means you will miss the ball completely!

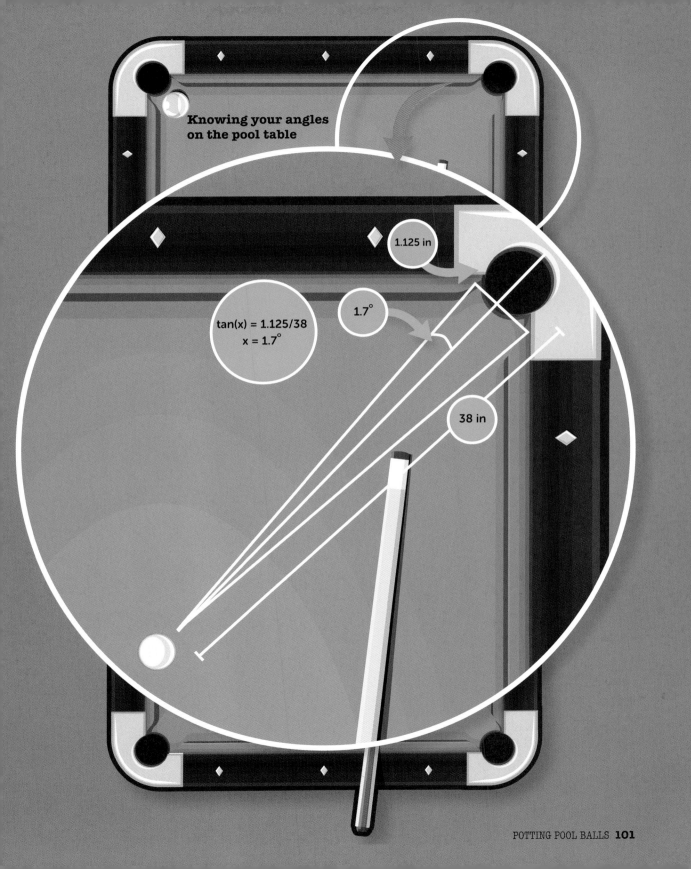

Knowing your angles on the pool table

1.125 in

$$\tan(x) = 1.125/38$$
$$x = 1.7°$$

1.7°

38 in

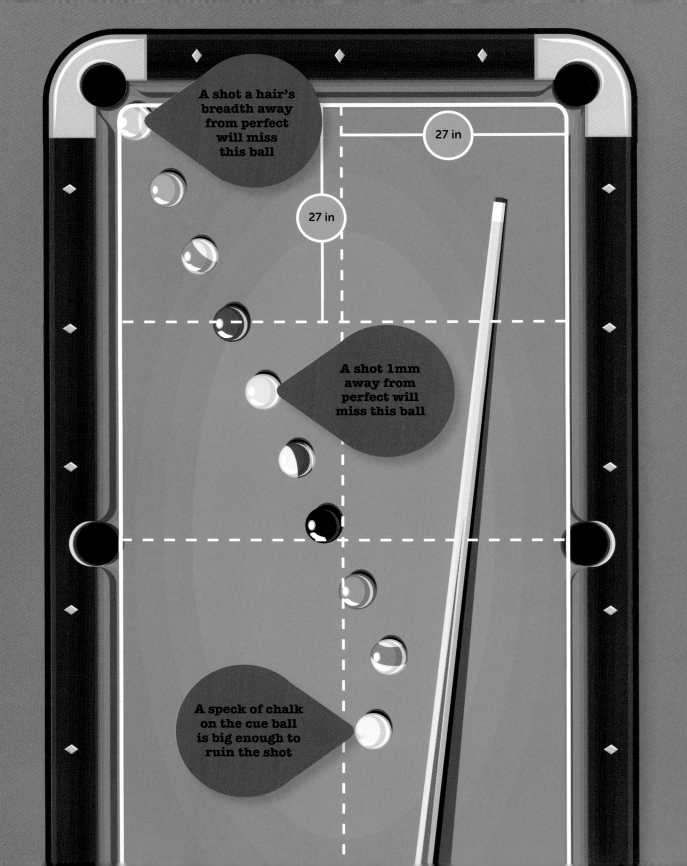

CAN YOU SINK A NINE-BALL PLANT?

Take nine pool balls and line them up on the table in a straight line pointing towards your favourite pocket. Leave a couple of pool-ball widths between each pair. Can you knock the first ball into the second so it knocks into the third and so on until the ninth ball goes into the pocket?

It looks like it ought to be simple. You can almost hear the balls tock-tock-tocking into each other, can't you?

However, I am going to go out on a limb and say that, no matter how good you are, and no matter how straight you play the shot, you are not going to make it. You will be lucky to even *hit* the ninth ball.

The trouble with plant shots like this is that errors get magnified very quickly. In this setup, being off by 1 mm in your aim means the contact between the first and second ball would be 2 mm off-target. Each subsequent contact is about twice as far off-target as the one before – so balls 2 and 3 would hit 4 mm away from centre, and ball 5 would miss ball 6 altogether.

So, how accurate would you need to be if you wanted to pot the ninth ball? Let us suppose you need the contact with the ninth ball to be accurate to within 2 mm. The contact before would need to be correct to within 1 mm. The one before that, half a millimetre. And so on, each sweet spot half of the size of the one before it. The first of the nine contacts would need to be within about a two-hundred-and-fiftieth of a millimetre – 4 micrometres. For comparison, a human hair is about 75 micrometres wide.

However, at that scale, hitting the first ball straight is not your only problem! This model also assumes that you can place the balls down in a perfectly straight line (even the slightest deviation will decrease accuracy – and if you can place a pool ball to micrometre accuracy, you have a steadier hand than me!) You would need the cloth to run perfectly smoothly. Even specks of chalk on the table are typically a few micrometers in size, enough to knock your ball off-track.

In short, you are not going to make the shot without a healthy dose of luck – but at least you have a huge number of excuses!

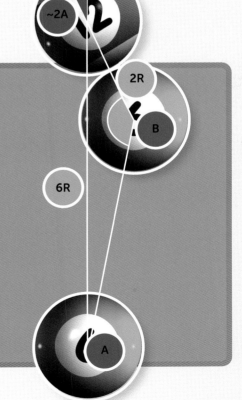

HOW ERRORS MULTIPLY

The geometry of a plant shot relies on a little bit of trigonometry. The centre of the object ball (which has radius R), the centre of the white when it is struck, and the centre of the white when the balls connect, form a triangle with sides $2R$ and $6R$ as marked, and an error angle of A.

Applying the sine rule, $2R/\sin(A) = 6R/\sin(B)$, which leads to $\sin(B) = 3\sin(A)$. Because it is a triangle, $A + B + C = 180°$, and the laws of trigonometry dictate that $\sin(B) = \sin(180° - B) = \sin(A + C)$, so $\sin(A + C) = 3\sin(A)$. If we use radians, we can use a small-angle approximation and say that this means $A + C \approx 3A$, so $C \approx 2A$.

The ball then moves about $4R$ (two ball-widths) on this trajectory, and strikes the other ball roughly $4AR$ away from straight-on. That is about twice as far away from straight-on as the previous contact was, so the next angle is approximately twice as big again.

The 18-foot Pole Vault

$$KE = \frac{1}{2}mv^2$$

Watching Usain Bolt coast home in the 200 metres, you would be forgiven for thinking that athletics was all genetics, body strength and technique. For sprinting, that is pretty much the case: you get out of the blocks as soon as you hear the gun, then run as fast as you possibly can until you reach the finish line.

Other events, though, involve much more interesting mathematics. How does Renaud Lavillenie manage all of the moving parts in an 18-foot pole vault?

In large part, the mathematics of the pole vault boils down to "the faster you run, the higher you can jump." As you gather speed in your sprint, you gain kinetic energy: if you are travelling at a speed of v, you have a kinetic energy of $\frac{1}{2}mv^2$ (where m is your mass). If you are a height of h above the height you started from, you have a gravitational potential energy of mgh, where g is your acceleration towards the earth (about 32 feet per second per second). The perfect pole vault converts all of your kinetic energy from sprinting into gravitational potential energy.

So, you have the equation $\frac{1}{2}mv^2 = mgh$, which simplifies to $v^2 = 2gh$. If you know how fast you are moving, you can calculate your maximum clearance height. A decent sprinter might travel at about 31 feet per second, and would be able to increase their height by $(31 \times 31)/(2 \times 32) \approx 15$ feet.

That is how far your *centre of mass* rises in a vault. If you are 6 feet tall, your centre of mass is probably around 3 feet off the ground when you begin, meaning you could reach a height of around 18 feet from the ground if you shape your body appropriately. This corresponds pretty well to respectable pole-vaulting: an 18-foot vault would have got you joint seventh place at the 2016 Rio Olympics.

...converting to gravitational potential...

Sprinting to gain kinetic energy...

Some ways you can improve your pole vaulting heights include:

running faster (every extra foot per second you can run gains you about a foot at this speed)

using a lighter pole (this does not make you go any higher; it just means you can run faster)

passing over the bar feet first in an up-side-down U-shape (this allows your body to pass over the bar while your centre of mass passes underneath it – without knocking the bar off!)

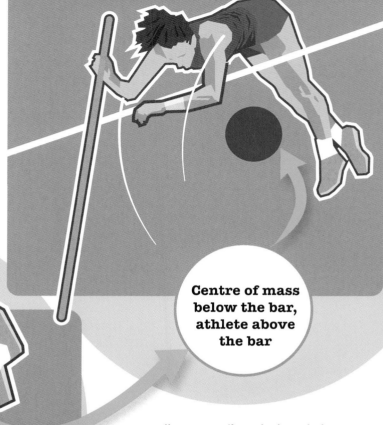

Catapult effect

Centre of mass below the bar, athlete above the bar

travelling more efficiently through the air (air resistance is not in this model, but certainly slows you down)

reducing gravity by moving further from the centre of the earth (for example, the shape of the earth means that nearly tropical Rio de Janeiro is slightly further from the centre of the earth than practically arctic London; gravity is a quarter of a per cent weaker in Rio than it is in London, meaning the same jump in Brazil would get you nearly half an inch higher).

If you get *really* good at the pole vault, you can do what Sergey Bubka did: repeatedly (35 times!) break the world record by a quarter-inch at a time, picking up massive bonuses for each new mark.

Winter Sports

Ski jumping is hurtling down a ridiculous hill before leaping as far as you possibly can and landing safely... well, the mathematics of being reckless enough to do it is probably as interesting as that of being able to do it without dying.

The 2018 Winter Olympics, in Pyeongchang, South Korea, are the culmination of a lifetime's training for many skiers, skaters, snowboarders, sledders, curlers and other winter athletes.

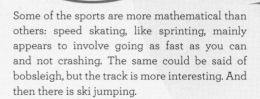

Some of the sports are more mathematical than others: speed skating, like sprinting, mainly appears to involve going as fast as you can and not crashing. The same could be said of bobsleigh, but the track is more interesting. And then there is ski jumping.

THE PERFECT SKI JUMP

It is an awfully long way down, and steep with it. Contrary to every survival instinct you have, you are to go down the slope as fast as you can, jump as high as you can, and – finally doing something sensible – come down to earth smoothly and safely.

If your personal safety is so insignificant to you that you want to be a champion ski jumper, then there is a fair amount of mathematics that *is* significant to you.

For example, to reach the highest possible speed on the ramp, you need to reduce air resistance as much as you can. Because air resistance is proportional to the cross-sectional area of your body moving forwards, ski jumpers crouch down as much as they can without endangering themselves. The *drag* force experienced by a ski jumper (or any other object) is $\frac{1}{2}CApv^2$, where C is an experimentally derived constant that depends on the shape of the object, A is the cross-sectional area, p is the air pressure and v is the speed. Since the cross-sectional area is the only one of these you can easily control, it makes sense to do that.

SKI LENGTH

There is even a mathematical formula for the length of ski you are allowed to use: $l = 1.46h$. If you are 183 cm (6 ft) tall, your skis would be about 267 cm ($8\frac{3}{4}$ ft) long.

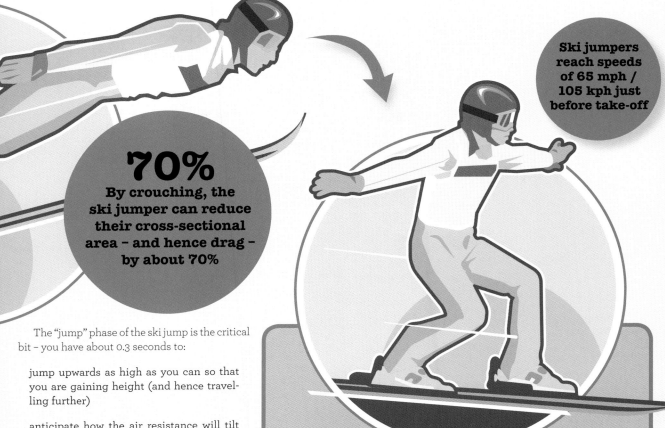

70%
By crouching, the ski jumper can reduce their cross-sectional area – and hence drag – by about 70%

Ski jumpers reach speeds of 65 mph / 105 kph just before take-off

The "jump" phase of the ski jump is the critical bit – you have about 0.3 seconds to:

jump upwards as high as you can so that you are gaining height (and hence travelling further)

anticipate how the air resistance will tilt you once you are in the air

tilt yourself forwards to counterbalance that effect, but not so far forward that you tumble

get into the right body shape to fly safely (at least, relatively safely) through the air.

Once you are in the air, drag is more of a friend than an enemy: the more you can slow down, the longer you can stay in the air – so you want to make yourself as big as possible after you jump. Within reason, of course: since you need to land cleanly, it is probably inadvisable to have your skis too far from parallel with the ground.

And then, at something a little less than 32 feet per second per second (because your suit has, by design, expanded mid-flight to slow down your descent), you touch down to relieved cheers from the crowd.

Then, in competition, you go back and do it again, because anybody can do it *once*. Doing it again takes proper courage.

HILL SIZE AND THE K-POINT

Ski jumps take place on hills of varying shapes and sizes – so the same distance is easier to achieve on some runs than others. To counteract this, ski jumping scores are given in points based on the *hill size point*, or *k-point*, of the hill, defined as where the hill is steepest.

If you land precisely on the line marking the k-point on a standard hill, you get 60 points; every metre farther from or nearer to the ramp gains you more or fewer points (the bigger the hill, the smaller the bonus/penalty). On ski flying hills, you get 120 points for reaching the k-point (and frankly, you deserve it). In principle, it is possible to end up with a negative score.

Depending on the wind conditions, your distance score is adjusted upwards or downwards as appropriate, to keep the conditions fair for all jumpers.

On top of your distance points, you are awarded up to 20 points by each of five judges for style – steady skis, balance, body shape and landing. You only get the three middle values, though; you would only get the maximum of 60 points if at least four of the judges awarded you full marks.

Bobsleigh tracks are generally 1200–1300 m in length

$$\text{drag}=\frac{1}{2}CApv^2$$

and must have at least 15 turns

BOBSLEIGH

Four people, two on each side, push the sleigh to get it up to about 25mph over 50 yards, before jumping in. Everyone apart from the driver puts their head down to reduce drag.

They then accelerate down the track with practically nothing to slow them down, hurtling around corners almost horizontally, and reaching speeds of up to 100mph or so.

It is OK to finish the race on your side or upside down, as long as you are all still inside when you cross the line.

There is a clear athletic requirement to the sport: you need to be a pretty good runner on ice to get the bob up to speed, but after that, it is a minimization problem! How do you choose a path to get your sleigh from the top to the bottom of the run in the shortest possible time, without tipping anyone out?

The main trade-off here is between speed and distance. Steer too low into a corner and you lose the benefit of the banked corners to accelerate you; steer too high and you have to travel further. For a race that is often decided by hundredths of a second, even a few inches can be the difference between success and failure.

Taking the shortest path (1) requires slowing down. The highest-speed path (3) means going further. The quickest path is in between (2).

The true heroes of bobsleigh, of course, are the designers: without a shape that reduces drag as much as possible, and runners that just barely meet specification, the best drivers and athletes in the world would not be able to compete.

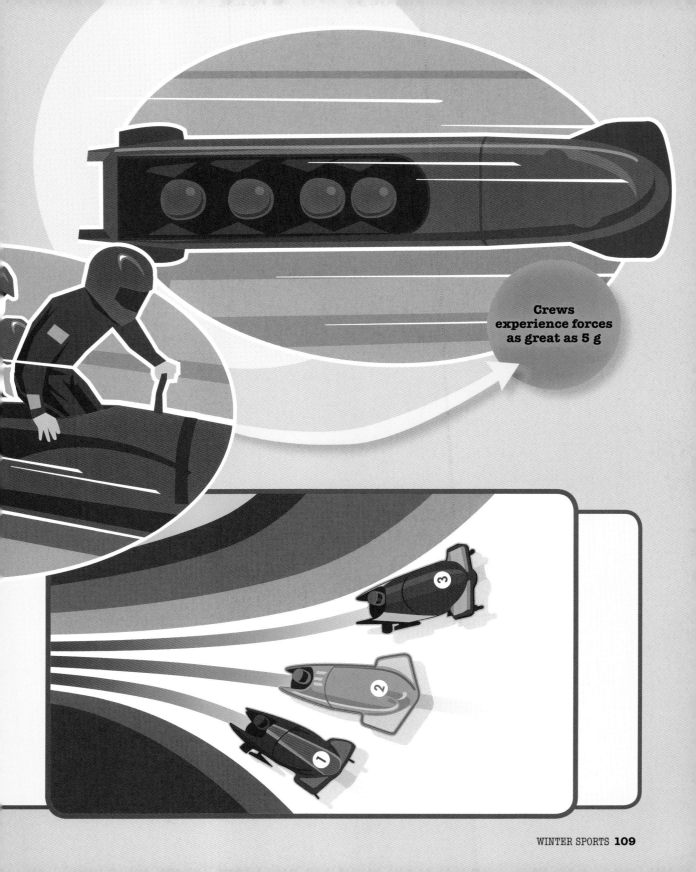

Crews experience forces as great as 5 g

Entertainment

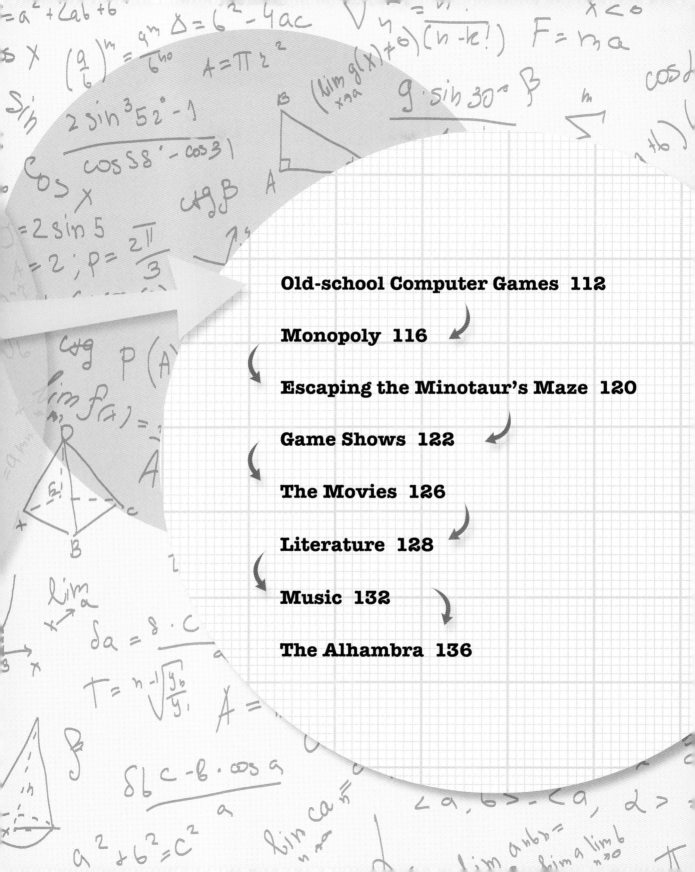

Old-school Computer Games

$$h = 16 - \frac{4\ln(p)}{9\ln\left(\frac{6}{7}\right)}$$

Graphics have developed dramatically in the last three decades or so, with game objects becoming ever more complex and realistic. So how do computers process something as ridiculously complex as a golfer's swing, or a sports car, or a terrifying dungeon monster?

GRAPHICS

Get a magnifying glass and look closely at your TV or computer screen. If you look closely enough, you will see separate dots in different colours – but those dots, at a distance, are adequate to show just about any shape you want to see in realistic detail. With enough pixels, you can approximate practically any two-dimensional picture.

You *can* do a similar thing in three dimensions, using voxels, but it gets very expensive. A high-definition TV has a resolution of 1920 by 1080 pixels, more than two million pixels. By contrast, two million voxels would give you a cube of about 128 pixels on each side

– less resolution, on the surface at least, than my trusty ZX Spectrum gave in the mid-1980s. So, to do three-dimensional graphics, you need a more efficient system. One based not on tiny cubes, but on arbitrarily sized triangles.

Triangles are the best shape there is. For sheer simplicity and versatility, no shape comes close to the triangle. Three points lie automatically in a plane, which makes it easy to calculate how light reflects off a triangle. Triangles can be joined together to make a good approximation to any surface you like – and, if necessary, broken down cleanly into smaller triangles if better resolution is required.

So, to model any shape, you keep track of a set of points on its surface, and all of the connections between them that make triangles. You might think it would make sense to use a three-dimensional coordinate system to model things in three dimensions – and you would be right, to an extent. You can model rotations using matrix multiplication, and movement by matrix addition – but there is a better way.

If you employ *projective geometry*, you can use a single matrix to rotate and move the shape as needed.

Instead of using the traditional three coordinates (x, y and z) to represent a position in 3D-space, projective geometry uses four (the fourth,

Improved computing and screen technology have dramatically improved the realism of computer games.

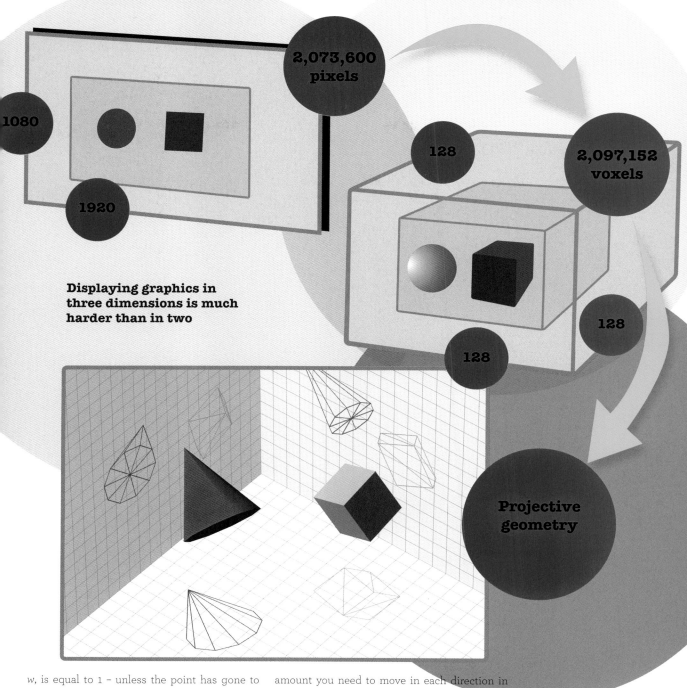

2,073,600 pixels

1080

1920

Displaying graphics in three dimensions is much harder than in two

128

2,097,152 voxels

128

128

Projective geometry

w, is equal to 1 – unless the point has gone to infinity, in which case it is 0). A rotation is represented by the same matrix as you would use in 3D, but it is padded in the last column and row with 0s (apart from a 1 in the bottom right). A displacement is simply a matrix with 0s everywhere except for 1s on the diagonal and the amount you need to move in each direction in the fourth column.

Why is that better? Well, if you need to do several different movements, you can combine them into one complicated matrix, rather than a much more complicated combination of multiplications and additions.

TETRIS TILES

The word Tetris is a combination of the Greek tetra-, meaning four, and tennis, game designer Alexey Pajitnov's favourite sport. All of the tiles in Tetris are made of four blocks – in fact, the seven blocks are (ignoring rotations but not reflections) the only possible connected four-block patterns.

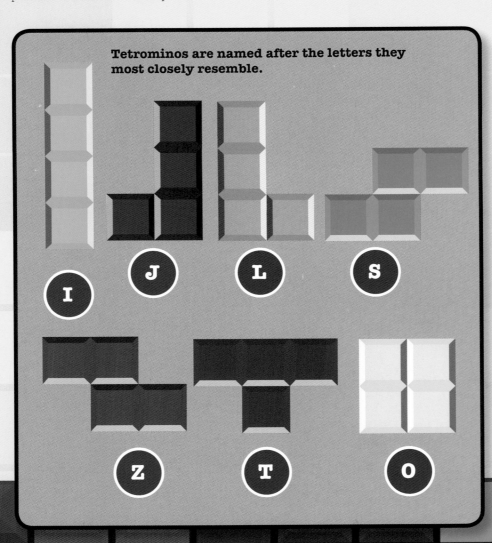

Tetrominos are named after the letters they most closely resemble.

I

J

L

S

Z

T

O

PROBABILITIES IN TETRIS

A product of the 1980s "simplicity is genius" approach to games, Tetris involves directing coloured pieces as they fall onto a stack of other pieces. If you fill a line all the way across the screen (ten blocks), the line disappears, and everything drops down in its place. You get a bonus for removing more than one row at a time, up to the point where you remove four rows at once by carefully dropping an "I"-shaped block. When the board – usually twenty blocks high – fills with tiles, the game is over. The key to playing good Tetris is to balance the need for "chimneys" you can drop I blocks into, against keeping the pile of tiles small enough that a bad run of tiles will not end the game.

So, the mathematical question is, what is the ideal height for you to have the blocks? At what point do you say "I have to cut my losses and take a few easy lines to reduce the height?" To work this out, we need to know how often we can expect to get an I-shaped piece, and how much space we lose if we get a different piece.

Useful pieces show up more or less at random. On average, that means one in seven tiles that drop will be an I.

If you get a non-I tile, it will fill up four spaces – assuming you can stack them neatly together, every extra piece takes up $4/9$ of a line.

You also do not want to reach a block height of 16 – that would not give you enough room to manoeuvre the piece into place.

If you are at a line height of h, you can afford to wait $N = (16-h)/(4/9)$ tiles before losing. The probability of getting that many non-I tiles in a row is $(6/7)^N$ – and the rest is just down to your risk tolerance.

If you are happy with a 50–50 chance of losing before you get an I, you would solve $(6/7)^N$ and find N is about 4.5 and $h = 14$; a row height of 14 is fine for living dangerously.

If, instead, you want a 1% chance of losing, we solve $(6/7)^N = 1/100$ and get $N = 30$ and $h = 3$. Playing so conservatively means you do not ever get a chance of removing four rows at once!

A more reasonable strategy is to keep the blocks somewhere about 10 units high, which would give you a 10% chance of losing if you carried on waiting.

To work out the correct height for your risk tolerance, p, use the formula

$$h = 16 - \frac{4\ln(p)}{9\ln\left(\frac{6}{7}\right)}$$

It is possible to come up with a more detailed model that takes into account where you would be after successfully clearing four rows, and how likely you are to get things back under control if you abandon your chimney-building – but this is not the place for that model.

Monopoly

Monopoly is the classic capitalist board game: a group of players start with the same assets and compete to reduce their opponents to bankruptcy. They move around the board, buying and selling property, developing houses and hotels, extracting rent and occasionally ending up in jail.

•••

It is a game where chance plays a role (an unlucky roll of the dice or an inopportune Community Chest card can turn a winning position into a losing one), but where skill and judgement generally prevail. And it is a game where a little mathematics goes a long way.

WHICH PROPERTIES TO BUY

The expected lifetime value of a Monopoly property is a tough thing to calculate. You need to take into account a large number of factors, including how much it costs, how likely you are to be able to develop it, how much rent it generates at each level, and how often you can expect your opponents to land on it.

Assuming the rent and costs are roughly in the same proportion for each property, and the probability of being able to develop is the same everywhere, the probability of landing on each square is the key variable. You might think you were equally likely to land on each of the board's 40 squares, but some are more likely than others: for example, you never really land on "Go To Jail" because you immediately go to jail. Many of the Chance cards move you elsewhere – particularly to Jail, the third red square (Trafalgar Square for the UK/Illinois Avenue for the US) and Go.

In fact, those three are the squares most commonly landed on, with about 3.95% of turns ending in Jail, 3.19% on the third red square and 3.10% on Go. The most common group to land on is the orange set, conveniently located for players just leaving Jail, but the railways are also a reasonable target: three of the four stations are in the top ten.

The least popular stops happen to be the cheapest ones on the board: Old Kent Road in the UK/ Mediterranean Avenue for the US (2.13%) and Whitechapel Road/ Baltic Avenue (2.16%).

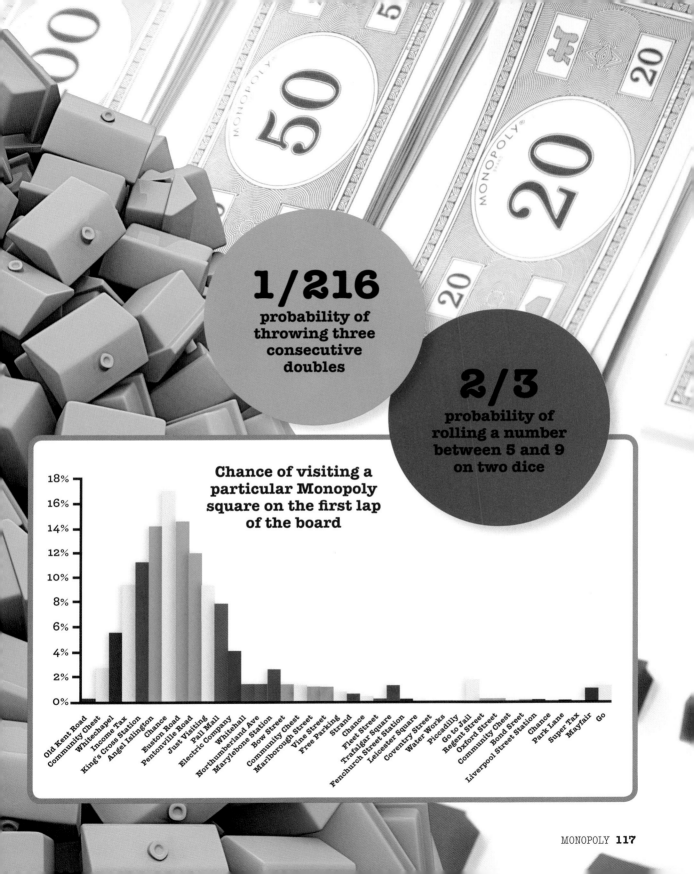

1/216
probability of throwing three consecutive doubles

2/3
probability of rolling a number between 5 and 9 on two dice

Chance of visiting a particular Monopoly square on the first lap of the board

18%
16%
14%
12%
10%
8%
6%
4%
2%
0%

Old Kent Road
Community Chest
Whitechapel
Income Tax
King's Cross Station
Angel Islington
Chance
Euston Road
Pentonville Road
Just Visiting
Pall Mall
Electric Company
Whitehall
Northumberland Ave
Marylebone Station
Bow Street
Community Chest
Marlborough Street
Vine Street
Free Parking
Strand
Chance
Fleet Street
Trafalgar Square
Fenchurch Street Station
Leicester Square
Coventry Street
Water Works
Piccadilly
Go to Jail
Regent Street
Oxford Street
Community Chest
Bond Sreet
Liverpool Street Station
Chance
Park Lane
Super Tax
Mayfair
Go

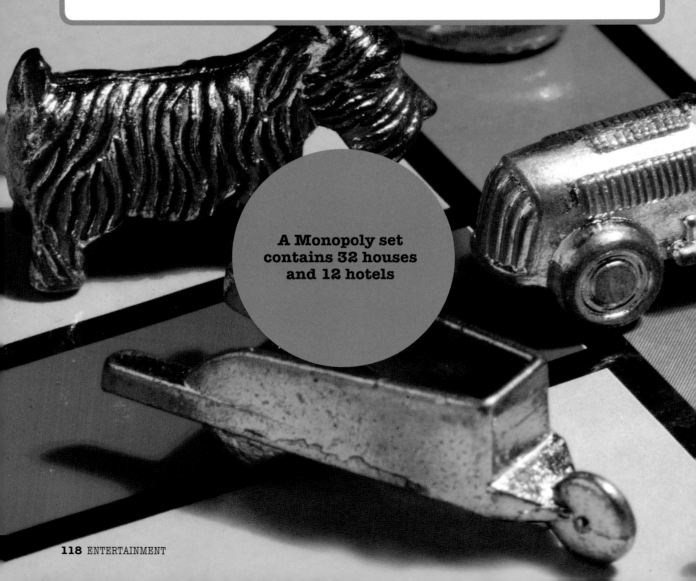

HOW LIKELY AM I TO GET OUT OF JAIL?

Supposing you do not want to pay the £50 fine or use a Get out of Jail Free card, if you are in Jail, you have three turns in which to roll a double.

Of the 36 ways a pair of dice can be rolled, six of them are doubles, so your probability of escaping on each roll is $\frac{1}{6}$. However, that does not mean that your escape chances are 50–50: in fact, they are slightly smaller.

The probability of escaping on your first roll is $\frac{1}{6}$, but you only need a second roll if you have not escaped on your first! That means the probability of escaping on your second roll is $\frac{5}{6} \times \frac{1}{6} = \frac{5}{36}$. Similarly, the probability of escaping on your third roll is that of missing your first two rolls and hitting the third, which is $\frac{5}{6} \times \frac{5}{6} \times \frac{1}{6} = \frac{25}{216}$. Altogether, that gives you a $\frac{91}{216}$ chance of escape, about 42%.

A simpler way to arrive at the same answer is to realize you would need to miss with all three rolls to fail to escape, the probability of which is $\left(\frac{5}{6}\right)^3 = \frac{25}{216}$ or 58%.

A Monopoly set contains 32 houses and 12 hotels

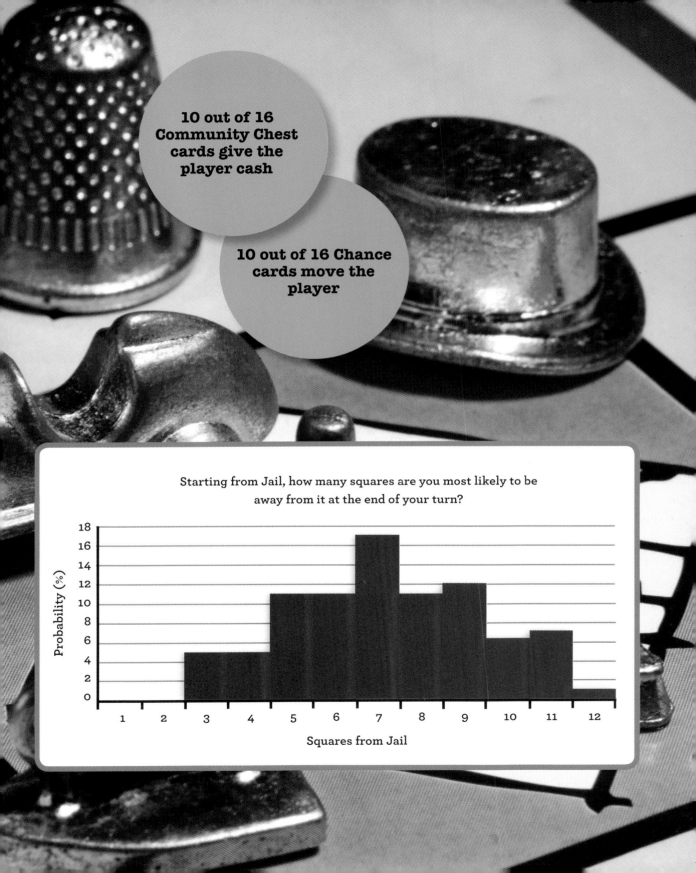

10 out of 16 Community Chest cards give the player cash

10 out of 16 Chance cards move the player

Starting from Jail, how many squares are you most likely to be away from it at the end of your turn?

Probability (%)

Squares from Jail

Escaping the Minotaur's Maze

You are trapped in a surprisingly well-lit maze with only a large supply of pebbles for company. You have left your trusty several-mile-long piece of thread at home, so how on earth are you going to find your way out?

To get out, you need a reliable method. There are many algorithms you could use, but I am a fan Charles Pierre Trémaux's.

His first rule is: every time you leave a passageway, you place a pebble at the exit to show you have been there; similarly, every time you enter a passageway, you place a pebble at the entrance. All of the other rules are about deciding what to do at an intersection.

If you arrive at an intersection for the first time (the only pebble is the one marking the passageway you just emerged from), you pick a random, unmarked passageway to explore.

If you arrive at an intersection where there are already pebbles lying around, and there was no pebble on your passageway before you came down it, you must turn back. (You will have put down two pebbles here: one as you exited, and one as you re-entered.)

If you arrive at an intersection and there is already a stone at the end of your passageway, pick a passageway with no stones in it (if there is one) or with only one stone in it if not.

If every passageway at your intersection has two pebbles at its end, bad luck: there's no way out of the maze. You have explored the whole thing.

THE RIGHT-HAND RULE

When I was a child, my dad taught me the right-hand rule: put your right hand on the wall and walk along so that your hand stays on the wall. It would, he claimed, guarantee finding the exit eventually. (Your left hand would work just as well.) Unfortunately, the right-hand rule does not always work: to take a simple counter-example, imagine the wall on your right happens to look like the one pictured: following it simply brings you back to where you started. (If you know that all of the maze's walls connect to each other, you should be OK.) It is also not all that great for mazes in three dimensions.

Jon Pledge came up with a method to get around the limitations of the right-hand rule in 2D: you leave the wall and walk forwards if you are facing the same direction as when you started *and* you have turned as much to the left as you have turned right. The Pledge algorithm prevents you getting caught in G-shaped traps, but is only guaranteed to work if the exit is on the outer wall of the maze.

If, on the other hand, you stumble on the exit, you have helpfully left a trail back to where you started: you can easily get back to your starting point by going through passageways with only one stone at the end.

Why does this work? "No stone" means a passageway is unexplored. "Two stones" means the passageway led to a dead end. "One stone" means you have been this way before, but do not automatically reach a dead end. The only puzzling rule is the "turn back at explored junctions" one: this appears to be to prevent you getting into a loop.

Game Shows

In the pivotal moment of TV game show *Let's Make A Deal*, the contestant would be faced with a choice of three closed doors. Behind one of the doors would be the star prize, a new car; behind the other two would be stinky cabbages.

SHOULD YOU SWITCH DOORS WHEN MONTY HALL ASKS?

As the contestant, you would pick one of the three doors. The genial host, Monty Hall, would then select one of the other doors to open – deliberately revealing a cabbage. He would then ask you whether you wanted to change your choice to the remaining closed door, or to stick with your original choice.

Well – would you?

Most people's initial instinct is to say "it doesn't make a difference!" After all, you have got two doors remaining, one of which has a car behind it, the other of which has a cabbage, so it must be 50–50. . . right?

The correct decision, speaking probabilistically, is to switch doors. Your initial guess is correct only $\frac{1}{3}$ of the time, so sticking with it only wins the car $\frac{1}{3}$ of the time. Switching gives you the car $\frac{2}{3}$ of the time, so that is what you should do.

Not convinced? I don't blame you. Read on.

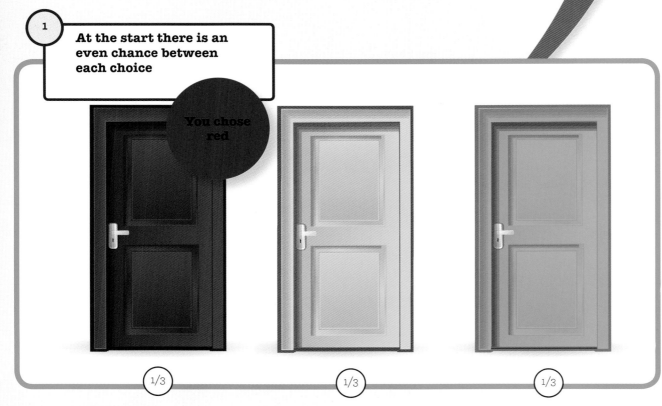

1

At the start there is an even chance between each choice

You chose red

1/3   1/3   1/3

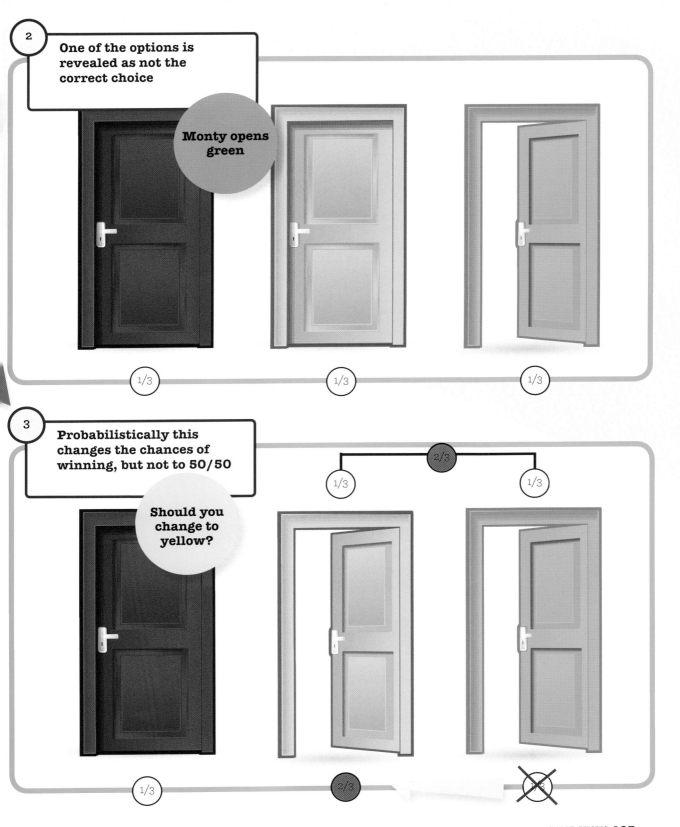

SHOULD YOU SWITCH YOUR CHOICE ON
WHO WANTS TO BE A MILLIONAIRE?

Suppose you are on *Who Wants To Be A Millionaire?*, and a question comes up that you have absolutely no clue about. All four of the answers look plausible, but you need the money, so you decide to take a guess. "I'm leaning towards answer A," you tell the host.

"Remember," he says, "you still have your 50–50 lifeline. Would you like to play it?"

Of course you would!

"Computer," says the host, "please remove two incorrect answers," and two wrong answers are duly removed. Your answer remains there.

"So," asks the host, "you were leaning to A – would you like to stick with that answer, or switch to answer D?"

Well – would you?

Having just read about the Monty Hall problem, most people now say "switch! switch! Now there's a higher chance of the answer being D!"

It turns out, there is a good reason the 50–50 lifeline is called 50–50: there is no benefit or loss from switching to the other answer in this scenario.

WHY NOT?

There is one key difference between the *Let's Make A Deal* situation and the *Who Wants To Be A Millionaire?* setup, and it has to do with how the wrong answers are removed.

The rules on *Let's Make A Deal* are that Monty Hall opens one of the *other* doors.

The rules on *Millionaire* are that the computer removes *any two* wrong answers – which means your original choice of answer could be removed. Another way to look at it, if you are not convinced there is a difference in the rules: if you had originally picked a different door on *Let's Make A Deal*, Monty's behaviour could have been different. If you had picked B, C, or D on *Millionaire*, the same two choices would have been removed – so there is clearly a difference.

In *Millionaire*, before you play the lifeline, there are twelve equally likely scenarios:

Correct answer	Computer removes	Probability
A	**BC**, BD or CD	1/12 each
B	AC, AD or CD	1/12 each
C	AB, AD or BD	1/12 each
D	AB, AC or **BC**	1/12 each

There are two equally likely scenarios (highlighted) that leave you with A and D – so the two answers are equally likely.

In *Let's Make A Deal*, by contrast, if the contestant picks door A, there are four possibilities – and they are not equally likely!

Correct answer	Monty opens...	Probability
A	B	1/6
A	C	1/6
B	C	1/3
C	B	1/3

If you played 300 games of *Let's Make A Deal*, guessing A each time, Monty would open B about 150 times. 50 times, there would be a cabbage behind door C; 100 times, a car.

By contrast, if you played 300 games of *Millionaire*, guessing A each time, A would be removed as a wrong answer 150 times, remain as a wrong answer 75 times and remain as the correct answer 75 times.

MONTY HELL

Mathematicians being mathematicians are not content to leave the rules of *Let's Make A Deal* alone, and have devised alternative versions of the game, perhaps inspired by the fact that Monty Hall did not *always* offer contestants the chance to switch.

The analysis on the previous page is fine, as long as you are given the chance to switch either every time, or completely at random. However, it might be that Monty is in a generous mood and only gives you the chance to switch if your initial guess is wrong (in which case, switching would ensure you won every time rather than two-thirds of the time).

Alternatively, if the host was feeling mean, he might only offer you the chance to switch if you were correct. Here, you would never win by switching.

You can dig deeper still: what if Monty always offers you the chance to switch if your initial choice of door is correct, but only half the time if you are wrong?

Well, in that case, the chances are back to 50–50 – for every three times you play, you expect to get the correct door once and be offered the choice; one time you will get the wrong door and you will be allowed to switch; and one time you will get the wrong door and have to take the cabbage behind it.

MARILYN VOS SAVANT

These days, you will encounter the Monty Hall problem in high school mathematics class, but it was largely unheard of until Marilyn vos Savant wrote about it for *Parade* magazine in 1990, explaining why switching doors was the correct choice.

If you found it counter-intuitive or difficult to understand, perhaps it will make you feel better to know that vos Savant's mailbag was filled with angry letters from readers – tens of thousands of them, many from people with PhDs in mathematics or statistics – telling her she was an idiot and should not spread this kind of garbage analysis. Even Paul Erdős, probably the greatest mathematician of the 20th century, refused to believe that switching made a difference until someone ran a computer experiment for him.

For me, this is one of the best things about mathematics: if you are right, and can prove it, then you are right.

228
American Marilyn Vos Savant, the woman with the world's highest IQ (228)

The Movies

Kevin Bacon, it has long been claimed, has worked with everyone in Hollywood. This led to a quiz-style challenge: take an actor, any actor, and find a chain of films connecting your actor to Kevin Bacon: the Bacon number.

● ●

BACON NUMBER

For example, there is a chain of three films connecting Al Gore to Bacon: he featured with Bill Clinton in *The Final Days*; Clinton played alongside Sean Penn in *Clinton Foundation: Celebrity Division*; and Penn and Bacon both acted in *Mystic River*. Al Gore has a *Bacon number* of 3. (Bacon himself has a Bacon number of 0; anyone who has been in a film with him has a Bacon number of 1; anyone who has featured with those actors but not the man himself has a Bacon number of 2, and so on.)

Kevin Bacon has, according to oracleofbacon. org, worked with 3,303 other actors in feature films (as of early 2017). Of the two million or so actors listed on the Internet Movie Database (IMDb), about 64% have a Bacon number of 3, like Gore. Only 34,000 or so have a Bacon number of 5 or higher; the site says that one person has a Bacon number of 10 – but not who it is! (I am curious to know, but not so curious that I will trawl through two million actors to find them.)

However, Bacon is not the best-connected actor to pick as the goal. In fact, he is a long way down the list. He comes in at #435, with an average *connection score* of 3.02. That is calculated, roughly speaking, as the average number of links between a random actor on IMDb and Bacon. The best centre (at the time of writing) is specialist villain-portrayer Eric Roberts (2.83), followed closely by Michael Madsen, Danny Trejo, Samuel L Jackson and Harvey Keitel.

There are variations of this game played in different fields. The *small world hypothesis* claims that any two people on the planet can be connected by a chain of no more than six mutual friends – the idea has been around since the 1920s, and it is said to have been Marconi who posited the number six. (Humans, of course, do not behave as they should: experiments to test this have generally failed because people lose interest after a few links.)

Lisa Kudrow has an Erdős-Bacon-Sabbath number of 15

Colin Firth has an Erdős-Bacon number of 7

Frank Sinatra has a Bacon-Sabbath number of 8

Tom Lehrer has an Erdős-Sabbath number of 14

BACON–ERDŐS–SABBATH NUMBER

In mathematics, the centre of the universe is Paul Erdős, who collaborated with around 1,500 other researchers over a long and productive career. Similarly to the Bacon number, Erdős's co-authors have an Erdős number of 1. (Mine is 5 or 6, depending on who you believe.)

In music, the traditional centre is Black Sabbath: anyone who has recorded and released a song with Ozzy Osborne or his mates has a Sabbath number of 1.

The true Renaissance people of our time are those who have an Erdős–Bacon–Sabbath number – that is, those who qualify in all three spheres get to add their numbers together and display it as a badge of pride. Any number at all is pretty impressive, but the record (so far as the internet knows) is 8: erdosbaconsabbath.com lists psychologist Daniel Levitin, inventor Ray Kurzweil and physicists Lawrence Krauss and Stephen Hawking as the leaders.

Marcus du Sautoy has an Erdős number of 3

Taraji P Henson has a Bacon number of 2

Literature

$$\pi \approx 3.14159265$$

You might think that, if there is one place you could avoid mathematics altogether, it is in the great works of literature. But no, you don't escape that easily. Even if they don't realize it, authors use game theory!

To build a credible story, characters must behave plausibly – they should not really make magical leaps of faith; the author needs to keep track of who knows what, and how they will figure out the things they need to know. That is game theory.

There have also been experiments in using mathematical ideas and techniques more explicitly in writing and we will look at some of the more serious and the more silly versions of mathematical literature.

THE JUDGEMENT OF SOLOMON

One of the most famous stories in the Bible involves a child custody dispute: two women argue in front of Solomon that the child is theirs. Solomon neatly solves the dispute by suggesting he chop the child in two and give them half each; one of the women screams and says "no, no, let her have the child," proving to Solomon that she is the real mother.

This is a basic example of comparing payoffs. Let us call the two claimants "Mother" and "Impostor." Before Solomon's suggested intervention, the payoffs looked pretty similar: for both claimants, winning the case would have been positive and losing negative. We can quibble about the relative amounts, but there's no easy way for a judge to tell the difference (see **Table 1**).

Solomon's suggestion, as barbaric as it sounds, is actually quite wise. While Impostor does not necessarily want the child to die, she also probably does not see a huge difference between losing the case and the child dying – death might be worth -2 points for her, and losing the case -1, compared to +1 for winning. For Mother, though, the death might be more like -1000, losing the case -10 and winning +10.

The section title pages of *Jurassic Park* contain iterations of the dragon curve.

Table 1: Before Solomon: stalemate

	Mother's payoff	Impostor's payoff
Mother wins	+10	−1
Impostor wins	−10	+1

Table 2: After Solomon: the claimants have different strategies

Payoff	Mother's payoff	Impostor's payoff
Baby dies	−1000	−2
Mother wins	+10	−1
Impostor wins	−10	+1

(The numbers are arbitrary.)

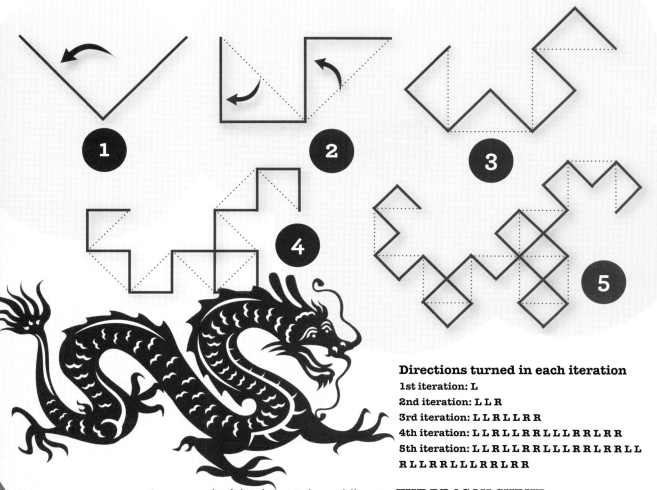

Directions turned in each iteration

1st iteration: L

2nd iteration: L L R

3rd iteration: L L R L L R R

4th iteration: L L R L L R R L L L R R L R R

5th iteration: L L R L L R R L L L R R L R R L L R L L R R L L R R L R R

Suppose each of the claimants has a different probability (M and I) of continuing the case (as opposed to withdrawing her claim). Differentiating Mother's payoff with respect to her probability gives $dP/dM = -1000I + 10$, which is negative if $I > 0.01$. if Mother believes Impostor has a greater than 1% probability of continuing her claim, she should reduce her probability (to zero, if necessary).

From Impostor's point of view, $dP/dI = -2M + 1$, which means that if Impostor thinks Mother has a greater than 50% chance of continuing the claim, she should reduce her probability, and otherwise continue.

In this scenario, almost any set of initial beliefs leads to Mother withdrawing her claim – Solomon, being the wise king he is, knows this, and on hearing her withdraw, immediately awards the child to her.

THE DRAGON CURVE

In the section title pages of Michael Crichton's *Jurassic Park*, one of the few books involving a mathematician (Ian Malcolm) there is something that looks like a doodle. The doodle gets more complicated as you get further into the book and gradually – if you squint a bit – begins to look like a dragon.

And that is its name, the Dragon Curve (also the Heighway Dragon), a kind of fractal. You can construct it yourself. Take a sheet of paper and fold it in half to the right. Then fold it in half to the right again. Then do it again, for as long as you can keep going. When you unfold it, making all of the folds right angles, you get the Dragon!

The idea of simple instructions leading to complex (and sometimes dangerous) consequences is a central theme of the book – and to chaos theory, Malcolm's field of study.

BORGES'S LIBRARY OF BABEL

Many authors have delved into the world of mathematics, perhaps most notably the Argentinian Jorge Luis Borges. His work is peppered with mathematical content, from the topological idea of bifurcations and chaos theory in *The Garden of Forking Paths* to infinity, which crops up (as you would expect) everywhere, including *The Book of Sand*, a book that grows as you read it.

However, my favourite bit of Borges mathematics is in the *Library of Babel*, which details a library containing every possible 410-page book. There is a colossal number of these (a ballpark figure of $10^{1,700,000}$), arranged in hexagonal rooms. I say arranged: they are in no discernible order, and the vast, vast majority of the books are complete gibberish. However, all possible useful information must exist in the library, from perfect predictions of the future to translations of classic works, to an index of the books themselves.

That said, there are more books full of incorrect predictions about the future, mistranslations of classic works, and erroneous indexes than correct ones – but the probability of finding even one of these is vanishingly small.

Above: Argentine writer Jorge Luis Borges (1899– 1986), photographed in 1943 by Gisèle Freund.

Right: This indoor maze, inspired by Jorge Luis Borges, was built using 250,000 books and created by Brazilian artists Marcos Saboya and Gualter Pupo.

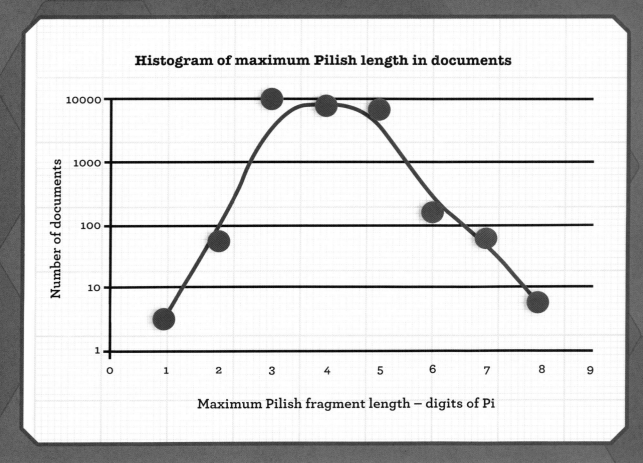

Histogram of maximum Pilish length in documents

Y-axis: Number of documents

X-axis: Maximum Pilish fragment length – digits of Pi

PILISH

Can I make a verse
Obviously be rather worse...

I think I should stop my attempt at *Pilish poetry* there, before I succeed with it. If you count the numbers of letters in each word of my "poem," you will find they are 3 1 4 1 5 9 2 6 5..., a number that will be familiar to anyone who has ever taken geometry.

Pilish is a form of constrained writing, in which the numbers of letters in each successive word are the successive digits of π. It can also be used as a mnemonic for the number: the anonymous piece of Pilish "How I need a drink, alcoholic in nature, after the heavy lectures involving quantum mechanics!" is both memorable and quite a reasonable reaction to quantum mechanics.

The record for writing Pilish, so far as anyone knows, is Michael Keith's novel, *Not A Wake*, which covers the first 10,000 digits of π.

One question that strikes the mathematician, though: how do you deal with zeros? Basic Pilish asserts that you can use a ten-letter word to represent zero. Standard Pilish extends the rules so you could use, for example, an eleven-letter word to represent the digits 1 1, rather than try to find a way to shoehorn two successive one-letter words together.

Incidentally, there is a good chance this book is, in fact, part of a series of Pilish works, many unwritten: it is widely believed that the decimal expansion of π contains every possible combination of numbers, which would mean that you would find the exact 50,000 or so letter-counts for the words I have used in this book.

Music

For all the talk of "two cultures," the worlds of mathematics and music are closer than you might naively expect. In fact, it is only fairly recently that the two were considered separate – for most of history, from Pythagoras to Mersenne and beyond, to be a mathematician was to be a music theorist, and vice versa.

$$\left(\frac{3}{2}\right)^{12}$$

Douglas R Hofstadter's astonishing book, *Gödel, Escher, Bach*, explores many of the similarities between Bach's music and advanced mathematics, while many mathematicians also happen to be accomplished musicians. For example, Per Enflo (who was famously presented with a goose on Polish TV for solving an especially tricky mathematics problem) is one of many mathematicians who are also concert pianists. And a substantial chunk of the theory underlying what makes good music is based on mathematics.

I focus on a few specific details about why certain music sounds good or bad: from a theoretical point of view, looking at structure and composition; and from a practical point of view, looking at recording and acoustics.

ON CHORDS, HARMONIES AND STRUCTURE

The basis of a musical note is its *frequency* – how many times per second the string vibrates,

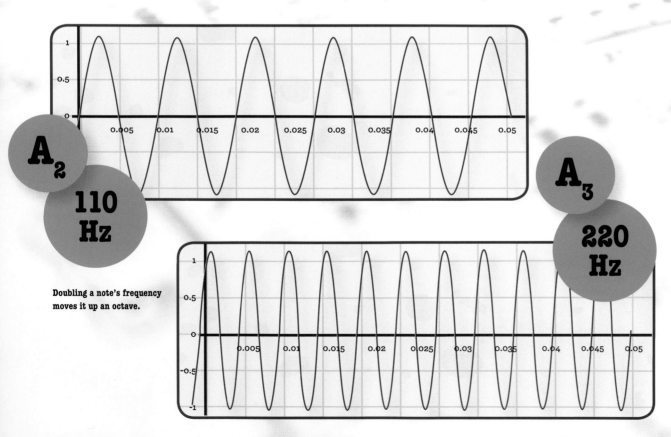

A₂

110 Hz

Doubling a note's frequency moves it up an octave.

A₃

220 Hz

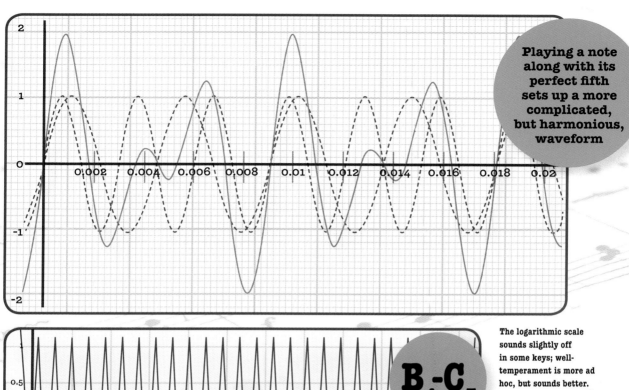

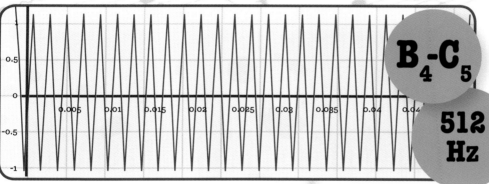

The logarithmic scale sounds slightly off in some keys; well-temperament is more ad hoc, but sounds better.

B₄-C₅

512 Hz

or the sound oscillates. A middle C has a frequency of 256 Hz, which means if you attached a microphone to an oscilloscope, you would see 256 peaks of the sound every second. A lowish A has a frequency of 110 Hz.

Where things get interesting is the relationship between the frequencies. If you double the frequency of a note – for example, by pressing a guitar string against its fretboard halfway along, you get the same note, an octave higher – the C above middle C has a frequency of 512 Hz, and the A above the previous A has a frequency of 220 Hz.

What about pressing down the string a third of the way along rather than halfway? This turns an A into the E above it. You have multiplied the frequency by 3/2 and the interval is known – for no obvious reason – as a perfect fifth. It's quite

a pleasant-sounding interval, and the two notes played together sound harmonious: because their frequencies are in a simple ratio, they match up very frequently – the oscilloscope would look something like the image at the top of the page. You can clearly see the peaks of the original A, the original E and (as an unexpected bonus), an E an octave higher – this is an overtone, or harmonic, that comes from the whole pattern repeating.

A similar thing happens with different ratios, all of which have bizarre, fractional-sounding names that have nothing to do with the ratios involved (or even the fraction of the way through the octave you are). A ratio of 4:3 takes your A to a D, a perfect fourth, which as an overtone of the D two octaves above.

THE CIRCLE OF FIFTHS

If you keep multiplying the ratio by 3/2, you keep moving up the scale: A to E, to B, to F#, to C#, to A♭, to E♭, to B♭, to F, to C, to G, to D, and back to an A seven octaves higher. Or, at least, nearly. You have multiplied the ratio by $(3/2)^{12}$, which is 129.75. The A seven octaves higher has a frequency 128 times higher – so we are off by a bit more than 1%. (This discrepancy is due, on a very fundamental level, to three not being even.)

What about all of the other notes? This, (thinks the mathematician) is a great excuse to use a logarithmic scale. On a linear scale, the octaves get further apart as you go up. If, instead, you plot the logarithm of the frequency, the octaves remain the same size.

That is useful if you want to subdivide the scale up into notes: you can simply chop the octave up into twelve equal parts on the logarithmic scale,

and work out the appropriate frequencies. Each note's frequency is about 18/17 the frequency of the note before. This works fairly well, if you are a busker – the correction for each note is on the order of a tenth of a per cent – but if you have perfect pitch, you can hear the difference between a logarithmic "perfect" fifth and a traditional one. It just does not work quite so neatly; some keys sound noticeably out of tune.

So, to find a compromise between the early mathematicians' approach (it is all ratios!) and the later mathematicians' approach (it is all logarithms!), musicians (in particular, Johann Sebastian Bach's predecessor, Andreas Werckmeister, in the late 17th century) shook their heads and came up with "well-temperament," which involves adjusting the notes in a slightly ad-hoc way, so that any key can be used without offending anyone's ears.

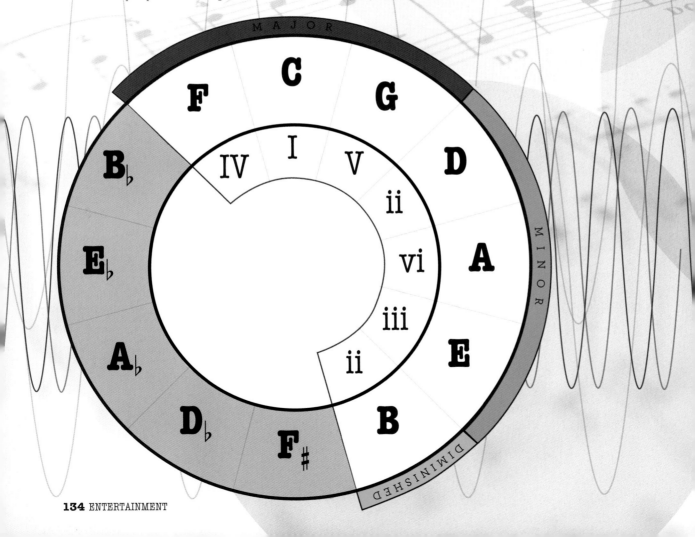

THE UGLIEST MUSIC EVER

So, if beautiful music relies on repetition and variations on a theme, it follows that ugly music does not follow any sort of pattern. And that is exactly what Scott Rickard did in 2011: he composed the world's first pattern-free sonata.

Now, pattern-free is not the same as random: if you played notes completely at random, you would occasionally get a couple of bars following some sort of pattern completely by chance. Rickard wanted to deliberately avoid patterns, which he managed (paradoxically) by following a pattern.

You can recreate this yourself. A piano has 88 notes, which you can label from 1 to 88. This makes much more sense than starting at C, if you ask me! The first note you play is 1. The second is 3, the third is 9, and so on, multiplying by 3 each time. When you run out of piano, as you would on the sixth note (243), you keep taking away 88 until you get back onto the piano – so the 6th note is 67. This continues until you get back to 1, 88 notes after you began.

But that is not all. To increase the patternlessness even further, Rickard introduced a mathematical method for the amount of time for which each note should be played. A *Golomb Ruler* is one where no pair of marks is the same distance apart; in Rickard's piece, the start time of each note is taken from such a ruler so that each note is a different length. Not only that, each consecutive pair or trio of notes is a different length (none of which coincide with the length of any single note), and so on. It is a marvel of patternlessness!

It's also practically unlistenable.

Golomb ruler of order 4, length 6

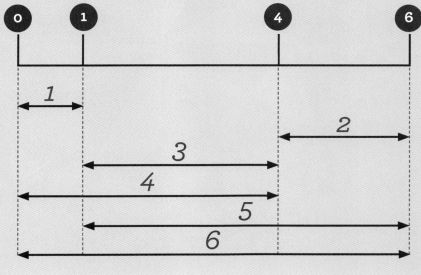

The Alhambra

What do the weird etchings and strange worlds of Dutch artist M C Escher and the beautiful 14th-century Islamic art of the Alhambra Palace have in common with something as mundane as wallpaper? The answer is tessellation.

THE ALHAMBRA, M C ESCHER AND ISLAMIC ART

If there is one place I would choose to revisit, anywhere in the world, it would be the Alhambra Palace in Granada, Spain. A Moorish palace completed in the 14th century, it is now a UNESCO World Heritage site best known for its beautiful tilings. Every room offers something different, and some of the visual deceptions are stunning (I am convinced I went up several flights of stairs and ended back on the same level as I started). And all of it is based on the intricate geometry of tessellation that has traditionally inspired Islamic art.

TESSELLATING SHAPES AND THE MATHEMATICAL ART OF M C ESCHER

The Dutch artist Maurits Cornelis Escher's etchings of bizarre, twisting worlds, of impossible shapes and of a blurred distinction between the real and the drawn have fascinated me from the moment I first saw them.

Escher described it as the *regular division of the plane*, and it involves picking a repeating pattern that covers the plane – for example, a set of parallelograms, hexagons or "I-bars" – squares with circular arcs added to the top and bottom and removed from the sides, or vice versa, making identical shapes in two different directions. By adding extra bits onto shapes while removing them elsewhere (according to the symmetry of the situation), a hexagon can be turned into a running person, or I-bars into angels and bats.

He also used deeper mathematical ideas. For example, his Circle Limit pictures draw heavily from hyperbolic geometry, a branch of mathematics that was thought impossible for several millennia until János Bolyai, Nikolai Lobachevsky and Carl Friedrich Gauss all discovered it at about the same time. Inspired by correspondence with Donald Coxeter, these woodcuts can be seen as beautiful representations of the Poincaré disk model of the hyperbolic plane.

In the Poincaré disk model, "straight" lines are circular arcs with ends perpendicular to the disk's circumference.

WALLPAPER PATTERNS AND ISLAMIC ART

Repetition is what makes patterns patterns, and there are only so many ways you can repeat a pattern (by shifting it – translation, reflecting it, or rotating it). As a result, there are only so many ways you can make a repeating pattern that covers the plane – 17, as it turns out.

The simplest of the patterns is what you would normally think of as tiling – the same pattern shifted and repeated, without any other kind of symmetry. Barely more complex are patterns with simple 180-degree rotational symmetry, with a simple reflection, or with glide symmetry – like stereotypical "crazy paving."

These can be combined in all sorts of ways, becoming more and more intricate, breaking into triangles and hexagons, using colour to allow or disallow certain symmetries.

It is said (and disputed) that the Alhambra contains examples of all seventeen groups; just as controversial is the idea that *girih* designs – more of a Persian thing than a Moorish one – can create aperiodic tilings, ones that appear to produce patterns but do not ever repeat.

Girih patterns are based on order-5 and order-10 symmetry, and are based on five tiles: a regular pentagon and a regular decagon, a rhombus, a slightly squished convex hexagon and a similarly squished concave hexagon, as pictured. All of these can be constructed using a straight-edge and compass.

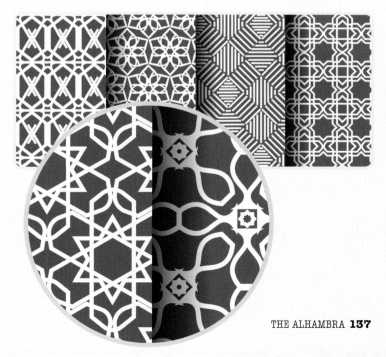

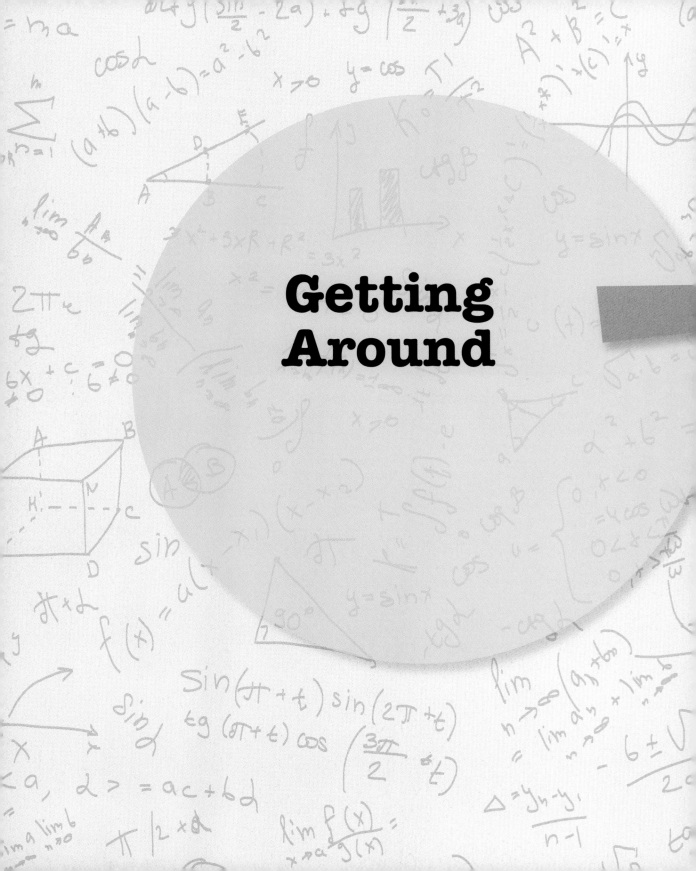

Getting Around

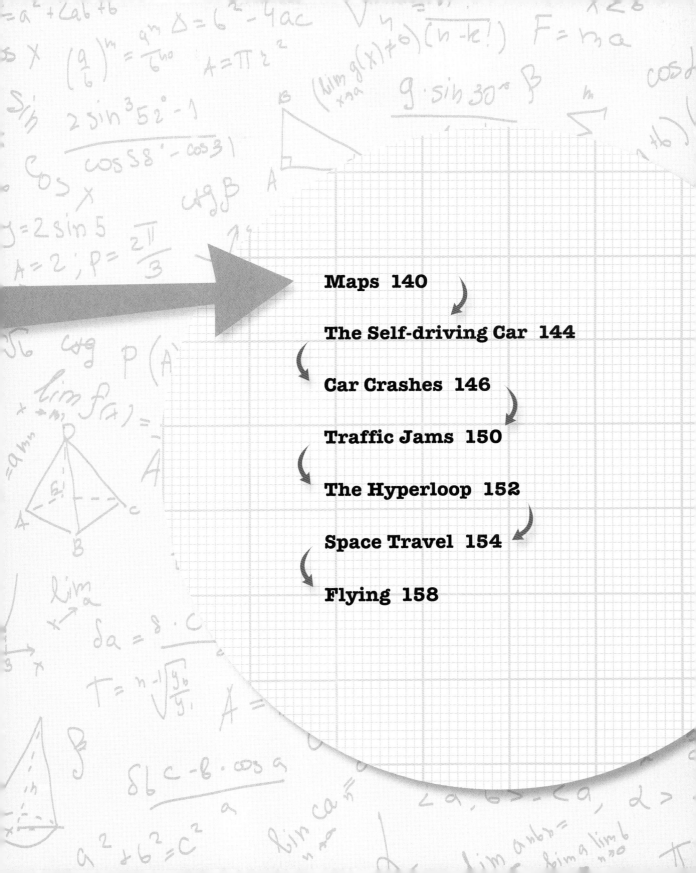

Maps

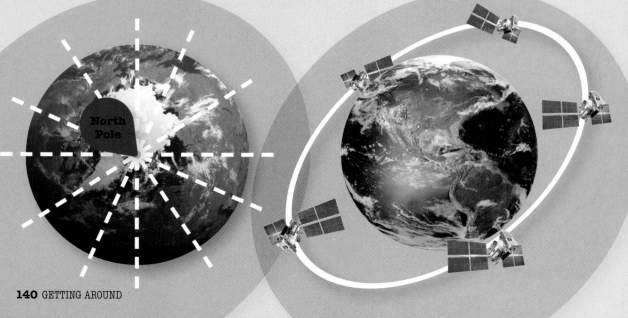

distance = speed of light × time

Twelve thousand miles above the earth, thirty satellites are arranged so that, wherever you are on the planet, at least four are visible (as long as you have a clear view of the sky.) These satellites are the Global Positioning System, or *GPS*, and they mean you can figure out fairly precisely where you are.

Each of the satellites sends out information about where it is, and what time it thinks it is, at regular intervals. When your device picks up one of these signals, it compares what time it thinks it is with GPS time to work out how long the signal has taken to reach it. Because the signal travels at a known speed (the speed of light), the device knows how far you are from the satellite: *distance = speed of light × time.* What this tells your GPS is that you are somewhere on a sphere with its radius centred on the satellite. While that has narrowed down where you are, it is typically quite a big range of possibilities.

A second reading gives you another sphere. If you know you lie on both spheres, you must lie on a known circle, which is a vast improvement.

A third reading gives you yet another sphere, which typically intersects your known circle in two points – one of which is normally inside the earth or in space and thus impossible.

A fourth reading narrows down which of the two possibilities it is – and gives an idea of the inaccuracy in your position. The more readings you have after the fourth, the more accurately you can figure out your position.

There is a slight wrinkle in the space–time continuum, though: the satellites are orbiting at such a high speed that you have to take *special relativity* into account (clocks moving at a higher speed appear to run slower), and the difference in gravitational pull is large enough that you have to take *general relativity* into account as well (clocks on the satellites appear to run faster). Although these effects work in opposite directions, there is no reason to expect them to cancel out, and the software on your receiver needs to make corrections to the observed times to get an accurate reading.

Strictly speaking, that is physics. The mathematics comes in making sure at least four of the 30 satellites are visible from any point on earth – they are arranged with five satellites on each of six equally spaced orbital planes – you should typically be able to pick up around ten at a time, which can give you position estimate correct to a few inches.

Below left: the 30 satellites are split between six planes.

Below right: in each plane, there are five satellites, at least two of which are visible from any point on the planet.

North Pole

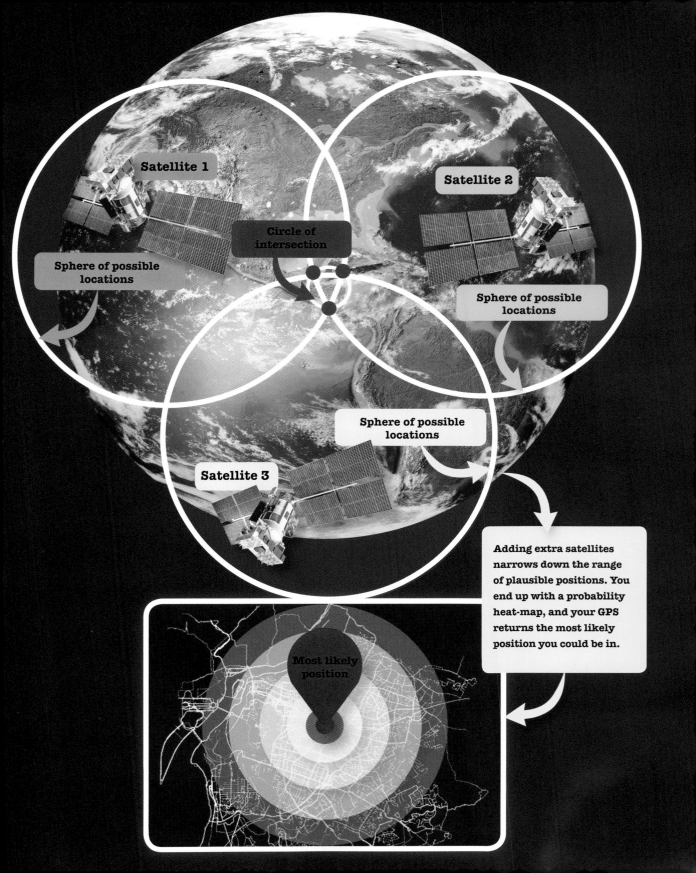

Satellite 1

Circle of intersection

Satellite 2

Sphere of possible locations

Sphere of possible locations

Sphere of possible locations

Satellite 3

Adding extra satellites narrows down the range of plausible positions. You end up with a probability heat-map, and your GPS returns the most likely position you could be in.

Most likely position

$$n! = n(n-1)(n-2)...(3)(2)(1)$$

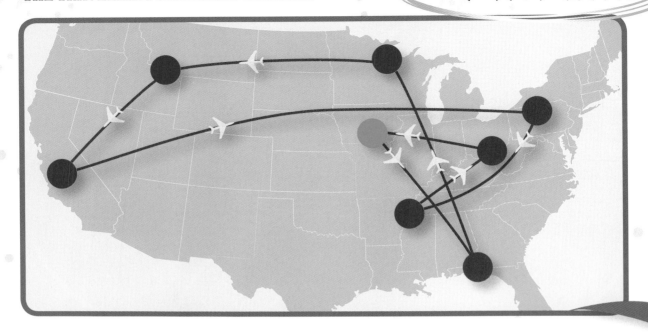

"Yes, boss, I'm in Des Moines, Iowa. And you need me to go where? Let me get a pen. Columbus, Ohio. Memphis, Tennessee. Buffalo, New York. Sacramento, California. Butte, Montana? Seriously? Yes, sir, sorry, sir. Duluth, Minnesota; Tallahassee, Florida... you could just email these to me, you know."

The poor travelling salesman: he has a long list of cities to visit, and an awful lot of possible orders in which to visit them. With a list of seven cities, there are over 5,000 ways to visit each of them in turn; for 20 cities, it is about 2,433,000,000,000,000,000. (In general, if you have n cities, you have $n!=n(n-1)(n-2)...(3)(2)(1)$ possible routes – a number that grows extremely quickly.)

This is an example of a *combinatorial explosion* – the number of possible permutations you need to check grows extremely quickly, even with fairly modest numbers. It makes it extremely difficult to plan a route through all of your specified cities so that it minimizes the amount of time taken or distance travelled. In fact, the *Travelling Salesman Problem* belongs to a class of problems known as *NP-hard*: there is no known algorithm that gives the optimal

solution in polynomial time. If you can find an efficient solution for the TSP, or any other NP-hard problem, you will have solved one of the Clay Mathematics Institute Millennium Prize Problems, known as P=NP, and won $1,000,000.

Luckily, although there are no perfect algorithms, there are some very good ones, and it is possible to find a route that gets within a few per cent of the optimal solution. One of the more interesting is called *Ant Colony Optimization*. An ant is sent out to explore the map at random, picking the next city to visit based on how far away it is, and how much "pheromone" has been left on the relevant road by previous ants. Once it has completed a circuit, it deposits an amount of pheromone on each of the roads it took. The shorter the route it has taken, the more pheromone it leaves.

A team led by William Cook of the University of Waterloo in Canada used a completely different method – a plane-cutting algorithm – to find the optimal walking tour visiting each of the United Kingdom's 24,727 pubs. You would need to cover about 28,400 miles (45,500 kilometres) – about 10% further than a complete circuit of the earth.

By changing the order of the cities, the amount of driving time can be significantly reduced. Finding the *optimal* route is difficult, especially for large numbers of cities.

HOW TO FIND A MISSING PLANE

On 8 March 2014, Malaysian Airlines flight MH370 vanished en route from Kuala Lumpur to Beijing with 227 passengers and 12 crew members on board. At the time of writing, only a few pieces of debris from the disappeared Boeing 777 have been found washed ashore. There is no sign of the plane itself after nearly three years of searching.

How hard can it be to find something as big as a Boeing 777 plane?

Finding MH370 is a trickier task than most air investigations have to deal with, because the flight communications equipment was turned off before the (presumed) crash. The plane was spotted over the Andaman Sea, north of Indonesia and west of Thailand, at around 2:22am Malaysian time; a satellite distance reading six hours later is consistent with it having then travelled roughly south into the Indian Ocean. The combination of the aircraft's flight speed and known distance suggests that it crashed into the ocean somewhere about 1,600 miles to the west of Perth, Australia.

It is about as far from populated land as it is possible to get – which makes the search site difficult to get to. It is also very deep – on average, the depth of the Indian Ocean is about 3,890 metres, about half the height of Mount Everest. And the priority search area,

the most likely place it could have been, covers an area of more than 23,000 square miles – about the size of West Virginia. (The *plausible* search area is twice the size of Texas.)

It is hard to visualize things that big, so let us shrink them down to something more easily imagined. Scaling the distances down by a factor of 2,500 would give a priority search area the size of a football field. On that scale, the water is 1.5 m deep, and the plane (assuming it is still in one piece) is about 2.5 cm long.

Oh, and the surface of the pitch is in total darkness, covered in molehills and under about 500 atmospheres of pressure, and you are about 0.064 cm tall. If it was anything other than a plane full of humans, the search would probably never have been attempted.

It is not even certain that the plane is in the priority search area (in fact, given that that is where they have looked most closely, it is becoming less and less likely that it is there). Different models for the aircraft's flight path put it in different places on or near the satellite arc, and drift analysis of where the debris that washed ashore could have come from appears inconsistent with the search area.

In summary, it is hard to find a missing plane because the ocean is huge and deep. It is even harder when you do not have good data about where it was when it crashed.

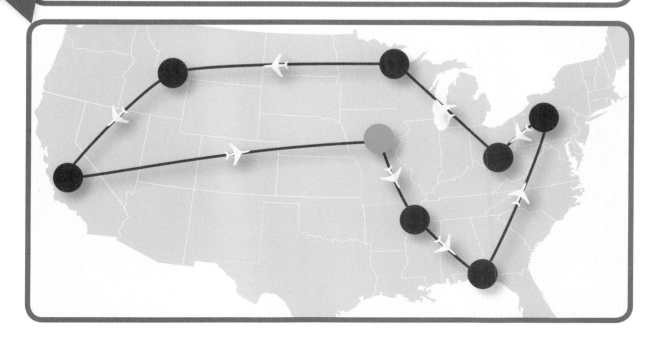

The Self-driving Car

$$f(x) = \sum_0^\infty A_n \sin(nx) + B_n \cos(nx)$$

The year is 2025. You step out of your front door, into the waiting car and say "Computer: take me to the stadium." You sit back, read a bit of the *The Maths Behind, Volume 8*, and before you know it, the computer pipes up: "You have reached your destination. Have a nice day!" before driving off to park itself.

• •

The amount of mathematics needed for that to happen is *staggering*.

The computer needs to figure out the words you used, by converting the sound signal into a vector using a *Fourier transform*, and using a hidden *Markov model* to determine the most likely sounds you made, before using that information to determine the most likely words you said.

It then needs to figure out what the words you used *meant*. It needs to understand not just that your destination is "the stadium," but also which stadium you mean. This most likely requires a *Bayesian analysis* of where you have gone before (if the only stadium you ever go to is the soccerdrome, it can be pretty sure that is where

you want to go; if you hate sports, it might figure out that The Stadium is a new Greek restaurant downtown and take you there instead).

Now it knows where you are going, it needs to plan a route. Google and other companies have spent vast sums of money converting the road network into a system that can be understood by computers – a weighted graph showing how long it typically takes to travel along each section of road. Updated with the current traffic reports, the computer will use a shortest-path algorithm such as A* to find the quickest way through the traffic to the ballpark.

The biggest difficulty is safely travelling along the planned route. The car needs to avoid other vehicles and road users; it needs to obey

From understanding the passenger's commands, to plotting a route, to avoiding other vehicles and obeying the rules of the road, self-driving cars use mathematics on every level.

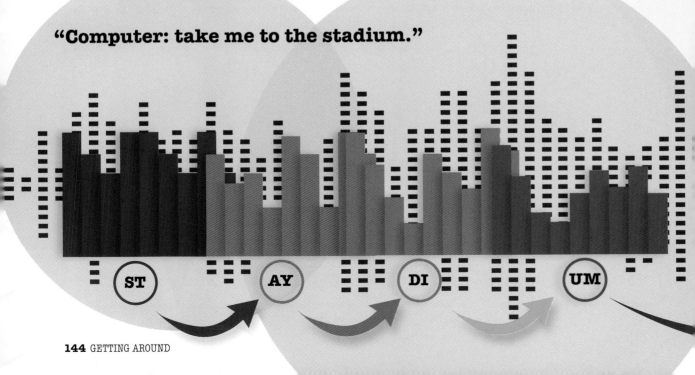

"Computer: take me to the stadium."

ST   AY   DI   UM

traffic signals and signs; it needs to react to weather conditions; and hardest of all, it needs to identify and safely avoid unpredictable obstacles in the road (it is obvious to you whether that white blob ahead is a plastic bag or a rolling rock – but not to a computer). All of these tasks come down to image processing: spotting something car-shaped, truck-shaped, bicycle-shaped or pedestrian-shaped involves all sorts of matrix algebra and probabilistic reasoning. For the car to respond to its environment requires decision and control theory: at this speed, in these conditions, can I swerve without endangering my passengers?

This brings us to one of the most philosophically interesting things about self-driving cars: if the safety systems fail and a crash becomes inevitable, how does the car minimize damage? Does it protect its own passengers, no matter who else it injures or kills in the process? Does it save the greatest number of lives it can, even if that means you die? Or does it leave it to chance, as would happen with a human driver? To a large extent, this calculus of ethics is still being developed – but you can bet it will have a mathematical basis when it is.

Car Crashes

$$KE = \frac{1}{2}mv^2$$

When a careless driver ran into the back of me at a stop sign, there were all sorts of questions running through my head: am I ok? Is he ok? Is the car ok? Did I do something wrong? Where are my insurance documents? What do I do now? And, most importantly, how does mathematics play into this scenario?

It turns out, there is a *huge* amount of mathematics involved in automotive collisions.

STOPPING SAFELY

On the back of the UK Highway Code, which is a sort of user's manual for roads, there is a chart of stopping distances. At 20 mph, it takes you about 40 feet to stop, in good conditions: 20 feet to react to what is going on in front of you, and 20 feet to bring the car to a halt. At 40 mph, you might expect it to take about double the distance but in fact it is three times as far, 120 feet. Because driving at 80 mph would be illegal, the stopping distance at that speed is not listed, but would be 400 feet, more than a football field, and ten times as far as the stopping distance at 20mph.

1.25m
annual worldwide road fatalities

34,000
annual US road fatalities
(10.6 per 100,000 population)

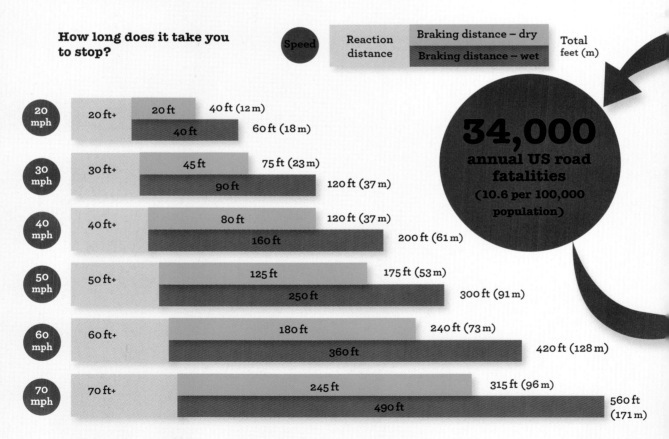

How long does it take you to stop?

Speed	Reaction distance	Braking distance – dry / Braking distance – wet	Total feet (m)
20 mph	20 ft+	20 ft	40 ft (12 m)
		40 ft	60 ft (18 m)
30 mph	30 ft+	45 ft	75 ft (23 m)
		90 ft	120 ft (37 m)
40 mph	40 ft+	80 ft	120 ft (37 m)
		160 ft	200 ft (61 m)
50 mph	50 ft+	125 ft	175 ft (53 m)
		250 ft	300 ft (91 m)
60 mph	60 ft+	180 ft	240 ft (73 m)
		360 ft	420 ft (128 m)
70 mph	70 ft+	245 ft	315 ft (96 m)
		490 ft	560 ft (171 m)

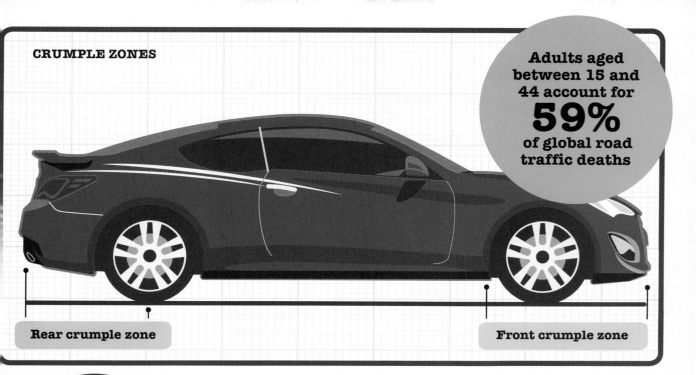

CRUMPLE ZONES

Adults aged between 15 and 44 account for **59%** of global road traffic deaths

Rear crumple zone

Front crumple zone

1827 annual UK road fatalities (2.9 per 100,000 population)

77% road deaths are among men

How is this worked out? Looking at the graphic, you will notice that the thinking distance increases in roughly a straight line – every extra mile per hour you drive means you take an extra foot to think about stopping. That makes some kind of sense: during the thinking time, you are travelling at a constant speed, and it does not take you any longer to react at highway speed than in slow-moving traffic. The thinking distance in seconds is simply:

your speed in feet per second × your thinking time in seconds

To convert miles per hour into feet per second, you need to multiply by 1.4666... – or, since you are trying to avoid a crash, let us call it 1.5 to make it simpler. You can deduce that a typical reaction time is about $\frac{2}{3}$ of a second.

Braking distance is a more complicated calculation – but you can see that doubling your speed roughly quadruples your braking distance. This is because of *kinetic energy* –

the amount of work needed to stop a vehicle (or anything else) is $\frac{1}{2}mv^2$, where m is its mass and v its speed. Work can be calculated as *force × distance*, so if you apply a constant force, the distance it takes your car to stop is proportional to the square of your speed. It turns out that squaring your speed (in mph) and dividing by 20 gives you your braking distance.

On highways, it is frequently recommended that you leave two seconds of gap between you and the car in front of you. That is not so you can stop in the distance between cars (at 70 mph, you travel 210 feet in two seconds, and you would still be going about 40 mph by the time you caught up to where the car in front was) – but you do not need to stop in that distance, because the car in front will have moved on in the same time. At those speeds, it is the *thinking* distance that is important; giving yourself a couple of seconds of space means you should have plenty of time to figure out the situation and stop before you tail-end somebody.

If only the guy at the stop sign had thought about that.

SURVIVING A CRASH

"Elliott, you've recovered from your injury – have you any words for the guy who ran into you?"
"Not really. I take some comfort from Newton's Third Law, in that I hit him just as hard as he hit me." American footballer Elliott Barnhart

Assuming you are strapped in, there are two main factors in determining how serious a collision is: how fast you are travelling when the accident takes place, and how long the collision takes. In mathematical terms, your kinetic energy (just like before) determines how much work it takes to slow you down, while the length of time the collision takes determines the force of the impact.

To imagine this, think about falling onto a hard floor (where you go from fast to stationary very quickly) against falling onto a foam mat (which slows you down more gradually). Which would you pick to land on? By spreading the impact out over a longer time, the mat allows the same amount of kinetic energy to be absorbed over a longer time – meaning you experience a smaller force, a less sharp deceleration, and hopefully a safer landing.

Similarly, passenger vehicles are designed so that, in the event of an accident, the impact is slowed down as much as possible. Your seatbelt tries to slow you down gradually. Your air bags slow down your interaction with the steering wheel. The front of the car crumples in a way that absorbs as much of the energy as possible, ideally without crushing your legs.

However, the best thing you can do to keep your collisions comparatively low-risk is to slow down. A collision at 50mph requires about half as much energy to be absorbed as a collision at 70mph does.

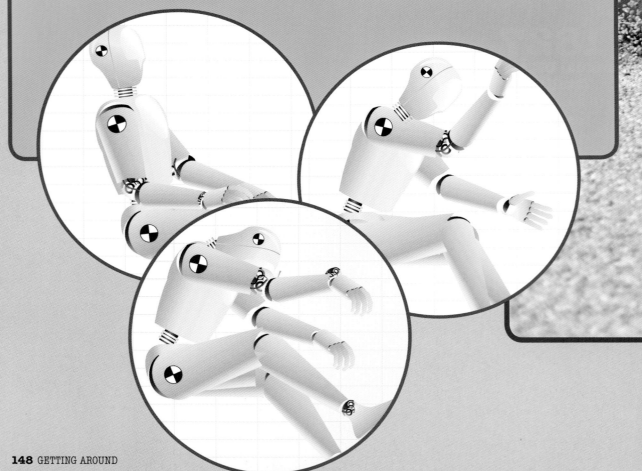

EMERGENCY RUNOFFS

In the 1981 movie *Chariots of Fire*, there is a famous scene of the Olympic hopefuls training by running along the beach at St Andrews, in Scotland. Have you ever tried that? How about riding a bike or pushing a buggy on sand or gravel? It is much, much harder than it looks.

On a hard surface, all the wheels of your car do is support you and push against the surface so you keep moving forwards. On a granular surface, several other things happen: you sink slightly, because the pebbles or grains can be easily moved around, which means that instead of running on the flat, your wheels are now continually trying to go uphill. Your wheels push the grains past each other rather than rolling nicely over them. You are also being pushed backwards by

the surface as you try to move forwards – the increase in the normal reaction force in turn increases the frictional force acting against your motion – all of which adds up to a much tougher ride than on the flat!

If you drive in the mountains, you will often see signs for "runaway truck ramp" or "escape lane" on steep descents. These appear to be giant gravel pits – and they are just about the safest way to stop an out-of-control vehicle in a hurry. Effectively, they turn a steep descent into what feels like a steep climb on a spongy surface, slowing the truck down in a controlled manner – not too quickly, so that there is not a big impact, but also not too slowly, so that the truck does not carry on careering down the hill.

Traffic Jams

Normally, when traffic flow returns to normal after a jam, you can see the cause of it: an accident, construction works, or even just a slow-moving vehicle. But sometimes, you emerge from the slowness without the faintest idea of what held you up. What held you up was probably a *jamiton*.

TRAFFIC JAMS

In free-flowing traffic, the distance between vehicles is generally quite large. When it gets smaller, something odd happens: it only takes a slight slowing down of one vehicle to cause a jam out of nothing – without stopping. Like a spring, the car behind has to slow slightly – but because it is closer than it would ideally be, it slows down more than it needs to. The car behind that does the same, and before you know it, the interstate is in gridlock.

There are several ways to model this, the most interesting of which (to me) is Kai Nagel and Michael Schreckenberg's *cellular automaton*.

They treat the highway as a list of cells which are either empty (no car) or contain a number (the car's speed). At each time step, they apply a set of rules to each car in the simulation: if it is driving slower than the limit, it accelerates; if it is too close to the car in front, it slows down; if a random incident occurs, it slows down; and if its speed is not zero, it moves forward that many spaces.

Outputs from the simulation show *beautiful* jamitons develop: the waves of slow-moving and stationary traffic move backwards along the highway at a predictable rate.

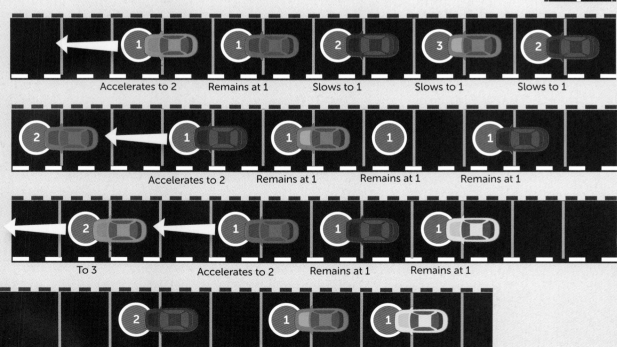

| Accelerates to 2 | Remains at 1 | Slows to 1 | Slows to 1 | Slows to 1 |

| Accelerates to 2 | Remains at 1 | Remains at 1 | Remains at 1 |

| To 3 | Accelerates to 2 | Remains at 1 | Remains at 1 |

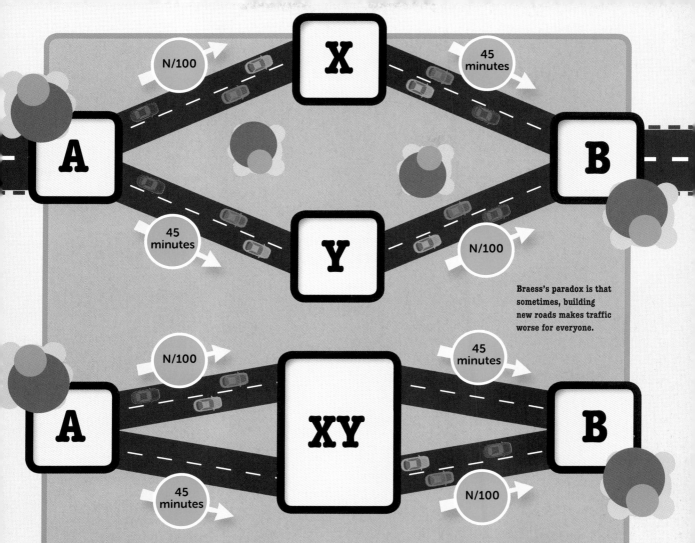

Braess's paradox is that sometimes, building new roads makes traffic worse for everyone.

BRAESS'S PARADOX

When Cheonggyecheon, a part of Seoul in South Korea, was regenerated in the early 2000s, a highway through the district was removed. Counter-intuitively, this led to an *improvement* in the traffic flow nearby. This is a real-life example of *Braess's paradox*: in some cases, adding a road to a network makes traffic worse rather than better, and vice versa.

Consider this road setup. The travel time from A to X and from Y to B depends on how heavy the traffic is: if *N* cars are on the road, it takes *N*/100 minutes to cover the route. From B to Y and A to X, travel takes 45 minutes, no matter how busy the roads are.

If 4000 cars want to get from A to B, and everybody behaves rationally, half of them will go via X and half via Y. Everyone will get there in 2000/100 + 45 = 65 minutes.

Now, some bright spark in the highways department decides to add a short linking route from X to Y that takes no time to drive along. Now the network looks like the diagram above, and everyone has a choice of routes from A to XY. Even with 4,000 cars on the road, it is quicker to take the top route, which takes 40 minutes. There is an identical choice from XY to B, and it is quicker to take the bottom route, which also takes 40 minutes. It now takes everyone 80 minutes to travel from A to B, despite the "improvement" to the road.

So, the next time you are stuck in traffic, you might consider writing to the highways authority and suggesting they close a few roads!

The Hyperloop

$$\frac{1}{2}CpAv^2$$

Elon Musk, the name behind Tesla cars, the SpaceX missions and all manner of alternative energy schemes, describes the Hyperloop as "a cross between Concorde, a railgun, and an air-hockey table."

Concorde was a luxury supersonic plane; a railgun is a weapon that uses magnetic induction rather than an explosion to accelerate its ammunition, and an air-hockey table uses air jets to reduce friction so the puck glides across it almost without friction.

The Hyperloop is (or rather, is planned to be) a transit system that runs extremely quickly, with a vehicle propelled by electromagnetic forces rather than combustion, through a practically frictionless (and air-resistance-less) tube. The initial concept suggests the train could run as fast as 760mph – slightly slower than the speed of sound in its environment, so there would be no irritating sonic boom.

As with ski jumpers, the aerodynamic drag on a train is $\frac{1}{2}CpAv^2$, where C is a constant depending on the shape of the train, p the air pressure, A is the cross-sectional area of the train and v is the speed of travel. Typically, high-speed train design focuses on A and C – making the cross-section smaller or a better shape, but running the Hyperloop in tunnels offers another avenue to pursue: reducing p. By pumping air out of the tunnels, the proposal is to lower the pressure to 100 pascals, compared to a typical air pressure of around 100,000 pascals at sea level. This would reduce air resistance

The Hyperloop would take passengers from LA to San Francisco in 30 minutes – instead of a six-hour drive.

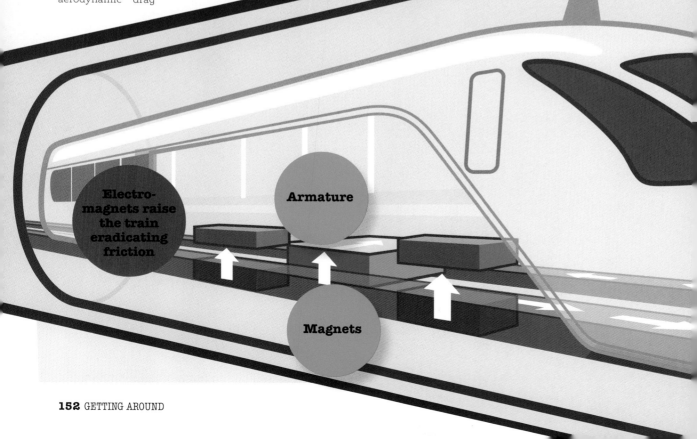

Electro-magnets raise the train eradicating friction

Armature

Magnets

by a factor of 1,000 – enough to run a train 30 times as fast as normal, all else being equal.

Of course, not all else is equal: running a train packed tightly inside a tube leads to some tricky physics problems. The short version is that even though there is not very much air in front of the train, it still needs to end up behind it – and get there smoothly. One possible solution is to use a giant fan to push the air *beneath* the train, which has the added benefit of lifting the train slightly from the rails and reducing friction – again, making the trains more efficient to run.

The whole thing – the electromagnets, the fans, the air pumps and the elevation jets – is to be powered by solar cells along the length of

the tunnel, and given that the track is running across the California desert, this seems like a smart move.

The project is not without its controversies – some doubt whether Musk's projections of cost are feasible; others think the whole thing is impossible, dangerous, and/or a ploy to derail other mass transit schemes in California – citing Musk's controlling interest in Tesla, an electric car manufacturer.

One of the safety concerns raised is about the stopping time for Hyperloop pods. It is proposed that pods should depart every 30 seconds, but the trains are designed to have a maximum acceleration of 0.5 g – so a train traveling at 760 mph (340 metres per second) – would take about 68 seconds to stop. If a train came to a catastrophic stop, the train behind would be unable to come to a safe halt in time, and the train behind that would likely also become involved in the wreck. Does this mean the trains would need longer between them, thus reducing the number of passengers that can be carried? Or does it just call for better emergency braking?

The Hyperloop has plenty of problems (mathematical, political and logistical), but it is still probably the most innovative infrastructure project of the last few decades.

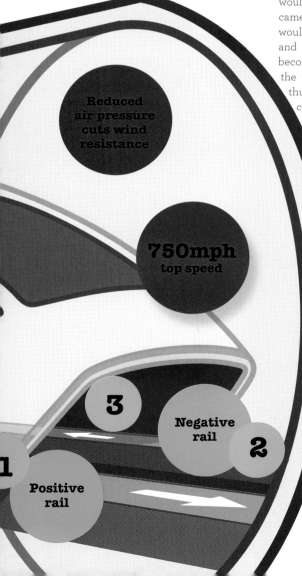

Reduced air pressure cuts wind resistance

750mph top speed

3

1 Positive rail

Negative rail

2

Rail gun technology

1 Electric current flows up the positive rail

2 The current flows across the armature and down the negative rail

3 The magnetic force is directed towards the end of the rails which drives the armature and the train forward

Space Travel

$$N = R^* \, f_p \, n_e \, f_l \, f_i \, f_c \, L$$

On 5 July 2016, the Juno probe arrived in orbit around Jupiter, after travelling 1.74 billion miles through space over the course of five years. It was a second behind schedule. How on earth – or rather, how *off* earth – can a route through space be planned so accurately?

To plot a route to another planet, you need several tools. First: a good working model of the solar system. Not just because you need to know where Earth and Jupiter are at the start and end of your journey, but because planets can also be helpful: you can use them to pick up speed.

Juno, after it left the Earth's atmosphere, followed an elliptical orbit around the Sun for a bit more than two years. During this time, it went out beyond Mars's orbit before catching up with Earth again for a *gravitational assist*.

Imagine you are gliding forwards on an ice-rink with your arms outstretched, and a small child is skating towards you. They grab your hand as they pass and you swing them back around in the direction they came from, slightly faster. You, meanwhile, slow down slightly as a result of the interaction.

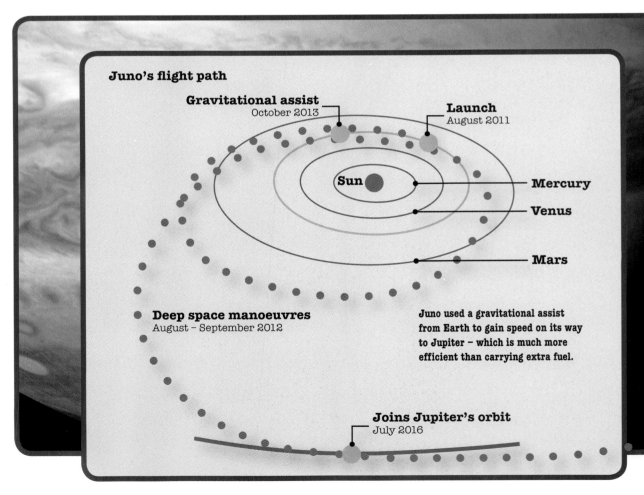

Juno's flight path

Gravitational assist
October 2013

Launch
August 2011

Sun

Mercury

Venus

Mars

Deep space manoeuvres
August – September 2012

Juno used a gravitational assist from Earth to gain speed on its way to Jupiter – which is much more efficient than carrying extra fuel.

Joins Jupiter's orbit
July 2016

That is roughly what happened in October 2013 when Juno flew by the Earth again: the spacecraft approached the Earth, and used its momentum to pick up speed. Because Juno is much smaller than the Earth, even though it borrowed more than 16,000 mph from the Earth, it only slowed the Earth down by about a ten-millionth of an inch per year. Juno's speed increase was enough to move it into a different orbit around the Sun, and one which would lead it to coincide with where Jupiter would eventually be.

As for planning all of this... well, it is exactly rocket science. However, it boils down to the kind of geometry you can do with GeoGebra (or similar mathematical software packages). Orbits around the Sun and around planets follow particular ellipses, and it is "just" a case of finding the ellipses that match up with where you want to be, when.

Once the operations team had a plan, they had a window of a few days when it would be possible to launch. Once the probe was in motion, it could more or less be left alone to follow its orbit (there is not an awful lot of friction or air resistance in the cold dark vacuum of space). When Juno approached Earth for its flyby, its rockets could be adjusted to make sure it came in at the correct angle and speed. When it reached Jupiter, its insertion into orbit needed to be very carefully managed, but the vast bulk of Juno's day-to-day navigation was pretty much on cruise control.

Why do it this way rather than fly on a straight-ish path to Jupiter? That is easy: doing it this way is much more energy-efficient and requires much less (relatively heavy) fuel. The less fuel you need to carry, the more room you have for interesting scientific equipment!

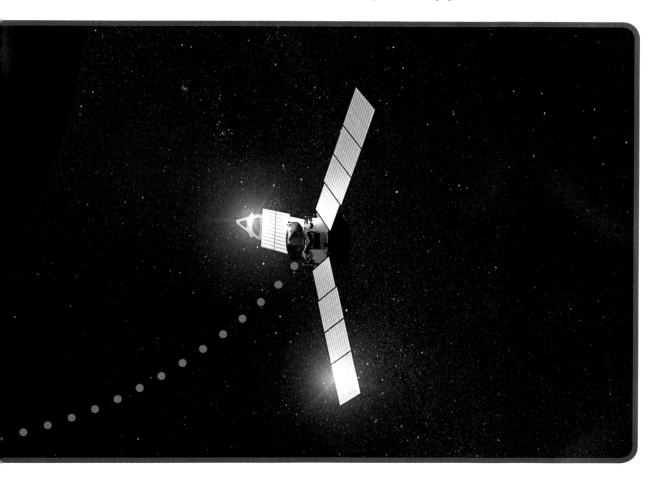

MEETING ALIENS

Will we ever meet aliens? The short answer is, "It depends what you mean." If you mean little green men who say "Take me to your leader," then no, it is unlikely we will encounter alien life. If you mean microbes, then yes, I would be surprised if a space mission did not come across aliens in my lifetime.

I am – quite obviously – not the first person to think about the likelihood of discovering extraterrestrial life. In 1961, just as the space race was hotting up, astronomer Frank Drake came up with an equation to approximate the number of alien civilizations we could conceivably encounter:

$$N = R^* \, f_p \, n_e \, f_l f_i f_c \, L$$

where:

R^* is the average rate of star formation

f_p is the fraction of stars that form planets

n_e is the average number of planets per star that could support life

f_l is the fraction of those planets where life does evolve

f_i is the fraction of planets with life where *intelligent* life evolves

f_c is the fraction of planets with intelligent life that have developed communications technology permitting them to broadcast their existence; and

L is the average length of time such communications survive for.

Unlike many "perfect formulas," Drake's equation makes perfect mathematical sense: it breaks down the number into coherent parts that multiply together to make the whole. The problem is, we do not really know what the numbers are, which means the uncertainties are too large for it to be especially useful.

Our current best guesses are that R^* is somewhere around 2, f_p is close to 1 (almost all stars have planets), and n_e around 0.4. The values of f_l, f_i, f_c and L are pretty speculative; f_l is likely to be close to 1, but f_i and f_c very small; humans have had radios for about 100 years and have almost destroyed themselves several times over in that time, so a reasonable value for L seems to be about 200.

That gives $N \approx 160 \, f_i \, f_c$, which is less than 1 for any reasonable "very small" values of f_i and f_c, meaning we are probably alone. If L is much larger (we expect radio transmissions to continue for thousands of millennia into the future), then N could be much larger.

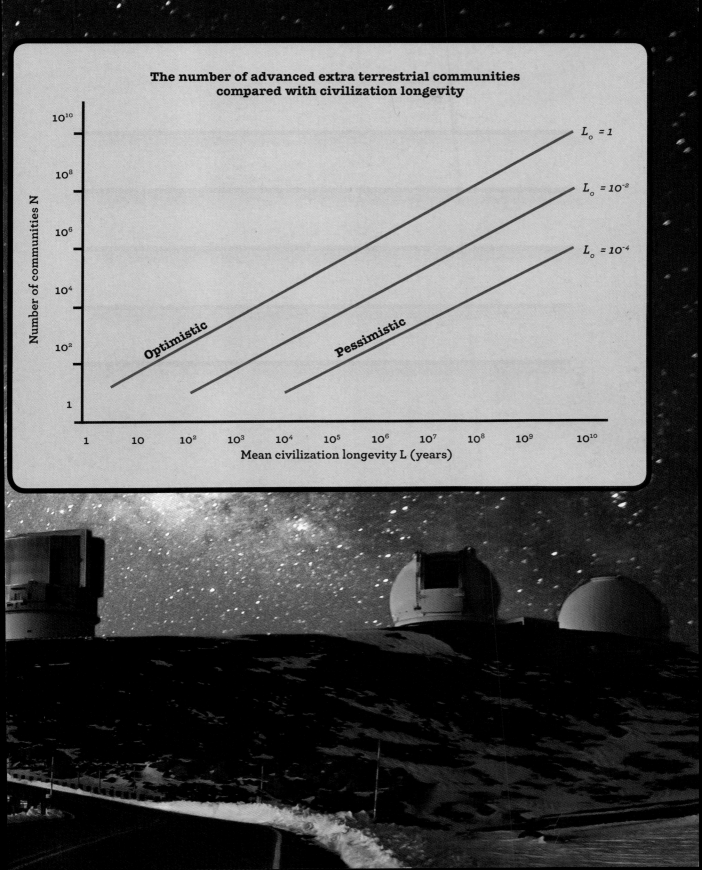

The number of advanced extra terrestrial communities compared with civilization longevity

Flying

One moment you are pelting along the ground, and the next minute your Airbus A380 – weighing nearly 600 tonnes, about as much as a dozen houses – is pitched backwards, up in the air, completely safely.

Put like that, it is incredible – barely a century ago, heavier-than-air flight was generally considered a crazy dream, and we have come a long way from the Wright Brothers bumping along for a few hundred feet in 1903.

The key idea behind air flight is that the shape of the wing changes how the air flows around it. A typical wing looks like **Figure 1**, although there are many variations. You could imagine trying to push this shape forwards in a ball pool, and it is hopefully obvious that it would be pushed upwards by the balls as you moved along.

The balls in front of the wing are pushed downwards. Sir Isaac Newton tells us that for every action, there is an equal and opposite reaction: this means that pushing the balls down (the downwash) results in the wings being lifted up. This accounts for about a third of the lift.

The bulk of the rest is from something that is a bit less obvious in the ball pool. Behind the wing, there are fewer balls than there are below it, meaning the wing is sucked upwards by the comparatively low pressure.

There is also an element of the balls being accelerated along the wing and "squirting" the air down and backwards; again, Newton tells us that the effect of this is to push the wing in the opposite direction, forward and upward. This is a result of air at high speed being slightly *viscous* – unlike the balls in the pool, it clings to the wing as it goes past.

> An aircraft more than 15° from the horizontal will tend to "stall"

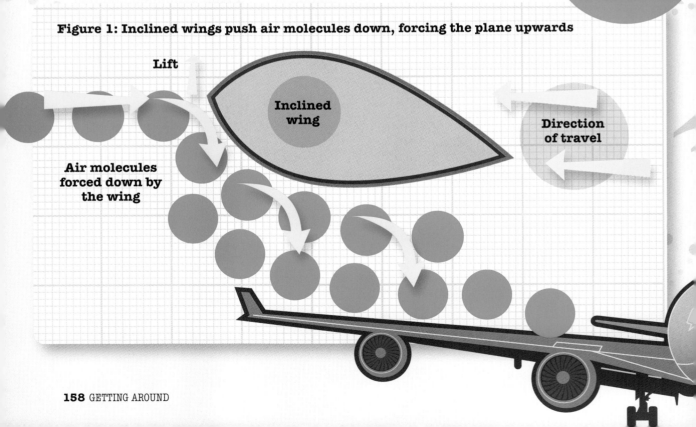

Figure 1: Inclined wings push air molecules down, forcing the plane upwards

Lift

Inclined wing

Direction of travel

Air molecules forced down by the wing

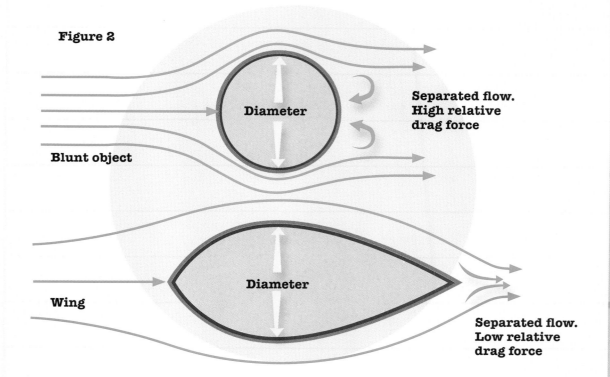

Figure 2

Blunt object

Diameter

Separated flow.
High relative
drag force

Wing

Diameter

Separated flow.
Low relative
drag force

D'ALEMBERT'S PARADOX

For Newton and those who came after, bird flight was a great mystery – and so human flight was at best wishful thinking. As far as anyone could tell from the sums, the whole thing was impossible: in 1752, D'Alembert showed that in inviscid (not sticky) incompressible (does not get squished) irrotational (does not form eddies) steady air flow, the equations of fluid dynamics do not allow wings to create either a lift force or a drag force. All of these assumptions were justifiable approximations – viscosity is fairly small, air is practically incompressible at low speed, and moving into effectively still air means you should not expect whirlwinds. Flight – according to fluid dynamics – was impossible; therefore (according to scornful mathematicians) fluid dynamics was hogwash.

Luckily, Martin Wilhelm Kutta and Nikolai Zhukovsky sorted out the problem in the end. They showed that lift was generated by circulation around the wing (so the assumption of irrotational flow was not correct), while Ludwig Prandtl showed that there was a viscous layer of air around the wing that provided drag, to the great relief of fluid dynamicists everywhere. (See **Figure 2**.)

While wings cause you to move up, they also slow you down. However, typically the drag force is about 5–10% the size of the lift force they provide.

Airfoils tend to work well as long as their *angle of attack* is no greater than about 15 degrees. At that point, the air stops flowing smoothly, and the turbulence causes the amount of lift generated to drop dramatically. When someone says a plane has stalled, they do not mean the pilot has lousy clutch control – they mean the pilot has tried to get the wings too steep for the conditions.

66 years
between first
powered flight
and landing on
the moon

WHY ISN'T MY ROUTE STRAIGHT?

If you are flying from, let's say, London to New York, you might look at a map and imagine flying in a nice straight line, taking you over Cornwall, then the Atlantic Ocean, then Long Island and you are there. If you check the flight path, though, it takes in Scotland, a fair chunk of Canada and the Atlantic coast. Why on earth would you take such a huge detour?

There are several parts to the answer. The first one is: the world is not flat, and the shortest distance on the surface (or a few tens of thousands of feet above it) is almost never a straight line on the map. Instead, it is an arc of a *great circle*, a circle on the earth's surface that splits the planet into equal halves. That circle is nowhere near the straight line on the map, because the projection of the spherical surface of the world onto a plane means everything gets distorted, the more so the further you get from the equator.

Different routes also take account of prevailing weather conditions – your pilot might be taking advantage of a tail wind, or avoiding an area of turbulence that could disrupt the flight.

Another practical reason is that flying over land is much safer than flying over water: if there is an emergency on board and the plane needs to land quickly, you are more likely to find an airport on land than in the ocean. Even if there is no airport nearby and you need to land on water, I would certainly prefer to do that close to the coast, where lifeboat stations are, than in the middle of the ocean, where they are not.

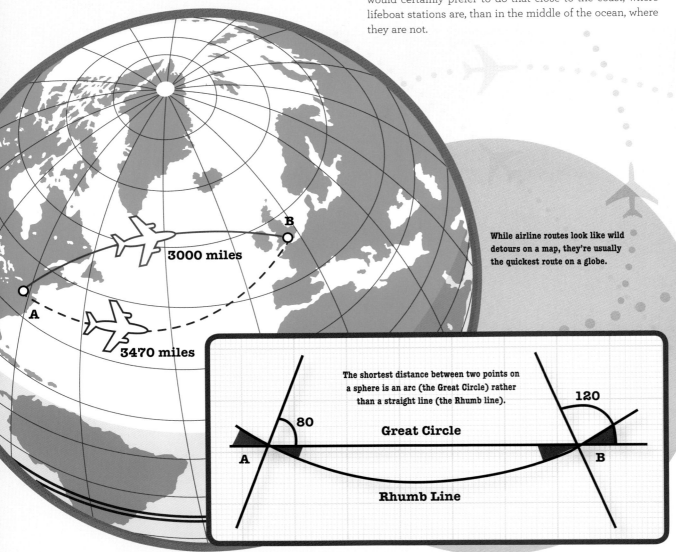

While airline routes look like wild detours on a map, they're usually the quickest route on a globe.

3000 miles

3470 miles

The shortest distance between two points on a sphere is an arc (the Great Circle) rather than a straight line (the Rhumb line).

80

120

Great Circle

A

B

Rhumb Line

A random boarding process is generally quicker than the way airlines do things

WHAT IS THE BEST WAY TO BOARD A PLANE?

If you are ever stuck standing in the aisle of an airplane waiting for some chump with carry-on the size of a small bus trying to cram it into a space in the overhead locker as big as a toy car, you might find yourself experiencing air rage. I urge you to calm yourself down by considering whether there may be a more efficient way to board a plane than the ones typically used by airlines.

Boarding from the front and moving backwards is about as boneheaded a way to arrange things as can be imagined, unless – for example – you were to encourage the elderly and families with small children to get on first. Oh, wait! They do that, too!

It turns out that even an entirely random boarding process is generally quicker than the way airlines typically do things just now.

A paper by Eitan Bachmat and his colleagues looks at some of the alternative possibilities for getting passengers on board quickly, and suggests that the *mathematically* best method is to board "outside-in" and back to front – so those with window seats in the back row are followed by those with middle seats and then aisle seats before moving on to the next-to-back row, and so on.

While this is great in principle, it would require a level of organization and cooperation from people who generally stand up to get off a good five minutes before the plane door is open.

The Everyday

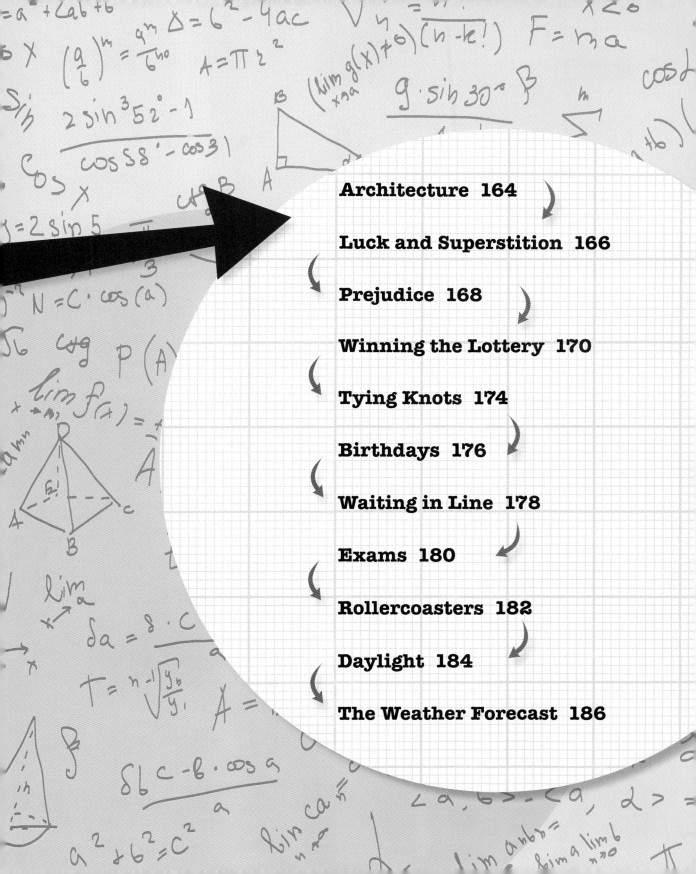

Architecture

Located at 30 St Mary Axe stands one of London's most iconic buildings, known to everyone as the *Gherkin*. It is 180 metres tall, round but not quite cylindrical (it bulges in the middle) and has a distinctive spiral design in its glass panes. Visually, it is striking; mathematically, it is fascinating.

Square-based skyscrapers cause severe whirlwinds at their bases. Mathematical models showed that cylinders, which are lacking in sharp corners, reduced these significantly; shapes with a bulge performed even better.

The stripes on the building are the result of each floor having six wedges cut into it for ventilation and lighting purposes. Rotating each floor 5 degrees with respect to the floor below allows better ventilation – and causes the spiral effect.

Of the more than 7,000 glass panels that make up the exterior of the Gherkin, only one (the lens at the very top) is curved. The others are almost all roughly parallelograms, which can be cut from glass with less wastage than can triangles.

Since the circumference of the tower comprises around 70 panels, each is offset by about 5 degrees from its neighbours – 70-gons appear circular, except on very close inspection!

The Gherkin's design reduces energy costs and whirlwind effects at street level.

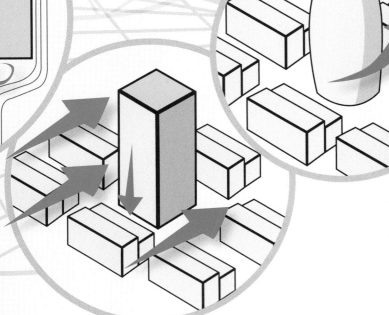

Cylinder-shaped buildings have reduced whirlwind effect

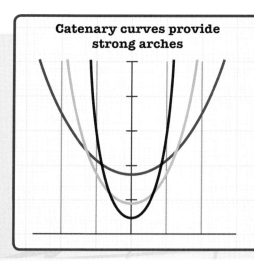

Catenary curves provide strong arches

THE SAGRADA FAMÍLIA

About as far removed from the smooth curves of the Gherkin as possible is Gaudí's still-unfinished masterpiece: the Sagrada Família Cathedral in Barcelona, Spain. It, too, is steeped in mathematics.

Much of the cathedral's design is based on two curves: the *catenary* and the *parabola*.

A *catenary* is the shape you get if you hang a rope or a chain between two supports; the canonical equation for one with its minimum at $(0, A)$ is $y = A \cosh (x/A)$. The catenary is an excellent shape for arches, as they are naturally self-supporting. Their weight is directed exactly along the curve, meaning the arch undergoes very little twisting.

A *parabola* is the shape you get from slicing diagonally into a cone, parallel to its other side; a typical equation is $y = Bx^2$. Qualitatively, parabolas and catenaries are very similar.

The pinnacles of the towers consist of precise geometrical shapes, including cubes, octahedra, tetrahedra and spheres, among others.

Gaudí invented an entirely new geometric structure for some of the cathedral's columns: a *variable transversal shape* consists of polygons that gradually increase their degree of rotational symmetry as they climb. For example, an octagon might be split into two squares, initially offset by 45 degrees, spiralling in different directions up the column. When the squares intersect, they are replaced by a pair of octagons behaving the same way – and so on, until the column is effectively circular in cross-section. This also

Hyperbolic parabola

allows the columns to branch off in a way that mimics a tree.

Many of the surfaces in the Sagrada Família make use of *ruled surfaces*, apparently curved shapes that can be made from only straight lines. For example, *hyperbolic paraboloids* are an excellent shape for collecting and diffusing light into a building, and for making saddle-shaped roofs that minimize the amount of material needed. There are also stairways in the form of *helicoids* – spirals built entirely from straight lines.

Gaudí made repeated use of simple ratios – for example, the height (in metres) of each column is double the number of points in the polygon at its base.

The Sagrada Família cathedral in Barcelona could justifiably claim to be the world's most mathematical building.

Luck and Superstition

$$\frac{2GMr}{R^3}$$

Is astrology plausible? Astrology suggests that the movement of distant planets across the heavens somehow affects our everyday lives. The exact mechanism by which they do this is never explained, of course, but there is only one force known to act at a distance: *gravity*.

• •

So, how much effect does a planet – for instance, Venus, the closest planet to Earth – have on our everyday lives?

This can be calculated using Newton's laws of motion: the acceleration on Earth due to the gravity of any body is $2GMr/R^3$, where G is the gravitational constant ($6.67 \times 10^{-11}\,\mathrm{Nm^2kg^{-2}}$), M is the mass of the body (for Venus, $4.87 \times 10^{24}\,\mathrm{kg}$), r is the distance from the centre of Earth ($6.37 \times 10^6\,\mathrm{m}$) and R is the distance to the body (at its very closest, about $3.8 \times 10^{10}\,\mathrm{m}$). Plugging those numbers into the equation gives $7.54 \times 10^{-11}\,\mathrm{N}$.

The weight of a feather is about $7.5 \times 10^{-1}\,\mathrm{N}$. The force due to Venus (our closest planet) at its very closest, is one ten-billionth of that.

If Venus has some sort of relationship with human characteristics or activity, it – or astrologers – have an awful lot of explaining to do.

THE GAMBLER'S FALLACY

If you toss a fair coin nine times in a row and get nine heads, what is the probability that the tenth toss will also be a head?

There are three types of answer to this. Two of them are mathematically reasonable; the third is not – but is still widely held by gamblers.

The first, literalist, answer is 50–50. The question told us the coin is fair, so it is no more likely to come up heads than tails or vice versa. A streak of nine heads is unusual, but not *that* unusual: it will happen once in every 512 experiments, slightly more likely than getting four-of-a-kind playing Texas Hold-'Em poker.

A second, Bayesian, answer is to say "there is some evidence for this coin being biased; the probability of throwing a tenth head is greater than a half." This is quite a sensible answer. It is certainly reasonable to be suspicious of a coin that is giving such unlikely outcomes.

The third answer – probably the most common one you will hear given by non-mathematicians – having thrown nine heads, it is much more likely to come down tails to start evening out the results. Unfortunately, coins do not have a memory. There is no mechanism by which a coin flip can take account of its past results and decide to act fairly. The idea of coins and other instruments of chance evening out imbalances is known as the *gambler's fallacy*.

The gambler's fallacy is easily confused with the *Law of Large Numbers*, which says something related but subtly different: over the long term, the results of a repeated random event will tend to approach the underlying probability of it – that is, if you flip a million coins, you can expect close to 50% heads and 50% tails.

How can it do this without a sense of justice? It happens naturally. Over the course of a run of ten coins, the probability of getting five heads and five tails is about one in four – and the probability of getting either that or a 6–4 split is almost two-thirds. The occasional extreme result (for example, a 10–0 split, which comes up about 0.2% of the time) is simply dwarfed by the large number of evenly-split outcomes.

In fact, the results of coin flips follow a *binomial distribution*, which – over a large number of flips – becomes more and more like a normal distribution with a mean of $n/2$ and a standard deviation of $\sqrt{n}/2$. If you flip a coin a million times, you would expect to get half a million heads, give or take 500.

Newton's laws show that other planets have no practical effect on the Earth.

Heads or tails: 50:50?

THE MATHS BEHIND WHY YOUR TOAST LANDS BUTTERED-SIDE DOWN

Mathematicians can be quite cynical about superstition in general, and about Murphy's Law in particular: if everything that could go wrong did go wrong, there would not be much of a planet left.

However, there is one aspect of Murphy's Law that has an element of truth behind it. Tradition claims that "the toast always lands buttered-side down," which makes a mess of both the toast and the carpet. While that is not entirely true, experiments and mathematics both show that – under certain conditions – the buttered side of a dropped piece of toast will hit the ground more often than the unbuttered one.

There are three critical factors to consider:

1. **Which way up you are holding the toast (normally, buttered-side up);**

2. **The height you drop the toast from; and**

3. **How fast the toast rotates.**

The height you drop the toast from is probably the height of your table. Let us say that is about a metre (3 feet 3 inches). Assuming no air resistance, the fall will then take $t=\sqrt{(2h/g)}$ seconds, with $h=1$m and $g\approx10$ m/s, a time of about 0.45 seconds.

If your slice of toast hits the ground before it completes a quarter-turn, it will land buttered-side up. If instead it completes between a quarter-turn and three-a quarter turn, it will hit the ground buttered-side down.

Less than a quarter-turn in 0.45 seconds would require the toast to rotate at less than 33 revolutions per minute, or a full turn every 1.8 seconds. The butter-down option would hold for any rate between 33 and 100 rpm, with each full turn taking between 0.6 and 1.8 seconds. A few experiments involving a careless toast-dropper (my two-year-old son) and a camera suggest a rate of around 80 rpm is typical.

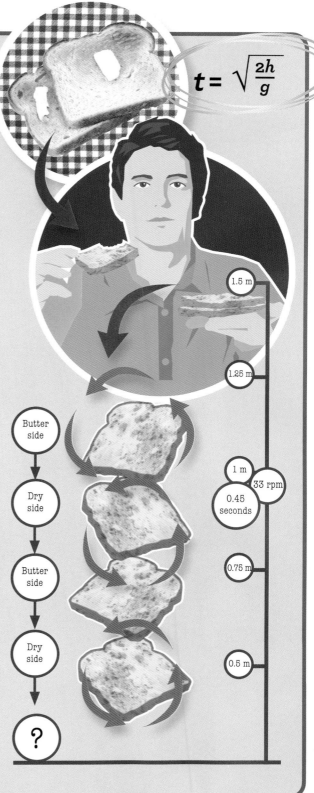

$$t = \sqrt{\frac{2h}{g}}$$

1.5 m

1.25 m

1 m · 33 rpm

0.45 seconds

0.75 m

0.5 m

Butter side → Dry side → Butter side → Dry side → ?

Prejudice

Why do minorities encounter more bias? One model of prejudice in the workplace (or elsewhere) gives an explanation of why any group that is in a minority experiences a disproportional amount of abuse – even if the majority is not any more prejudiced than the minority group.

Imagine that out of 100 people working at a firm, 90 are right-handed and 10 left-handed. Let us suppose that 10% of each group are hostile and abusive once a week to someone who writes with the other hand. What happens?

Nine of the right-handers abuse a random lefty; one of the southpaws is nasty to a random right-hander. But in terms of experiencing abuse, the ten left-handers experience nine incidents of abuse each week (so you would expect every one of them to experience an abusive incident within a little over a week). By contrast, only one of the 90 right-handers is on the wrong end of abuse in any given week; on average, a right-hander would go nearly two years without being abused by a lefty.

The expected number of abusive incidents one group receives is:

$$\frac{\textit{other population} \times \textit{other population's rate of prejudice}}{\textit{your population}}$$

and the ratio between the two is:

$$\frac{\textit{larger pop}^2 \times \textit{larger prejudice rate}}{\textit{smaller pop}^2 \times \textit{smaller prejudice rate}}$$

This idea is known as the *Petrie multiplier* (it is mathematically similar to Lanchester's Laws for battles). The imbalance can be reduced by employing a higher proportion of left-handers. Although the expected number of incidents would remain the same, fewer anti-left-hander incidents would be spread between more people, while the increase in anti-right-hander incidents would barely register for the average employee. A better solution is to reduce the prejudice rate and for everyone to see the merits in the other hand.

The Petrie Multiplier effect explains why, even if everyone is just as prejudiced, the minority experiences more unpleasant incidents.

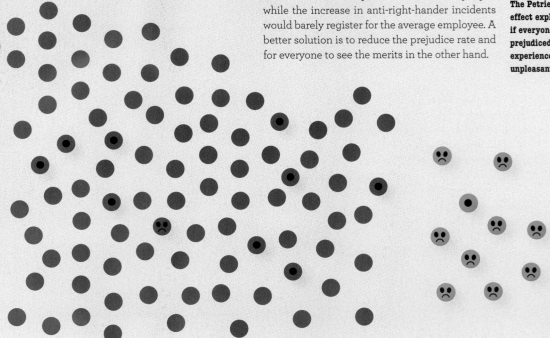

WHY DO NEIGHBOURHOODS BECOME MORE SEGREGATED?

Few people like to think of themselves as racist. Most of us are warm and friendly to others, regardless of skin colour or religious beliefs. We would be horrified to learn that our preferences somehow led to segregated communities.

However, a playable demonstration by the brilliant Vi Hart and Nicky Case, based on work by late Nobel Prize-winning economist Thomas Schelling – *The Parable of the Polygons* – shows that even a small bias towards just not being in the minority leads to exactly that.

They set up an experiment involving squares and triangles; each group is perfectly happy so long as at least one in three of their immediate neighbours is like them. They *like* diversity – but if they feel heavily outnumbered, they move elsewhere... and before long, the shapes are split into groups of triangles and groups of squares with very few mixed zones. It is uncanny.

Hart and Case also demonstrate that once a place is segregated, even if nobody has any opinion about their neighbours, it does not naturally desegregate. Instead, to get mixed neighbourhoods, the polygons need to have a preference for diversity, and to move if their neighbours are too similar to them.

(For the full experience, I recommend visiting http://ncase.me/polygons/.)

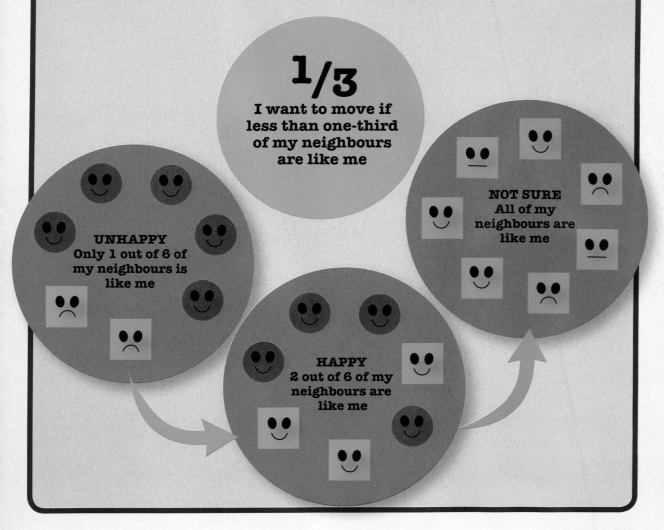

1/3
I want to move if less than one-third of my neighbours are like me

UNHAPPY
Only 1 out of 6 of my neighbours is like me

HAPPY
2 out of 6 of my neighbours are like me

NOT SURE
All of my neighbours are like me

Winning the Lottery

You have essentially no chance of winning the lottery jackpot. The odds of winning the UK lottery is about the same odds as tossing 25 coins and all of them coming up heads, or guessing three people's birthdays correctly. If you played every day for 85,000 years, you would have a roughly 50–50 chance of winning the jackpot.

In the UK's National Lottery, a £2 ticket entitles you to pick six numbers from 1 to 59. If those six numbers emerge from the lottery machine, you win the jackpot. Your chances of matching the first ball are 6 in 59 (a bit better than one in 10). Also matching the second ball carries odds of 5 in 58 (about 1 in 12), because you have five choices left on your ticket and the machine only has 58 balls left in. The subsequent balls have odds of 4 in 57 (1 in 14 or so), 3 in 56 (1 in 17), 2 in 55 and 1 in 54. The product of these gives your chances of winning: it is 720 in 32,441,381,280, or 1 in a little more than 45,000,000.

So, how can you improve your chances of winning the lottery?

Well, the bad news is you can't. It is random. The whole point of it is that no number is any more likely to come up than any other, so picking different numbers does not change your chances of winning.

What you *can* do is improve your chances of winning *big*, given that you do hit the jackpot.

The first thing that you can do is wait until times when the prizes are bigger. The bigger the jackpot, the bigger your payout if you win (although you may have to share it with more people, on average.)

The second thing is to pick unpopular numbers. Because the jackpot is shared between however many people pick those numbers, you want to minimize the chances of anyone else having your numbers. Most people, when playing the lottery, make their choices based on lucky

First ball odds:
6 in 59

Probability of matching all six balls:
720 in 32,441,381,280

Second ball odds:
5 in 58

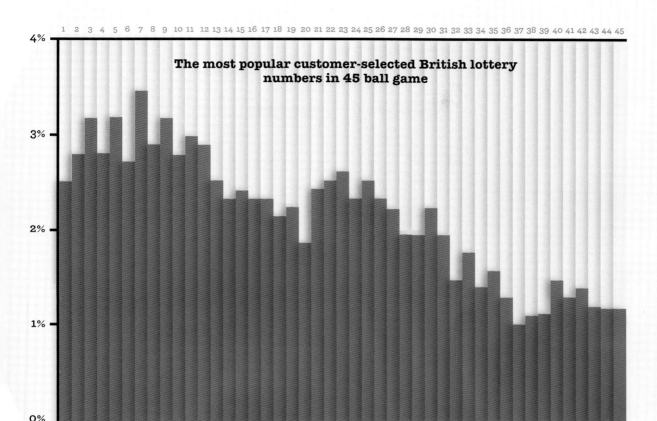

The most popular customer-selected British lottery numbers in 45 ball game

numbers, family birthdays, or numbers that look nicely spread out – so you want to exploit those patterns by doing the opposite:

Avoid lucky numbers. Do not pick 7, that is ridiculous. 42? It may be the answer to Life, the Universe and Everything, but it is probably not the answer to "What number should I put on my lottery ticket?" Unlucky 13 might be a better bet, but...

Pick high numbers, for preference. 45 is just as likely to emerge as 7, but is much less frequently picked.

Pick unremarkable numbers. Who cares about 53? You care about 53.

Avoid obvious patterns. There are people who pick 1-2-3-4-5-6 every week because

they know it is as likely as any other sequence. Others might draw a pattern of straight lines or diagonals on their ticket – avoid those patterns, too.

Do not be too mixed-up. People trying to pick at random will come up with something that deliberately avoids numbers next to each other, for example.

Instead, mix up short runs of high numbers with ugly numbers elsewhere on the ticket. You will still be almost certain to lose, but you will feel better about it.

Of course, every other lottery player reading this will now adopt the same strategy, so your edge may diminish significantly...

HOW TO CHEAT THE LOTTERY (MATHEMATICALLY)

Most known attempts to beat the lottery have focused on rigging the draw: in the Pennsylvania Lottery in 1980, news anchor Nick Perry conspired to replace the usual balls with weighted ones, guaranteeing that the number 6-6-6 would be drawn. Sadly for Perry, he was caught and sentenced to seven years in prison. Similarly, the Milan Lotto somehow lost hundreds of millions of dollars in the 1990s when the balls were tampered with so that the blindfolded children making the draw could select the "correct" ones.

Mohan Srivastava's case is different, though. In 2003, his squash partner gave him a couple of scratch-cards from the Ontario Lottery as a joke. Being a statistician, he wondered how the numbers on the cards were generated: they could not be random, because the lottery needed to control the number of winners – so they had to conform (he reasoned) to some sort of pattern.

The tickets consisted of eight tic-tac-toe grids, and each square of each grid contained a number between 1 and 39. The lottery-player would scratch off a panel to reveal a set of 24 numbers to check, and if any of those numbers formed a three-in-a-row pattern in any of the grids, the ticket was a winner.

Srivastava's insight was to ignore the *numbers*, and think instead about their *frequency distribution*. Because there are 72 spaces and only 39 numbers, some of them have to be repeated, but some appear only once – he called these *singletons*. The hidden numbers often happened to be singletons, so if Srivastava could find tickets with three singletons in a row on any of the grids, he figured those would be likely winners.

Putting his theory to the test, he found it worked around 90% of the time. He had – completely legally – cracked the lottery!

Doing some more analysis, though, he realized he could expect to make about $600 a day from his discovery – which was roughly what he was making as a consultant, doing far more interesting work than analyzing scratchcards. Instead of plundering the game, he notified the authorities, who pulled the game.

Of course, we only know about the weakness in the Ontario Lottery because Mohan Srivastava spoke up, and we only know about the 6-6-6 Fixers and the Milan Lotto because the perpetrators were caught. It is entirely possible that other lotteries suffer from similar flaws and have been cracked – legally or otherwise – by people who do not have another lucrative job to keep them honest.

1 in 500
chance of being born with extra fingers or toes

1 in 2,000
chance of being bitten by Luis Suárez

1 in 10,000
chance of finding a four-leaf clover

1 in 12,000
chance of finding a pearl in an oyster

1 in 700,000
chance of being crushed by a meteorite

34
is the least popular number in a 50-ball lotto (according to available statistics)

1 in 14 million
chance of winning the 49-ball lottery jackpot

1 in 11.5 million
chance of getting attacked by a shark in the US

1 in 10 million
chance of getting hit by a falling aeroplane part

1 in 3.5 million
chance of dying of a snake bite

1 in 1 million
chance of getting struck by lightning in the US

THE FUNDAMENTAL THEOREM OF GAMBLING

Any bet you make has an *expected value*: it is the number you get if you add up the probability of each payout, multiplied by the amount of the payout, then take away the cost of the bet from the total. (For example, if you have a lottery with $1 tickets that pays out $50 one percent of the time, and $2 ten percent of the time, the expected value would be $(0.01 \times \$50 + 0.10 \times \$2) - \$1 = -\$0.30$.)

The *fundamental theorem of gambling* states that if the expected value of the bet is positive, playing will tend to make you a profit over the long term; if it is negative, it will tend to make you a loss.

Except in exceptional circumstances such as rollovers and special events, lotteries almost always have a negative expected value – as do most bets at casinos and bookmakers. If you want to win big, you need to think outside of the box.

Tying Knots

How many ways can you knot a tie? It may surprise you to learn that mathematicians have written books and scientific papers working out the number and have developed formal languages to describe the knots.

If, like me, you went to a school with a traditional uniform, tying a tie was probably part of your childhood. To tie a basic tie knot, you:

1. Pass the fat end over the thin end;
2. Wrap it all the way around the thin end to form a loop;
3. Move the fat end through the gap under your chin and through the loop;
4. Finally, pull it tight.

You now have a passably smartly knotted tie.

I remember being surprised when my dad showed me how to tie a *Windsor knot*, which is wider and sturdier than the basic one, but even then it did not really occur to me to ask about other ways of tying ties. How many are there? That is the kind of question you need mathematicians to answer.

In 2000, Cambridge mathematicians Thomas Fink and Yong Mao came up with a formal language to describe the tying of ties. It uses three capital letters (**L**, **C**, and **R**) to describe the movement of the fat end of the tie, along with a lower-case letter to describe whether the move is towards the body (**i** for in) or away (**o** for out).

There's also **T**, which means "through" – threading the tie through the loop.

In this notation, the traditional knot described by the method at the beginning is **Li Ro Li Co T** – the first **Li** is step 1, moving left and towards the body; the next moves (**Ro Li**) are step 2 – outwards on the right, but back inward on the left to make a loop. **Co** corresponds to step 3 – moving outwards in the centre of the Y-shape the tie now forms – and **T** means the final step, finishing the knot.

Fink and Mao determined there were 85 reasonable knots using their language – of which "just over a dozen are sufficiently handsome or different from each other to be worn."

The Windsor knot, apparently, is **Li Co Ri Lo Ci Ro Li Co T** but be warned: James Bond thinks it the sign of a cad, and (according to Fink), it is popular among Communist leaders and dictators.

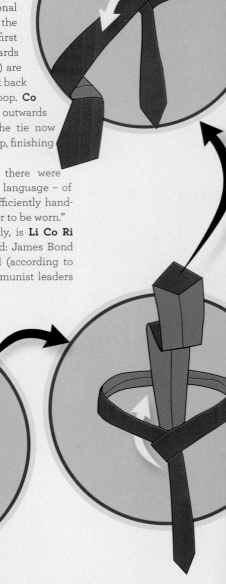

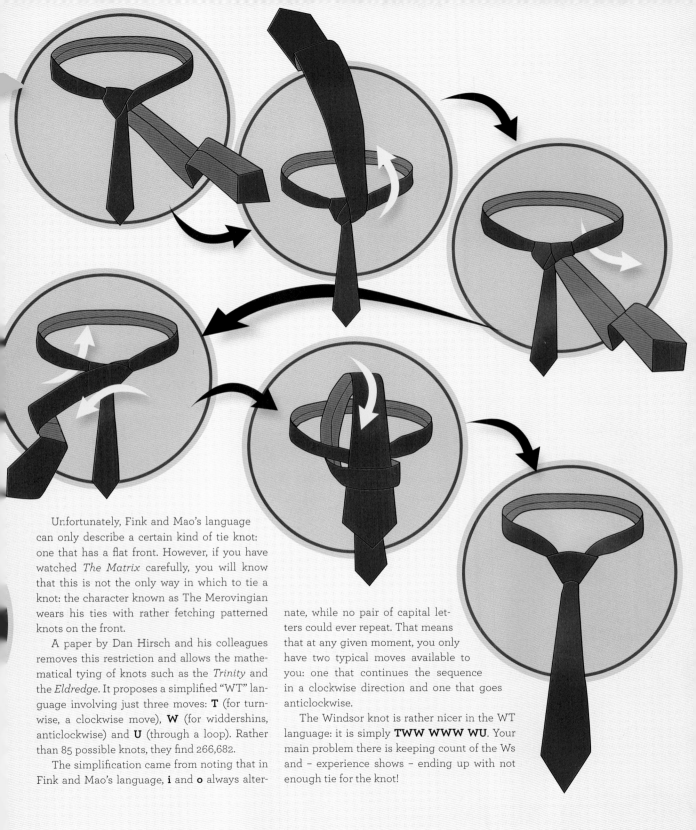

Unfortunately, Fink and Mao's language can only describe a certain kind of tie knot: one that has a flat front. However, if you have watched *The Matrix* carefully, you will know that this is not the only way in which to tie a knot: the character known as The Merovingian wears his ties with rather fetching patterned knots on the front.

A paper by Dan Hirsch and his colleagues removes this restriction and allows the mathematical tying of knots such as the *Trinity* and the *Eldredge*. It proposes a simplified "WT" language involving just three moves: **T** (for turnwise, a clockwise move), **W** (for widdershins, anticlockwise) and **U** (through a loop). Rather than 85 possible knots, they find 266,682.

The simplification came from noting that in Fink and Mao's language, **i** and **o** always alter-nate, while no pair of capital let-ters could ever repeat. That means that at any given moment, you only have two typical moves available to you: one that continues the sequence in a clockwise direction and one that goes anticlockwise.

The Windsor knot is rather nicer in the WT language: it is simply **TWW WWW WU**. Your main problem there is keeping count of the Ws and – experience shows – ending up with not enough tie for the knot!

Birthdays

You can use probability to look at birthdays. Consider your Facebook friends. How many friends do you need to have before two of them share a birthday? How likely is it that more than two will share a birthday?

When you open up Facebook, it typically tells you something like "Chris Jones and four other friends have their birthday today."

At the time of writing, I have around 400 friends on Facebook. It would be sensible to expect that any given day would likely be one, or occasionally two, of my friends' birthdays. After all, birthdays are more or less evenly spread through the year.

So, is it unusual for there to be a day with five (or more) birthdays? Is it unusual for there to be a day with *no* birthdays?

A BRIEF ASIDE ON THE BIRTHDAY "PARADOX"

A classical question in birthdays asks "how many people do you need to have in a room before you would expect some pair of them to share a birthday?" Because there are at most 366 days in the year, you need 367 people to be *certain* two of them share the same birthday. Obviously, you do not need quite so many for it to be *likely* that a pair of them are the same. But how many?

You can do an experiment to see. Find a list of people with their birthdays – a sports team's roster, or a list of Academy Award winners might be good examples – and go through it until you find two with the same birthday.

I picked the US Men's National Soccer Team's roster for the 2016 Copa América and among the 23 players, Chris Wondolowski and John Brooks share a birthday on 28 January.

In fact, 23 is the magic number: if you have 23 people, it is a slightly better than 50–50 chance that two of them could throw a joint birthday

You might expect birthdays to be spread evenly through the year - but some days get many, and others none. The binomial distribution explains why.

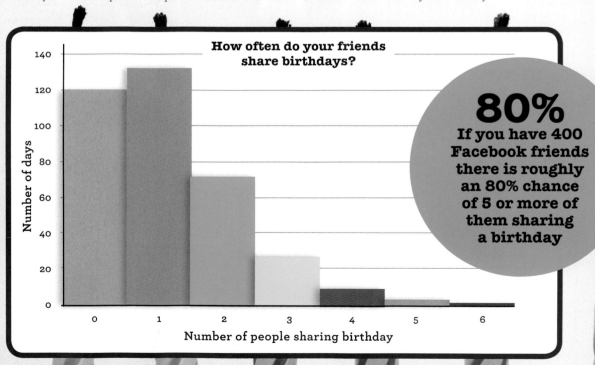

How often do your friends share birthdays?

80% If you have 400 Facebook friends there is roughly an 80% chance of 5 or more of them sharing a birthday

Number of days

Number of people sharing birthday

party. This does not seem like very many people – so why this number?

As with many probability problems, it is a bit easier to work out the chances of something *not* happening than to work out the chances of it taking place.

If we ignore leap years, the probability of the first and second person in the list having different birthdays is 364/365 – there is about a 99.7% probability of them matching.

The probability of the third person also having a birthday that matches neither of the first two is 363/365 × 364/365, down to 99.2%.

As more people are added, the top of the fraction continues to fall, and the probability begins to drop more and more quickly: once you have ten people in your list, you have about a one in eight chance of two of them matching; another five makes the chance a quarter... and between 22 and 23 people, the probability of everyone having missed flips from over 50% to below.

And if you have 50 people in a room, there is only about 3% probability that all of them have different birthdays – and at 96 people, it is a one-in-a-million chance!

BACK TO FACEBOOK

Working out the probability of having a day with multiple birthdays, though, is a bit tougher. If we take a random day – say 15 November – each person in the list has a 1/365 chance of having that birthday. This situation can be approximated using the *binomial distribution* – if you have 400 people, each having a 1/365 chance of that birthday, you will get no hits almost exactly a third of the time; 36.7% of the time, you get one birthday. Two birthdays is a one-in-five shot, and three birthdays 7.3% of the time. 2 per cent of the time, a day would have four birthdays on it, and five birthdays crop up on 0.4% of days – which I will call p.

However, the chances of such a day not happening over the whole of the year are $(1-p)^{365}$, which works out to be barely 20 per cent: which means, if you have 400 Facebook friends, there is roughly an 80% chance that five or more of them share a birthday.

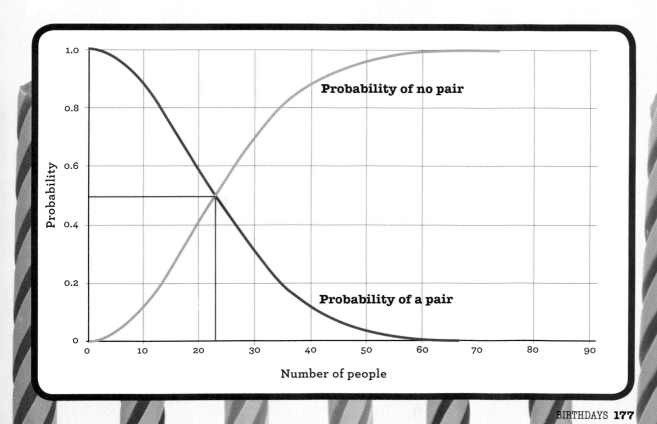

Waiting in Line

$\rho = \lambda t$

Agner Krarup Erlang worked at the Copenhagen Telephone Exchange in the early 20th century. He was concerned with how quickly the exchange could process incoming calls – and how long callers would have to wait for a connection.

He made some assumptions to turn the problem into one he could approach mathematically:

Callers arrive at random following a *Poisson distribution* with mean λ , which means that on average λ new callers join the queue in each hour.

Once at the front of the queue, callers take a fixed amount of time to be connected.

There is one person responsible for connecting the calls, and they can only deal with one call at a time.

This first model, known as M/D/1 (the M stands for *memoryless* – the callers join the queue with no knowledge of what has happened before; D is *deterministic*, meaning the service time is fixed; and 1 is simply the number of servers) was

solved by Erlang in 1919. He determined that the key parameter was the *utilization*, $\rho = \lambda t$. If this was smaller than 1, everyone in the queue would eventually be served, but if it was greater than 1, the queue would grow without limit. This makes sense: if the average time to serve a customer is longer than the average time it takes for the next customer to arrive, you cannot expect the queue to decrease!

Erlang also calculated the average length of queue, $\rho^2/2(1-\rho)$, and the average wait time to be served, $\rho t/2(1-\rho)$. For example, if an average of 10 callers joined the queue every hour and each took 5 minutes ($1/12$ of an hour) to be served, the utilization would be $10 \times 1/12 = 5/6 \approx 0.833$ – meaning that the queue will not grow out of control. On average, there would be a shade more than two people in the queue ($25/12$ to be precise), and the average wait time would be $5/24$ hours, or 12.5 minutes.

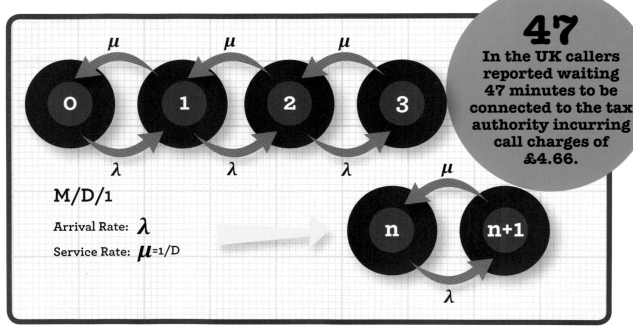

M/D/1

Arrival Rate: λ

Service Rate: $\mu = 1/D$

47

In the UK callers reported waiting 47 minutes to be connected to the tax authority incurring call charges of £4.66.

GETTING PEOPLE THROUGH CHECKOUTS

When you are in a supermarket, it is often difficult to decide which checkout to pick. Unlike Erlang's simple model, there are many factors to consider, including:

How many people are in each queue?

How much shopping does each person in the queue have?

How talkative is the cashier?

Is there a closed checkout nearby that could potentially open?

Is it quicker to have the cashier scan the shopping than to use a self-checkout?

However, there is a simple and elegant solution stores can adopt to save their customers from having to think about this at all.

The mathematically optimal way to design a queuing system is not to allow customers to choose a till (except, perhaps to make a choice between "premium" and "standard," or "self-service" and "cashier service"). Instead, a *snake* treats everyone fairly. Rather than have 20 distinct lines, there is one big line; at the end, a sign directs the next person in line to the first available cashier.

The one apparent disadvantage is that the snake looks like an extremely long line; however, it is moving 20 times as fast as the average line in the traditional layout. If there is a delay at one checkout, it holds up everyone behind them slightly – but there are still 19 other cashiers getting people through quickly, and nobody gets impatient with them. And, if you join the queue before someone else, you get served before them: a queue that treats people fairly is a good queue.

Exams

$$x_i - x_j = \ln\left(\frac{p_{ij}}{1 - p_{ij}}\right)$$

Most students approach exams the same way: start with the first question, proceed to the second, etc, until they reach the final question, or run out of time. Not *that* bad a strategy, especially if the questions are arranged in rough order of difficulty. However, especially on difficult tests, it pays to be smart about which questions you choose to do.

You can treat the exam a little like a shopping trip: you are spending something (time) to acquire something (points), and you want to make sure you get the best value out of your trip. If you know roughly how many points you can expect to pick up on each of the questions, and how long you expect to take on each, you can figure out which questions are bargains – ones that get high marks quickly – and prioritize these high-value questions over the "expensive" ones.

This type of problem is a variant on the *knapsack* problem – how to pack a set of items of different weights into a set of knapsacks with different capacities so that you either use as few bags as possible, or balance the bags as evenly as possible, or ensure as great a weight is carried as possible. In general, such problems are extremely hard to solve analytically, but there are some short-cuts you can take.

Pick the most efficient questions for you first. By doing the questions that make the best use of your time first, you make sure you do not miss out on the cheap questions if you run out of time.

Prefer questions with a big point-count. Obviously, it makes sense to tackle the hard questions before you get tired, but that is not the reason: it is the same reason as you pack large objects into your suitcase first. You want to make sure they fit in!

Watch your time. If your time estimate is off, do not be afraid to skip onto another question and come back to it later. Do not throw good time after bad!

HOW DO THEY MAKE EXAMS FAIR?

Broadly speaking, there are two traditional models for making sure an examination gives fair results.

One is the idea of "grading to a curve," which is often used in the USA. The professor looks at the scores of everyone in the class, finds their mean and says "that's the boundary between B- and C+." She then figures out a measure of the spread in the scores, the *standard deviation*, and picks grade boundaries that should, theoretically, ensure about 20% of the students get an A, 30% a B, and so on.

This relies on the assumption that test scores are *normally distributed* – that they are spread out roughly like a *bell curve* – and with enough students, that is probably not a bad approximation. However, there are problems with it.

For a start, if 20% of the students in each class are expected to get an A, a moderately bright student in an underperforming class may get a higher grade than a smarter student in a class that is doing well, simply because of the statistics. A tough class with one extremely capable student may end up with only a smattering of As and Bs. There is also no immediate way to measure changes from one year to the next.

A second approach, which is more standard in Europe, is more statistical. The people in charge of exams consider how students have historically fared with various types of questions, and set the grade boundaries based on how they expect the various percentiles of students to do – without necessarily looking at anyone's performance on these specific questions! The disadvantage of this system is that it is a lot more work than plugging a few numbers into

Grading a class's exams to a curve ensures a reasonable distribution of grades.

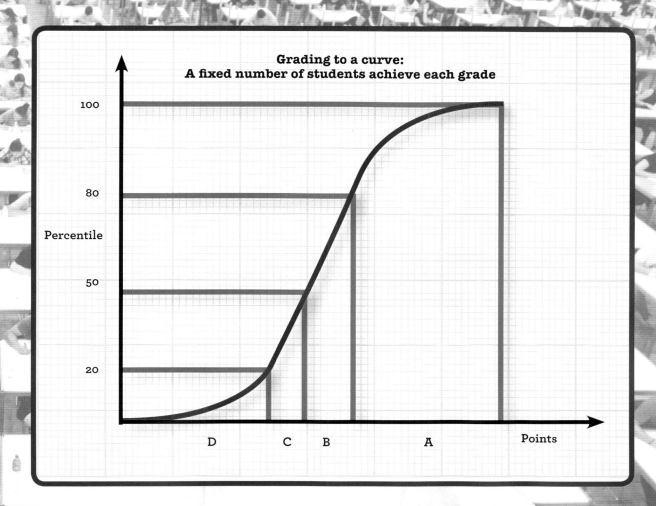

Grading to a curve:
A fixed number of students achieve each grade

Percentile: 100, 80, 50, 20

Points

D   C   B   A

a spreadsheet; the advantage is that it is less dependent on individual performances, and allows for exams of comparable quality to be set each year without simply setting the same paper over and over again.

However, there is a third model gaining some traction, known as *Adaptive Comparative Judgement*. Instead of being marked, exam scripts are simply compared one against another: in the opinion of the evaluators, which of the two is better? By comparing papers against those with a similar score, the system determines how likely it is that any given paper is "better" or "worse" than another.

A possible model for Adaptive Comparative Judgement is the *Bradley–Terry Model*, which uses these probabilities to assign relative scores to papers following the equation:

$$x_i - x_j = \ln\left(\frac{p_{ij}}{1 - p_{ij}}\right)$$

That is to say, if paper i has a probability of p_{ij} of being better than paper j, it scores $(x_i - x_j)$ more points than paper j. For example: if a paper had an 80% chance of being better than another, it would score $\left(\frac{0.8}{0.2}\right) \approx 1.39$ points more.

Once this is done, the scores can be compared to a curve, or even to previous papers in a similar exam, and given the appropriate grade without needing to quibble over each individual point on the mark scheme.

Rollercoasters

$$F = \frac{mv^2}{r}$$

The rollercoaster car pauses for a fraction of a second at the top of the GateKeeper at Cedar Point, just long enough for the thought to go through your mind: is this safe? How can the cars go upside-down without falling off? How can they make the cars go as fast as possible?

And you are lurched out of your thoughts, because you are suddenly accelerating at around 32 feet per second per second towards the ground several hundred feet below. Fingers crossed they have got the sums right!

As you hurtle into the rising phase of a loop-the-loop, it feels like you are being thrust down into your seat. As you reach the top, you feel weightless, and in danger of falling out. How can you be going upside-down without falling out? The shoulder straps are not *that* strong.

The key to not falling off a loop-the-loop is to make sure you are going fast enough. While my high-school physics teacher (correctly) drummed into me that centrifugal force is not a thing, it is a useful fiction when dealing with rollercoasters: you can consider the three main forces acting on your car as its weight (straight downwards), the centrifugal force (acting outwards, where m is your mass, v is your speed and r is the radius of curvature of the track – the smaller it is, the tighter the loop) and the normal reaction force of the track acting on the car.

As long as the centrifugal force is greater than the effect of your weight towards the centre of the circle, you stay on the track.

The shape of the loop means that the radius of curvature also becomes smaller, which tends to increase the centrifugal force. However, you lose speed as your height above the ground increases, meaning that the centrifugal force becomes smaller as you reach the top of the loop. The smaller that force, the closer to weightless you feel: a well-designed rollercoaster leaves you with just enough speed at the top to safely make it around.

The shape of the track and the speed of the cars keep you in your seat while upside-down.

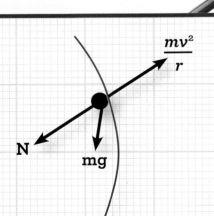

CENTRIFUGAL FORCE

"Centrifugal force" does not physically exist. Instead, to stay on a curve, you need to have a net acceleration along the radius of curvature of v^2/r. Rather than try to account for this, and get muddled up between forces and accelerations, not to mention keeping track of signs, it is simpler to make up a force to counterbalance it. The sums work out the same.

$$\frac{mv^2}{r}$$

N

mg

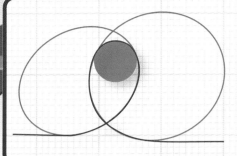

CLOTHOIDS

Rollercoaster loops are generally not circles, but *clothoids*. Moving from a straight section of track to a circle at high speed can be quite uncomfortable, and a smooth transition between the two reduces the jerk. The track's radius of curvature changes smoothly as you go along it, making for a comparatively comfortable ride.

RADIUS OF CURVATURE

You are probably familiar with the idea of a circle's radius, the distance from its centre to its edge. The idea can be extended to any kind of curve: at any point on the curve, there is a unique circle that is *tangential* to it on the inside – the circle just grazes the curve. The radius of that circle is the curve's *radius of curvature* at that point: the smaller the radius of curvature, the tighter the curve. If the curve is straight, though, the radius of curvature becomes infinite; we pretend that that is completely OK.

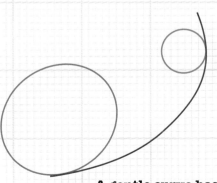

A sharp curve has a small radius of curvature

A gentle curve has a large radius of curvature

Daylight

If you are lucky enough to live in the tropics, you probably do not notice how the amount of daylight you get varies through the year. At the equator, you get a more or less constant 12 hours of daylight every day, and if you visit Miami, you will find the shortest day is only 97 minutes or so shorter.

The amount of daylight you get on any given day depends mainly on your *latitude*. Imagine a globe, and a skewer from where you are to the middle of the planet. Imagine another skewer from the middle of the earth to the point on the equator directly south of you. The angle between those skewers is your latitude – the North Pole is at 90 degrees north and the South Pole is at 90 degrees south.

Because the earth's axis is tilted at about 23 degrees to the plane in which it orbits the Sun, everywhere between 23 degrees north (the Tropic of Cancer) and 23 degrees south (the Tropic of Capricorn) has the Sun more or less overhead at some point during the year. By contrast, there are places where the Sun does not rise at all some winter days: those are inside the Arctic and Antarctic circles, and have latitudes greater than about 67 degrees north or south (respectively). The upside is that some summer days do not have a sunset – which is why Norway is sometimes called the Land of the Midnight Sun.

There is a formula to describe the theoretical amount of daylight you should get any day of the year. If you are at latitude L degrees, and it is t days after your winter equinox (around 21 December in the northern hemisphere, and around 21 June in the south), you need to work out a value, C, which is:

$$C = \tan(L)\tan\left(23\cos\left(\tfrac{360}{365}t\right)\right)$$

This is the distance, at your latitude, between the *terminator* – the line that divides day from night – and the earth's axis, scaled to the radius

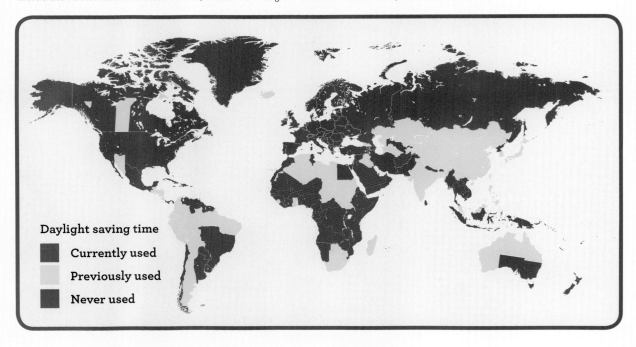

Daylight saving time

- **Currently used**
- **Previously used**
- **Never used**

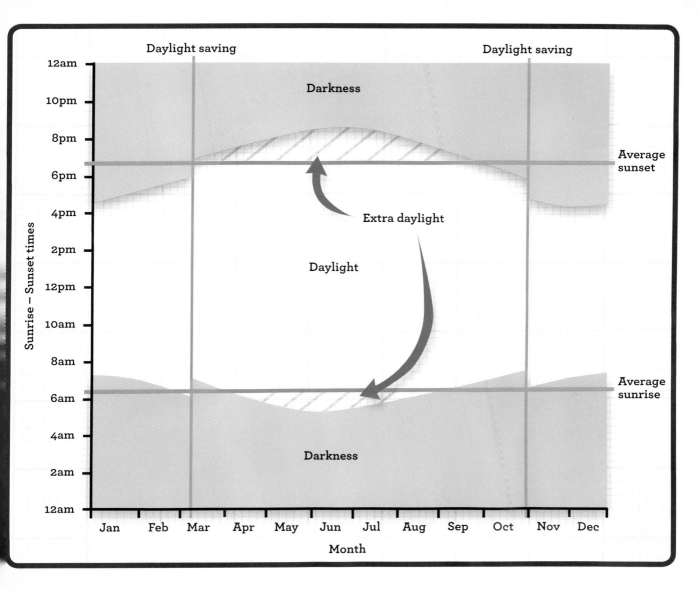

of the circle you revolve in. If that is greater than 1, it is very simple: you have a full day of daylight. If it is the wrong side of -1, it is also simple: you have no daylight at all. (This can only happen inside the Arctic or Antarctic circles.)

If C is between -1 and 1 (which it will be for most readers) the amount of daylight you get is 24/180 arccos (C) hours.

Someone in Rio de Janeiro (34 degrees south of the equator), wondering how much sunlight they would have 60 days after winter solstice, would work out:

$$C = \tan(34)\tan\left(23\cos\left(\tfrac{360}{365}\times 60\right)\right) \approx 0.14$$

That's between -1 and 1, so we need to work out 24/180 arccos (0.14) ≈ 10.92 hours. There would (in theory) be just short of 11 hours of daylight.

The actual amount of daylight you get is usually slightly more than the formula predicts – light refracts through the atmosphere, bending downwards, which means you can see the Sun before it physically crosses the horizon as it rises, and after it physically sets.

The Weather Forecast

The news finishes, and the newscaster says something like "The weather today: temperatures in the 60s under mostly cloudy skies, with a 30% chance of rain." So, depending on where you live, you take a light or heavy jacket, and... you have a dilemma about your umbrella.

A 30% chance of rain? It is more likely than not to stay dry, but all the same, that is a pretty significant chance of getting drenched. You can make a decision by asking "how much sadness would taking an umbrella cause me?" and "how much sadness would getting wet cause me?" in whatever units you like. For me, getting wet is at least ten times as miserable as taking an umbrella. If I take an umbrella, it costs me 1 unit of sadness, whatever happens. If I do not take it, I will remain completely happy 70% of the time, but lose 10 sadness units 30% of the time.

Over 100 similar days, I would lose 100 sadness units by taking the umbrella, but 300 by leaving it behind – so, on balance, I ought to take it. This is an example of using a *utility function* (here, sadness) as a way of making decisions.

WHAT DOES 30% CHANCE OF RAIN MEAN?

The idea of "what would happen over 100 similar days?" is exactly the way to think about statements like "a 30% chance of rain." It all comes from the weather forecasters' simulations.

On huge banks of computers, meteorologists run thousands upon thousands of simulations of what could reasonably happen, given the time of year, the recent weather, temperature, wind direction, atmospheric pressure, laws of physics, and everything else that goes into a sensible weather model. Each of the simulations is one possible reality based on the original setup.

If they ran 10,000 simulations and your city got rained on in around 3,000 of them, the forecast would predict a 30% chance of rain.

This can be broken down by hour, or into any chunk of time you like. The mathematics of reading a weather forecast gets interesting when you compare two hour-by-hour forecasts

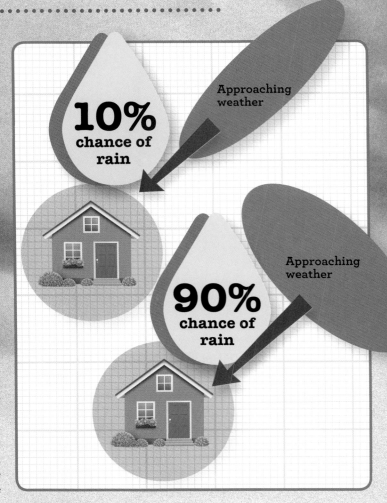

that list a 10% chance of rain in each hour, but different chances of rain during the day – say 10% and 90%. In the first case, you know that it is unlikely to rain, but if it does, it is likely to set in for the day; in the second case, you know rain is almost certain, but can infer it is likely to be only a short shower.

HOW GOOD IS PUNXSUTAWNEY PHIL?

Every winter ever since the 1880s, a groundhog based in Punxsutawney, Pennsylvania has made a meteorological prediction based on whether he can see his shadow on 2 February. If it is sunny enough for a shadow, that suggests a long, cold winter; otherwise, the prediction is for an early spring.

The National Climatic Data Center has collected Phil's predictions from 1988 to 2015, alongside whether temperatures in February and March were above, slightly above, below or slightly below average in each year.

In 8 of the 28 years, Punxsutawney Phil predicted an early end to winter – and none of those predictions were wrong! Four times, both months were warmer than average, and the remainder had a mixture of warmer and cooler months.

Unfortunately, his predictions of long winters were not anything like as good: the only unambiguously correct one was 2014, which had below-average temperatures in both February and March.

In fairness to the groundhog, 2014 was the *only* year in the range when both months were cooler than the historical mean, while 12 of the 28 were both warmer. All the same, Phil's hit rate was about 38 per cent, slightly lower than you would get by flipping a coin, and much worse than predicting an early winter every time.

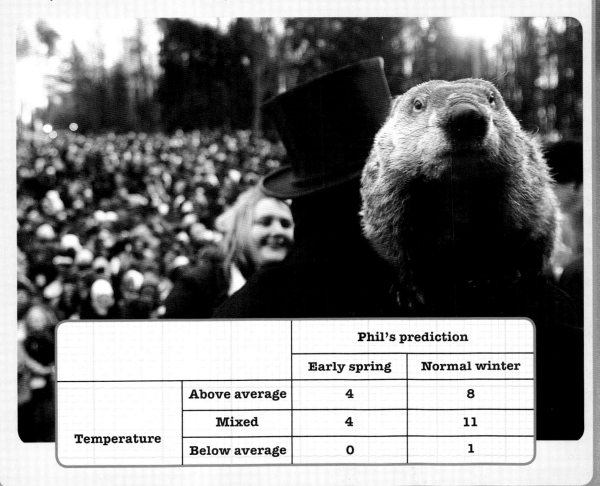

		Phil's prediction	
		Early spring	**Normal winter**
	Above average	4	8
	Mixed	4	11
Temperature	**Below average**	0	1

Acknowledgements

This book is warmly dedicated to my sons, Bill and Fred. May the numbers always fall kindly for you both.

Thanks as always to my patient and supportive family — Linda Hendren and Nicky Russ for making it possible for me to write, Ken and Stuart Beveridge for their unwavering belief in me, and Laura Russ for tolerating my antisocial work patterns.

Picture credits

123RF Denis Ismagilov 8–9, 34–5, 60–1, 86–7, 110–11, 138–9, 162–3. **Alamy Stock Photo** Brian Harris 81 left; Chutikarn Wongwichaichana 137 below; Damien Loverso 72–3; Derya Duzen 164 left; dpa picture alliance 118–19; Granger Historical Picture Archive 78 below, 130 left; Guillem Lopez 136–7; Heritage Image Partnership Ltd. 81 right; Ian Shipley SP 149; Images & Stories 165 above right; Jason Cohn/Reuters 187; Justin Kase zsixz 130 right; Keystone Pictures USA 6 left, 23 left; Lebrecht Music and Arts Photo Library 128; Michelle Chaplow 137 above; Roger Bacon/Reuters 125; Sergio Azenha 112; The Ohio Collection 182–3. **Dreamstime.com** Alvin Cha 112 inset; Americanspirit 28–9 background; Anan Punyod 129 below; Andreadonetti 132–3 background, 134–5 background; Andrey Armyagov 141 above left; Andrey Gudkov 36 background; Angelo Gilardelli 32–3; Brad Calkins 176–7; Daniel Schreurs 126–7; Designua 56; Drserg 62 above; Georgios Kollidas 23 right, 166 above; Grandeduc 116–17; Haiyin 145 right; Intrepix 140 left; Isselee 36–7 below; Kathrine Martin 116, 117; Klausmeierklaus 30; Lajo_2 100 above, 100 below, 103 above, 103 below; Liz Van Steenburgh 167 above right; Mark Eaton 6 right, 42; Meryll 74; Michael Brown 142–3, 158–9 background, 160 background; Mihai-bogdan Lazar 59 above left; Pixattitude 95, 98 left, 99 left; Raphaelgunther 167 background above; Skypixel 7 left, 44–5; Stephen Girimont 59 above right; Stuartbur 167 above left; Valentin Armianu 156–7; Vampy1 154–5; Victor Zastol`skiy 186–7; Viktor Bobnyev 114–15. **iStockphoto.com** cyrop 148; reinobjektiv 80 right. **Science Photo Library** T-Service 49. **Shutterstock** Antony McAulay 50 left, 50 centre, 51 above right, 51 left, 57 centre, 59 centre right, 59 below left, 59 below right; Bagrin Egor 121 below; bibiphoto 180–1; FXQuadro 19; Inked Pixels 99 right; lisheng2121 144–5 background, 145 left; Rawpixel.com 40–1; Rozilynn Mitchell 79; Somchai Som 50 right, 51 below right, 57 left, 58, 140 right, 141 above centre.